In Search of Hospitality

Theoretical perspectives and debates

Edited by

Conrad Lashley
and
Alison Morrison

BUTTERWORTH
HEINEMANN

OXFORD AMSTERDAM BOSTON LONDON NEW YORK PARIS
SAN DIEGO SAN FRANCISCO SINGAPORE SYDNEY TOKYO

Butterworth-Heinemann
An imprint of Elsevier Science
Linacre House, Jordan Hill, Oxford OX2 8DP
225 Wildwood Avenue, Woburn MA 01801-2041

First published 2000
Reprinted as a paperback edition 2001
Reprinted 2002

British Library Cataloguing in Publication Data
A catalogue record for this book is available from the British Librar

ISBN 0 7506 4562 8

For information on all Butterworth-Heinemann Publications
visit our website at www.bh.com

Composition by Genesis Typesetting, Rochester, Kent
Printed and bound in Great Britain by Biddles Ltd,
www.biddles.co.uk

Contents

Hospitality, Leisure & Tourism Series

v

Foreword

I began reading this volume in a somewhat anxious state of mind. I'd accepted the invitation to write a foreword without having any very clear idea in my mind about the meaning of 'hospitality' or about how the subject might engender the 'theoretical perspectives and debates' which were promised in the sub-title. I need not have worried. As soon as I began to read I realized that this was not only an area of study which connected with many of my own sociological interests in the 'escape attempts' provided by holidays and tourism but also provided me with a nice justification for further pursuing the amateur obsession I've had over the years with hotels and guesthouses.

This interest was initially prompted by my friendship with the first editor of *The Good Hotel Guide*. I remember spending hours talking with Hilary about the possibility of such a guide and about whether it would be possible to persuade a sufficient number of people to write in with highly personal accounts of the places where they'd stayed. As it turned out, Hilary's optimism about the venture was entirely justified and now, like so many others, I find myself not only racing out to buy the latest edition but positively longing for the moment when I can settle back and savour the thousands of lovingly written independent reports on hotels, inns, guesthouses and B&Bs which make up its content.

What makes the guide so fascinating is the insight it provides into the distinctive idea of hospitality held by the British middle classes. Every year, for example, the 'note for new readers' announces that most of the entries are for small establishments run by resident owners. Even though the bulk of hotel rooms in the country are to be found in large hotels run by managers, the guide knows its audience well enough to confidently dismiss their claims in a single sentence: 'We don't object in principle to large hotels . . . but in our experience they often fail to provide the welcome and care for guests' comfort that can be found in the best of the small individually-owned hotels'.

Now, it would be difficult to argue with the idea that any self-respecting hotel or guesthouse should provide a reasonable welcome and show a concern for its guests' comfort, but even the briefest glance at any of the entries in the guide shows that these words are being used in an exclusive and specialized sense. No matter how enthusiastic the welcome provided by the reception-ist at a Hyatt or a Hilton, no matter how much concern for a guest's comfort is evidenced by the furniture and fittings within a Marriott or Moat House, there is no way in which such establishments can meet the distinctive welcome and comfort requirements of the typical guide reader.

What exactly are these requirements? I can't pretend to have done a systematic content analysis of the 750 essays that make up the guide but there are several descriptions which regularly recur whether the facility under inspection is a five-bedroom B&B or a grand thirty-bedroom mansion. Guide readers almost always relish any establishment with a 'homely feel'. They like to feel 'at home', enjoy the sense of being in a 'private house', and relish a degree of 'informality'. Great emphasis is also placed upon the personality of the owners. They should above all be 'enthusiastic' (even 'exuberant'), 'friendly', 'unfussy', 'generous', 'kind', 'infor-mal', free of snobbery and pretension, and as proud of their establishment as they are knowledgeable about its history and setting. There's no need to go on. What we have here is a simple exercise in projection. Guide readers expect their hosts and hostesses to correspond as closely as possible in an imperfect world to their own idealized self-conceptions. They must provide a refreshing and reassuring reminder of the core middle class values which are so difficult to live up to in today's frenzied material world as well as preside over a 'traditional home' free from the disunity and fragmentation of contemporary domestic life. Above all they must contrive to give the impression, even on the morning when the final bill is presented, that they are not so much motivated by a desire for personal gain as living out a vocation.

At this point I must draw a line under my own speculations and trust that the academics who have contributed to this collection of essays on the nature of hospitality will forgive my intrusion into their specialist area. My intention was solely to demonstrate a personal fascination with the subject matter of their research, to reinforce the view so often articulated in this volume, that hospitality is a concept which has not only been much neglected in the literature of social science, but also one which is well capable of taking its place alongside such other more familiar intellectual areas of enquiry as 'stratification', 'deviance', 'social mobility' and 'leisure'.

All these now familiar areas of enquiry were preoccupied in their infancy with defining the exact nature of their subject area. This volume shows 'hospitality' going through a similar process and it was refreshing to find Elizabeth Telfer asking the question which at least implicitly preoccupies the editors of *The Good Hotel Guide*: 'Can a commercial host be hospitable?'. As she observes, 'On a superficial view this seems to be ruled out on the grounds that he or she always has an ulterior motive, namely the profit motive'. The Guide's resolution of this dilemma is to reserve the word 'hospitable' for those institutions where the profit motive is better concealed than others but as I have already indicated, in so doing, it is forced to ignore those larger hotels which may provide their guests with exactly what they require in terms of service, comfort and efficiency. Telfer avoids this trap by arguing that 'if a commercial host looks after his guests well out of a genuine concern for their happiness and charges them reasonably rather than extortionately for what he does, his activities can be called hospitable . . . To say that a commercial host cannot be said to behave hospitably simply on the ground that he is paid for his work is like saying that doctors cannot be said to behave compassionately because they are paid for what they do'.

It's a neat point but I'm unhappy about that weasel word 'genuine'. How on earth are we to measure such 'genuine concern'? All we have to go on is the behaviour of the particular host and if this behaviour seems genuine enough to visiting guests, should the news that it was entirely learned during a six-week course on hospitality lead us to withdraw the epithet? What is important to hotel guests is surely a successful 'show of hospitality' in much the same way that patients visiting their local GP are delighted to find an appropriate display of compassion.

This perspective is fruitfully adopted by Jane Darke and Craig Gurney in their analysis of hospitality as performance. By drawing upon Goffman's theory of presentation they avoid the need to question the 'genuineness' or otherwise of the hospitality that is being offered. As far as Goffman is concerned all self-presentation is accomplished by recourse to a variety of techniques which have affinities with the way an actor successfully brings off a role on stage. There is no more point in asking whether the motive behind the hotelier's successful performance of hospitality is genuine than in seeking to discover whether or not John Gielgud really was Hamlet.

This perspective has two other advantages which are well exploited by Darke and Gurney. It allows for a very fruitful comparison between domestic and commercial hospitality in terms of what is required for successful accomplishment in both spheres as well as highlighting the dangers of the hospitality industry drawing too freely upon domestic metaphors. More importantly, it provides a basis for understanding the range of embarrassments and anxieties which lie around the practice of hospitality. As they write: 'The performance of hospitality is fragile and precarious'.

There's one other critical way in which Goffman helps us in the characterization of hospitality. At the centre of all his work on presentation and performance lies the notion of reciprocity and exchange. Visitors to a hotel are not merely passive observers of the staff's attempts to provide them with hospitality, they provide the conditions for that performance by colluding with the presentation. They have, in other words, a vested interest in the performance being successful in that its breakdown creates an embarrassment which denies them their chance to carry off their own role of hotel guest. The running joke in *Fawlty Towers* is not John Cleese's incapacity to perform successfully the role of hotel manager but the manner in which this failure creates havoc among guests who persist even in the face of the most appalling insults and provocation in continuing to cling to their own circumscribed role of hotel guest.

Although Brotherton and Wood do not draw upon Goffman in their conceptual chapter on hospitality and hospitality management, they are commendably insistent upon placing the idea of exchange (economic, social and psychological) at the heart of their synthesis. As they suggest, this emphasis promotes an 'exploration of trans-historical and cross-national studies of hospitality as well as immediately raising questions about the relationships between 'private/domestic and public/commercial hospitality'.

I hope I've said enough to indicate that I find much of the discussion in this text to be important and timely. There have been occasions in my regular column in the *Times Higher Education Supplement* when I've rather lazily used 'Hospitality Studies' as shorthand for all those new-found university courses which seem to be prompted rather more by student fashion and the requirements of the job market than any deep seated intellectual curiosity. I will take more care in future. This book amply demonstrates that the study of hospitality is as intellectually valid as any other area of human relations. It is also of the moment. The massive expansion of the tourist industry and the dramatic increase in the use of private homes as sites for dinner parties and weekend stopovers means that most of us are now regular consumers as well as purveyors of hospitality. Anyone who is curious about the implications of these developments for our notions of interpersonal reciprocity, gender relations, hyperreality, and public and private space now has a valuable work of reference. As essential hotel reading it sure as hell knocks spots off the Gideon Bible.

Laurie Taylor

Introduction

This book aims to both reflect and open up a number of debates between academics working in the field of 'hospitality management' and academics from the wider social sciences. As Airey and Tribe show in Chapter 15, hospitality management is a relatively new academic discipline that has been largely concerned with the hospitality industry. In many ways 'hospitality' has been used as a term to describe activities that were called 'hotel and catering' in earlier times. The study of 'hospitality' presents avenues of enquiry that the more prosaic title of hotel and catering tends to discourage yet which are essential for understanding host and guest relationships. When the possibilities are explored, hospitality and hospitableness can be studies in private and in wider social settings.

There have been a number of recent books dealing with food and social aspects of eating. For example, the work of Visser (1991), Mennel, *et al.* (1992), Wood, (1995), Beardsworth and Keil (1997) all address aspects of eating and meals. With few exceptions, these texts rarely touch on or mention hospitality and relationships between guests and host through a study of mutual obligations and the practice of hospitableness. Telfer's work (1996) and Heal's (1990) exploration of hospitality in early middle England are notable in providing analysis that can inform future study.

Current interest in defining hospitality as an academic subject outlined in this book stems from a meeting held in Nottingham in April 1997. The meeting aimed to explore subjects of common interest amongst some of the leading researchers and writers in

Hospitality, Leisure & Tourism Series

hospitality subjects within the UK. This text draws together some of the ideas both presented in discussion papers written by colleagues, and in some of the other texts mentioned earlier. The book is therefore exploratory, intended as a medium for dissemination, debate and future directions of work in the discipline.

By the very nature of the project, the contents are eclectic. Chapters have been commissioned, in some cases because authors were already working in a discipline that had a contribution to make about the nature of hospitality. In other cases, chapters have been volunteered by those involved in research activities that shed insights into the topic. In some cases, authors write from different philosophical and epistemological perspectives, and the book deliberately aims to reflect a plurality of views in which some individuals do not agree with others.

Our aim in selecting chapters has, therefore, been concerned with reflecting insights into the study of hospitality that encompass the commercial provision of hospitality and the hospitality industry, yet at the same time recognize that hospitality needs to be explored in a private domestic setting and studies hospitality as a social phenomenon involving relationships between people. It is our hope that these chapters will each in their own way encourage further research and study. The book is, therefore, not intended as the final word, but more a beginning from which the subject will develop and grow.

Conrad Lashley

School of Tourism and Hospitality Management, Leeds Metropolitan University

Alison Morrison

The Scottish Hotel School, University of Strathclyde

References

Beardsworth, A. and Keil, T. (1997) *Sociology on the Menu*. London, Routledge.

Heal, F. (1990) *Hospitality in Early Modern England*. Oxford, Clarendon Press.

Mennel, S., Murcott, A. and van Otterloo, A.H. (1992) *The Sociology of Food: Eating, Diet and Culture*. London, Sage.

Telfer, E. (1996) *Food for Thought: Philosophy and Food*. London, Routledge.

Visser, M. (1991) *The Rituals of Dinner*. Toronto, HarperCollins.

Wood, R.C. (1995) *The Sociology of the Meal*. Edinburgh, Edinburgh University Press.

Hospitality, Leisure & Tourism Series

About the authors

Amel Adib is a research student in the South Bank Business School at the University of the South Bank

David Airey is Professor of Tourism Management in the School of Management Studies for the Service Sector at the University of Surrey

Hazel Andrews is a research student in the Centre for Leisure and Tourism Studies at the University of North London

Stephen Ball is Principal Lecturer in Hospitality Management in the School of Leisure and Food Management at Sheffield Hallam University

David Botterill is Director of Research and Enterprise in the School of Hospitality, Tourism and Leisure at the University of Wales Institute, Cardiff

Bob Brotherton is Principal Lecturer in the Department of Hotel, Catering and Tourism Management at Manchester Metropolitan University

Jane Darke is Lecturer in Housing in the School of Planning at Oxford Brookes University

Craig Gurney is Lecturer in Housing at the Centre for Housing Management and Development at the University of Wales

Yvonne Guerrier is Professor and Head of the Division of Leisure and Tourism in the South Bank Business School at the University of the South Bank

Peter Jones is Forte Professor of Hotel Management in the School of Management Studies for the Service Sector at the University of Surrey

Keith Johnson is Professor of Human Resource Management in the Business School at the College of Ripon and St John

Conrad Lashley is British Institute of Innkeeping Professor in Licensed Retail Management in the School of Tourism and Hospitality Management at Leeds Metropolitan University

Andrew Lockwood is Professor of Hospitality Management in the School of Management Studies for the Service Sector at the University of Surrey

Paul Lynch is Senior Lecturer in the Department of Hospitality and Tourism Management at Queen Margaret's University College

Doreen MacWhannell is Senior Lecturer in the Department of Sociology at Queen Margaret's University College

Alison Morrison is Director of Research in the Scottish Hotel School at the University of Strathclyde

Sandie Randall is Senior Lecturer in the Department of Hospitality and Tourism Management at Queen Margaret's University College

Tom Selwyn is Professor of the Anthropology of Tourism, Centre for Leisure and Tourism Studies at the University of North London

Elizabeth Telfer is Reader in Philosophy in the Department of Philosophy at the University of Glasgow

John Tribe is Principal Lecturer in Tourism in the Faculty of Leisure and Tourism at Buckinghamshire Chilterns University College

John K. Walton is Principal Lecturer in Urban History in the Department of Historical and Cultural Studies at the University of Central Lancashire

Alistair Williams is Senior Lecturer in Marketing in the Division of Hospitality Studies at the University of Huddersfield

Roy C. Wood is Professor in Hospitality Management in the Scottish Hotel School at the University of Strathclyde

Towards a theoretical understanding

Conrad Lashley

School of Tourism and Hospitality Management,
Leeds Metropolitan University

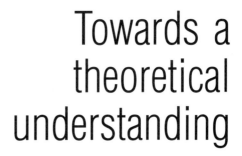

Key themes

- Background to the book
- Hospitality in the social domain
- Hospitality in the private domain
- Hospitality in the commercial domain

For a couple of decades now, both higher education providers and industrial organizations in English speaking countries have used 'hospitality' to describe a cluster of service sector activities associated with the provision of food, drink and accommodation. Reflecting changes in the industrial descriptor used by practitioners, both academic and industry journals have adopted the notion that hospitality was a term which better described activities which had previously been known as *hotel and catering*. The academic community have increasingly used 'hospitality' in degree course titles, and in several countries, educators describe their professional association using this term. Without wishing to explore the emergence of hospitality and its appeal to both practitioners and academics, it does open up potential avenues for exploration and research about hospitality which *hotel and catering* discourages. That said, the current research agenda and curriculum could still be described as hotel and catering under a new name. It is the contention of this chapter that the topic of hospitality is worthy of serious study and could potentially better inform both industrial practice and academic endeavour.

In the UK, several senior academics from universities across the country have been considering the meaning of hospitality as an academic discipline. This chapter attempts to co-ordinate and expand the themes which have been emerging from our discussions and papers written by various colleagues keen to build a theoretical framework for the study of 'hospitality' and hospitality management. There have been a number of attempts to define hospitality in the past, for example the work of Burgess (1982) explores some of the social psychology of mutuality and reciprocity associated with hospitality. Cassee (1984) suggests that the study of hospitality needs to be both multi-disciplinary and informed by an array of social sciences. More recently, the work of Heal (1990) examines issues associated with hospitality in early modern England. A number of writers not immersed in hospitality education have written other texts within the discipline of anthropology, sociology (Mennell *et al.*, 1992), philosophy (Telfer, 1996) and culture (Visser, 1991), though none have brought these contributions together into one unifying schema.

This chapter aims to distil some of the arguments and debates which have emerged amongst UK academics, and draw together other writings from the wider social sciences. It suggests a number of lines of enquiry for future research and indicates a range of perspectives that may further develop the discipline. Fundamentally, the industrial provision and management of hospitality services can be better focused when informed by a broad understanding of hospitality and acts of hospitableness. At root, studies need to establish a breadth of definition which allows analysis of hospitality activities in the 'social', 'private', and 'commercial' domains.

Background to the book

Several recent definitions of hospitality activities are interesting because they confirm the current preoccupation with commercial provision. The hospitality industry's umbrella organization, The Joint Hospitality Industry Congress, for example, defines hospitality in its 1996 report as *'The provision of food and/or drink and/or accommodation away from home'* (p.13). Similarly the Higher Education Funding Council – England's Hospitality Review Panel – defined hospitality as *'The provision of food and/ or drink and/or accommodation in a service context'*. Even the Nottingham group (see Introduction) started with a definition which stated that *'Hospitality is a contemporaneous exchange designed to enhance mutuality (well being) for the parties involved through the provision of food and/or drink, and/or accommodation'*. All these definitions are located in what academics have traditionally perceived of, researched, and taught about hospitality. It is a definition largely determined by hospitality as an economic activity – sets of consumers and suppliers, market niches, and occupations.

These definitions also, to varying degrees, reflect the origins of the academic study of hospitality as it is currently researched in universities and colleges. The HEFCE's (1998) *Review of Hospitality Management* was set up to explore the distinctiveness of the subject, and particularly the funding needs of programmes in this academic subject. At the time of the study, there were two somewhat contradictory strands of concern about the hospitality management provision in higher education. In some universities academics felt that hospitality management was not a suitable academic subject, it was 'just cooking' or 'learning how to boil an egg'. Other critics were not convinced that the subject was different from business studies and therefore required only the same levels of funding as straight management programmes. The HEFCE's report described hospitality management as '. . . a small but distinctive part of higher education provision which serves a large, rapidly growing and increasingly diverse industry' (Chairman's Summary).

The links between research activities by academics and the curriculum in hospitality management programmes, and the 'hospitality industry' is an important feature of the antecedents of the subject. Originally most managers within hotel, restaurant and catering businesses were developed through experiential

Hospitality, Leisure & Tourism Series

learning at work, and practical experience was highly valued in manager training. The first degree courses started in the late 1960s and reflected the wishes of many in the industry to combine a thorough appreciation of the industry's practical skills together with a suitable grasp of an array of management disciplines. In Chapter 15, Airey and Tribe's provide a detailed account of the origins of hospitality management programmes and the curriculum of programmes in the subject as these have been devised thus far.

As a result of the debates flowing from the Nottingham meeting (see Introduction), chapters provided by contributors from within and external to the hospitality management educational community have encouraged the consideration of hospitality in the wider social, anthropological and philosophical contexts. Thus hospitality can be conceived as a set of behaviours which originate with the very foundations of society. Sharing and exchanging the fruits of labour, together with mutuality and reciprocity, associated originally with hunting and gathering food, are at the heart of collective organization and communality. Whilst later developments may have been concerned with fear of and need to contain strangers, hospitality primarily involves mutuality and exchange, and thereby feelings of altruism and beneficence.

Fundamentally there is a need for a breadth of definition which allows analysis of hospitality activities in 'social', 'private', and 'commercial' domains. Put simply each domain represents an aspect of hospitality provision which is both independent and

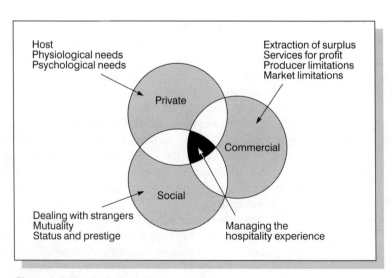

Figure 1.1 Hospitality activities.

Hospitality, Leisure & Tourism Series

overlapping. The *social domain* of hospitality considers the social settings in which hospitality and acts of hospitableness take place together with the impacts of social forces on the production and consumption of food/drink/and accommodation. The *private domain* considers the range of issues associated with both the provision of the 'trinity' in the home as well as considering the impact of host and guest relationships. The *commercial domain* concerns the provision of hospitality as an economic activity and includes both private and public sector activities.

Figure 1.1 attempts to show these relationships in visual form. This Venn diagram is perhaps somewhat crude, and may ultimately prove to be an early stage attempt to map these settings and the potential domains of the subject. The following discussion expands on the diagram and hopes to build an agenda through which the boundaries of hospitality can be extended.

Hospitality in the social domain

The social domain of hospitality activities suggests the need to study the social context in which particular hospitality activities take place. Writing about hospitality in early modern England, Heal (1990) makes an important general point, 'Whilst hospitality was often expressed in a series of private actions and a particular host, it was articulated in a matrix of beliefs that were shared and articulated publicly' (p.2). With the exceptions mentioned earlier (Burgess, 1983; Cassee, 1984) few hospitality academics have, until this text, considered hospitality and hospitableness from historical, cultural or anthropological perspectives. Again, consideration of hospitality and the value placed on being hospitable to strangers varies through time and between societies. Thus current perspectives and definitions of hospitality represent but one of a range of possibilities. This section aims to provide a flavour of some of the issues which might add theoretical perspectives to the study of hospitality and provision of food, and drink and accommodation.

Current notions about hospitality are a relatively recent development. In pre-industrial societies hospitality occupies a much more central position in the value system. In the UK and other Western societies, '... hospitality is preponderantly a private form of behaviour, exercised as a matter of personal preference within a limited circle of friendship and connection' (Heal, 1990, p.1). In contemporary pre-industrial societies, and earlier historical periods in developed Western societies, hospitality and the duty to entertain both neighbours and strangers represents more of a moral imperative. Frequently the duty to provide hospitality, act with generosity as a host and to protect visitors was more than a matter left to the preferences of individuals. Beliefs about hospitality and obligations to others were located in views and visions about the nature of society and the natural order of things. Thus any failure to act appropriately was treated with social condemnation. The centrality of hospitality activities have been noted in a wide range of studies of Homeric Greece, early Rome, medieval Provence, the Maori, Indian tribes of Canada, early modern England and Mediterranean societies (Heal, 1990). Selwyn (Chapter 2, this volume) notes that even in 'hunting and gathering communities' there are rituals and values associated with receiving strangers in to the band, reflecting 'a slight but significant act of hospitality signifying the acceptance by the band of a new member'.

One rich strand in the study of hospitality relates to the treatment of strangers. Beardsworth and Keil (1997) state, 'In all the social anthropological and historical accounts of traditional societies there is strong emphasis on the importance of hospitality. Such hospitality would extend to travellers (many societies had particularly strong culturally defined obligations to welcome strangers)' (p.101). Certainly anyone who has been the recipient of the lavish hospitality extended by people off the main tourist trails in southern European countries can testify to the genuine and universally shared cultural commitment to being hospitable to strangers. Heal (1990) states that there is a link between these societies' strong belief in the integrity of the household and the honour given to alien visitors as a way of expressing that belief.

The duty to not only be charitable to strangers but offer them protection is also an important feature of this strand of hospitality. In many cases this was seen as a sacred duty of the host to protect not only immediate family but also guests. In Bedouin communities, these duties were taken to include all threats to the guest, and this was extended to include relationships afterwards. People who had eaten salt together would not fight each other (Visser, 1991).

Heal (1990) also points to the significance of hospitality and particularly the treatment of travellers as an important value in early modern England. She reminds us of the status accorded to Julian the Hospitaller whose name was frequently invoked as an exemplar. Particularly, 'His qualities of charitable giving and selfless openness to the needs of other, were those constantly commended in late medieval and early modern England whenever hospitality was discussed' (1990, p.vii). Certainly contemporary audiences to Shakespeare's play would have recognized a dimension to Macbeth's regicide which would have made the crime more heinous, perhaps lost on modern audiences. That is,

Duncan is killed whilst a guest in Macbeth's house. Thus the villain is guilty of not only failing to protect his guest but actually doing him harm. The idea that the host has a solemn duty to protect the guest is well established in many myths and legends. Telfer reminds us of Wagner's opera *The Valkyrie* in which Hunding the jealous husband cannot kill Siegmund whilst the latter is a guest in his house. Siegmund must leave the house before Hunding can pursue him (Telfer, 1996).

The expression of hospitality in early modern England (1400–1700) had much in common with classical Rome. A powerful ideology of generosity was formulated in an *ius hospitii* but which was based on practical benefits. It assisted in the integration of strangers and through the inclusion of guests-friends formed a necessary part of the system of clientage. In both Rome and early modern England, 'good entertainment provided a necessary part of the everyday behaviour of leading citizens' (Heal, 1990, p.2). Even today in contemporary Turkey, many traditional families still lay an extra place at table, 'in case Allah sends us a stranger'.

Heal highlights a number of roles which hospitality played at the time. Apart from values relating to the treatment of strangers and travellers, hospitality played an important part in the local political economy. The redistributing food and drink to neighbours and to the poor helped to build social cohesion. Feasts played an important part in ensuring that mutuality and social obligation were met in medieval England, and the 'open door' was given high social value. Hospitality assisted in maintaining power relationships based on elite families; by feeding neighbours, tenants and the poor, the feudal lords were able to expect a mutual obligation from the recipient. Chapter 2 in this volume explores in more detail, the significance that hospitality plays, specifically the sharing and giving of food, in reproducing and reinforcing social relationships between status groups in society.

With one notable exception (Wood, 1995) hospitality academics have not engaged with sociological and cultural dimensions of human food and drink systems, nor with the role which the consumption of food and drink plays in communicating the consumer's position in the social world (Corrigan, 1997). Apart from the general cultural expectations about hospitality made above, Telfer (1996) states that ' . . . food is of central importance in hospitality' (p.83). First, related to the general duty to protect travellers, the needy and the unprotected, food is an essential part of what they need. Second, the giving and receiving of food is of a symbolic significance that hints at a bond of trust and closeness between host and guest. Apart from meals in domestic settings, the business lunch continues to have a symbolic role. Third, giving food is an act of friendliness. In particular, the added symbolic role of food and the rituals associated with it create an added significance to the occasion. In addition food needs to be a key element in academic study of hospitality because of the significance the avoidance of hunger and celebration of plenty plays in human social and cultural life.

The production and consumption of food and drink, and to a lesser extent accommodation, play a deep seated role in establishing important differences between human beings and the rest of the animal world. The role of food production, distribution and consumption, in particular, has significance in defining some essential features of 'humanness' and differentiates humans from other creatures. 'Civilisation itself cannot begin until a food supply is assured' (Visser, 1991, p.2). Fundamentally, the act of contributing to and sharing in the collective food supply are the foundations of obligations and rights which underpin hospitality: 'Sharing food is the foundation of civilised behaviour; it is what links individuals, families, villages and tribes' (Visser, 1991, p.53).

Activities associated with eating and drinking help to establish many basic human characteristics. Kinship and family groups are based round those who share and eat together. Language develops for discussing food and planning future supplies. Social rules and structures are established round the distribution of food and the ethical/moral principles to be applied. The application of technology in the gathering, preparing and consumption of food and drink is also a fundamental differentiating feature of human communities.

It is not incidental, for example, that even the most simple forms of hunting and gathering societies involve some rituals round food consumption. Feasts or fasts associated with particular religious ceremonies, times of the year, or other significant events; food taboos; or foods consumed by particular sections of the community are features of most societies. Patterns of food and drink consumption are some of the activities which assist societies in defining who they are, and in distinguishing 'civilized' behaviour.

Food and drink, in particular, perform an important role in defining the identities of groups, communities and societies, and in defining the relationship between individuals and the wider social context. 'You are what you eat' is a truth that extends beyond the nutritional. Through consumption of food and drink, and the rituals and norms associated with their consumption, individuals express their connectedness or disconnectedness with the wider community. Selwyn's ethnography of a Hindu meal in Chapter 2 provides a rich example of the role that feasts play in reflecting social status and differing roles in the social system. Frequently those who reject the values of the majority community symbolize their differentiation by exercising taboos on certain types of food and/or drink and/or accommodation (Beardsworth and Keil, 1997).

Given social expression in public arenas, individuals display both their connectedness to the society and display their culture and understanding of shared norms. Hospitality related activities, in the form of eating and drinking, provide opportunities for the social evaluation of individuals and for social and status displays. In addition, hospitality activities assist in the development of social bonds with others and the subsequent satisfaction of social needs. Similarly, in a domestic setting, individuals inviting strangers to their homes are meeting an array of social positioning and personal needs.

Anthropological and sociological studies of societies frequently describe them in terms of the means by which they produce food – hunters and gatherers, slash and burn farmers, herders, simple farming, etc. The current hospitality industry, for example, is fundamentally a feature of industrialization and the intensive farming methods which replace human and animal energy inputs with those of cheap but finite fossil fuels. The availability of cheap energy and food to the population of a small number of Western developed economies has had a fundamental impact not only on the growth of the tourism and hospitality industries, it has led to changes in diet both within these societies and globally (Corrigan, 1997).

In hierarchical societies, social class differences between people are frequently expressed in the way different groups consume food and drink, and accommodation. When food production is labour intensive and food relatively scarce, ruling elites often display their wealth in the form of obesity, or in the consumption of rare and exotic foods, and set the aspirations for the lower orders. In the past, a high meat diet was the luxury of a few but became available to more people through intensive farming methods. Paradoxically, in today's era of cheap and plentiful food in Western societies, it is socially fashionable to look to the diet of southern European peasants for low cholesterol and 'healthy' dishes. Similarly, travel and staying in paid for accommodation as status goods have become available to wider sections of society through reduced operating costs, though the patterns of consumption are often founded on images of elite consumption – the holiday in the sun – the room with ensuite facilities, etc. Again it is possible to detect some interesting trends in these experiences as those with perceived social status attempt to

Hospitality, Leisure & Tourism Series

distance themselves from other sections of community by the way they consume food and drink, and accommodation (Corrigan, 1997).

A study of the social domain of hospitality could provide some interesting theoretical perspectives through which to inform our understanding of the activities which comprise the hospitality industry. Clearly much current understanding is informed by economic concepts. It is possible to enrich these through an analysis of hospitality from sociological, anthropological and historical perspectives. Current notions of hospitality and consumption of hospitality goods and services can then be set against former historical periods and social situations.

Hospitality in the private domain

Most of the contributions to the study of hospitality have thus far tended to downplay the provision of food, drink and accommodation in domestic settings; this chapter asserts that hospitality academics need to include this private domestic arena in a number of ways. In Chapter 5, Darke and Gurney's piece on 'putting up' occasions confirms that the domestic and private arena involving essentially the nuclear family provides a key forum for social learning about hospitality activities. The nurturing and altruistic motives of those who cook, serve beverages, make beds, and create a safe environment, shape to some extent expectations of the non-domestic provision of hospitality activities. The provision of en suite and other room based facilities in hotels could be seen as a response to customers' demands for their own personal 'domestic' space in the hotel. Indeed the balance of usage between public and private areas of a hotel may reveal differences between social groups and differences in the degree of privateness which they value. The nuclear family introduces individuals to the rules, rituals, norms and mores which shape hospitality activities in a social setting. To better understand hospitality activities we need to understand the provision of food, drink and accommodation in the nuclear family.

The domestic setting in the provision of hospitality related activities can be the forum for the inter-relationship between the domestic and the social arenas. The receiving of guests into domestic settings provides opportunities for placing the individual and the family in a context of 'civilizedness'. To some extent, guests perform a role in evaluating the social connectedness of individuals and families. From the host's point of view these events provide opportunities for hosting, for social display, for developing social relationships, meeting social and status needs, etc. The receiving of guests therefore performs important social roles in binding individuals and groups together. Darke and Gurney show that these occasions can also be the source of tension and stress, where differing expectations of the rules and taboos result in behaviour that causes offence to the other party.

The private setting also helps us to consider some of the issues related to the meaning of hospitality, hosting and 'hospitableness'. The several definitions given above imply that hospitality involves supplying food, drink, and accommodation to people who are not members of the household. Obviously, much current research and published material focuses exclusively on the commercial, market exchange occurring between the recipient and supplier of hospitality, but the domestic setting is revealing because the parties concerned are performing roles which extend beyond narrow market relationships, with exception of those situations discussed in Chapter 6 by Lynch and McWhannell. The provision of food, drink and accommodation represents an act of friendship, it creates symbolic ties between people which establish bonds between those involved in sharing hospitality. As we have seen, in pre-industrial societies the receiving and kindly treatment of strangers was highly valued in most societies, though as Heal (1990) indicates, the motives were not always solely altruistic. Receiving strangers into the household helped to monitor the behaviour of strangers. Visser (1991) links the relationship between the host and the guest through the common linguistic root of the two words. Both originate from a common Indo-European word (*ghostis*) which means 'stranger' and thereby 'enemy' (hospitality and hostile have a similar root), but the link to this single term, 'refers not so much to the individual people, the guest and the host, as to the relationship between them' (p.91). It is a relationship based on mutual obligations and ultimately on reciprocity. Ultimately, the guest becomes the host on another occasion.

Telfer (1996) makes a valuable distinction between being a host and being hospitable. Being a good host implies more than specific behaviours such as ensuring drinks are full and guests have plenty to eat. It requires a genuine desire to please guests and make them happy. Hence, genuine hospitable behaviour requires 'an appropriate motive' and a hospitable person is thereby, 'someone who entertains often, attentively and out of motives appropriate to hospitality' (Telfer, 1996, p.86). These appropriate motives might include a desire for the company of other people, the pleasure of entertaining, the desire to please other people, concern or compassion to meet people's needs, and a perceived general duty to be hospitable. Ulterior motives might be concerned with trying to win favour with others, or seduce them, or, in commercial contexts, with winning greater exchange value. Is the attentive waiter, or manager, genuinely wanting to please the guest or just win a fatter tip, or bigger sale?

This distinction between being a good host and being hospitable is an important one. It opens up for discussion and analysis their motives and behaviour. It is possible, for example, for someone to be a good host, but not hospitable because the actions of the host may be driven by ulterior motives. Similarly, Telfer argues, the genuinely hospitable person may not be as skilful as a host with ulterior motives. 'Hospitable motives, are those in which concern for the guests' pleasure and welfare, for its own sake, is predominant ... And hospitable people, those who possess the trait of hospitableness, are those who entertain often for one or more hospitable motives ...' (1996, p.90).

The link between the domestic arena and hospitality activities is well established both in the historic origins of modern hotels, restaurants and pubs, and in the current practice in bed and breakfast establishments, and, moreover, the domestic nuclear setting also provides the venue for the commercial reception of guests. Specifically, the study of hospitality will be considerably enriched by an examination of hospitableness as a moral virtue and the ideal of hospitality. 'This ideal is found in a sense of the emotional importance of the home and food, and the special benefits which sharing them can bring' (Telfer, 1996, p.101).

Hospitality in the commercial domain

The commercial provision of hospitality takes place in most Western societies in a context where hospitality does not occupy a central position in the value system. For the most part hospitality is a private matter for individuals and there is no dominant requirement to be seen as beneficent or charitable. In some cases, acts of hospitality are entertained for calculative reasons; the business lunch, or office Christmas party are not primarily redistributive or undertaken for reasons which primarily value 'generosity and good behaviour as a host' (Heal, 1990, p.2).

In addition to this claim that hospitality is somewhat marginal to core values in Western industrial societies, there are those who would agree with Dr Johnson that, 'There is no private house in which people can enjoy themselves so well as at a capital tavern' (Telfer, 1996, p.101). The commercial and market driven relationship which allows the customer a freedom of action that individuals would not dream of demanding in a domestic setting is one of the benefits claimed for the 'hospitality industry'.

Guerrier (1997) for example argues that the lack of hospitality and anonymity of large hotels is in part their attraction. Thus 'guests' can use the facilities without fear of mutual obligation to the host other than those demanded of the market relationship, that is, to pay the bill. Telfer suggests that although it is possible to feel some sympathy for these views, 'This kind of hospitality is not very hospitable' (1996, p.101). On receiving genuine hospitality, the individual feels genuinely wanted and welcome. This is not the same as being welcomed as a valued customer.

Clearly our current concerns are, in part, to establish a robust understanding of the breadth and significance of hospitality related activities so that we can better understand their commercial application. Without wishing to deny the benefits that commercial provision of hospitality activities brings in the form of opportunities for travel, intercourse with others, etc., the commercial provision of hospitality activities is chiefly driven by the need to extract surplus value from the exchange. That commercial 'capitalistic' imperative creates a number of tensions and contradictions that become apparent when we develop a better understanding of the 'social' and the 'private' domains of hospitality activities. At root, the 'hospitality industry' suggests 'an immediate paradox between generosity and the market place' (Heal, 1990, p.1).

Commercial providers are often attempting to square circles, or at least provide hospitality, *but not too much*, in their operations. Harvester Restaurants supplies an interesting example of the paradox. The instruction given to the front of house personnel was, 'Treat the customers as though they were guests in your own home'. Bearing in mind links with the private domain of hospitality it is possible to understand the thinking, but the needs of a modern branded business for strict brand, portion and cost control limit the hospitality experience for both the server and the served. It would be a pretty rum domestic host who offered a guest another glass of wine so long as they paid for it. The difficulties that many branded hospitality service operators face in offering a brand which meets guest security needs yet at the same times meets customers' desires to be provided with personalized service is one outcome of the tensions present in commercialized hospitality.

Commercial hospitality provision depends on a reciprocity based on money exchange and limits on giving pleasure to guests which ultimately impact on the nature of hospitable behaviour and the experience of hospitality. Both host and guest enter the hospitality occasion with a reduced sense of reciprocity and mutual obligation. For the host, motives for being hospitable are mostly ulterior, the desire to supply just that amount of hospitality that will ensure guest satisfaction, limit complaint and hopefully generate a return visit whilst turning a profit. For the guest, there is little sense of the mutual obligation of the domestic context. The guest rarely has a sense that roles will be reversed and that guest will become host on another occasion. The exchange of money absolves the guest of mutual obligation, and loyalty.

At the same time many commercial hospitality providers are desperate to establish a substantial base of loyal customers. Though estimates vary, every sector of the hospitality industry reports that there are substantial savings to be gained from building repeat business from existing customers. Carper (1992) estimated that in the hotel sector it costs seven times more to attract new customers to the business than to attract existing customers. Similarly, customer reactions to service breakdown can be very costly when customers operate in the context of non-mutuality and loyalty. The market place relationship encourages many customers to seek an alternative supplier when they encounter a service problem. One estimate suggested that it costs an average of £11,032 for every lost customer in the licensed retailing sector (Leach, 1995).

Clearly, individual hospitality organizations can not change the social domain of hospitality nor run their operations as in the private domain, but they might be better able to build a community of customers more robustly loyal if they better understood hospitality in these contexts. For example, the mutuality of the elite and their 'subjects' was closely linked to values of generosity, beneficence and reciprocity. Without wishing to suggest that profit driven organizations would be willing to give away product, a judicious consideration of how regular customers can be rewarded with extra benefits which celebrate their importance and uniqueness as individuals could be successful. The key here is to making the giving seem like acts of genuine generosity rather than the formulaic 'give-aways' typical of many branded hospitality businesses.

In the same way, consideration of the distinction between being a host and being hospitable can be important for developing loyal customer relationships. Developing staff and management in the values of hospitableness could be useful in overcoming the commercially imposed impression of calculative hosting. Identifying, recruiting, developing and empowering individuals to be hospitable will be essential in building a sound base of loyal customers.

In the hospital catering sector, there has been recognition that the catering services need to understand and link back to patients' experiences in the private domain of hospitality. Hepple *et al.* (1990) demonstrate the importance of helping patients to 'feel at home' for reducing patient anxiety and aiding recovery through the provision of hospitality services.

These tensions and contradictions, touched on very briefly above, are fundamental to understanding the difficulties which hospitality industry operators and customers face. The use by providers of an array of controlling, quality assurance, hosting, marketing, human resource and management techniques in part stem from the nature of the commercial exchange where both the host and guest enter a relationship which requires little mutuality and reciprocity.

Conclusions

Industrial and commercial definitions such as those articulated by the Joint Hospitality Industry Congress (1996) and the Higher Education Funding Council – England (1998) are useful in that they describe a cluster of services provided by a variety of organizations in different sectors of the industry. These definitions are essentially economic in that they describe hospitality through the supply of goods and services. They help establish an understanding of the similarities and differences between hospitality provision in different sectors and encourage the consideration of the service context in which hospitality takes place. That said, these economic definitions are essentially limited and flawed by their preoccupation with the here and now.

A wider understanding of hospitality suggests firstly that hospitality is essentially a relationship based on host and guest. To be effective, hospitality requires the guest to feel that the host is being hospitable through feelings of generosity, a desire to please, and a genuine regard for the guest as an individual. Consequently, calculative hosting where the guest senses an ulterior motive can be counterproductive. This chapter has argued that some of the difficulties experienced by hospitality providers in retaining customers can be explained in these terms.

A second point flowing from this wider understanding is that the current commercial provision of hospitality provides but one avenue for the exploration of hospitality. The social domain assists in setting the study of hospitality and the component elements in a wider social context. The value placed on being hospitable, caring for strangers, assisting the poor and providing hospitality to those in need, within a society's value system, is an additional and fruitful line of enquiry. Similarly, the relationship between guest and host still takes place in private settings. These private domestic settings can be revealing because many of the commercial operations have grown from early domestic settings. The private domain of hospitality continues to be an important forum for establishing commonality, mutuality and reciprocity between host and guest.

A third reason for developing this wider understanding of hospitality activities flows from this second point, namely, current expressions of hospitality in Western industrial societies represent but one of a number of possibilities. The wider study of hospitality in both contemporary pre-industrial settings and earlier historical periods could reveal much to better understand current hospitality activities.

Bearing in mind these points, the definition devised by Brotherton and Wood in Chapter 8 has much to commend it. 'A contemporaneous human exchange, which is voluntarily entered into, and designed to enhance the mutual well being of the parties concerned through the provision of accommodation, and/or food, and/or drink.' This definition does allow for a focus which considers the relationship between guest and host, though it does limit consideration of the notion of reciprocity. It may also discourage consideration of hospitality in a wider social and private setting. As a starting point however, the definition has value. It is hoped that future discussion and debate will further build a definition to be used as the basis for the future academic discipline of hospitality.

This chapter has attempted to indicate how the study on hospitality in a wider context enriches and enhances the study of commercial applications of hospitality activities. There may be those in the practitioner community who regard these discussions as arcane and somewhat sterile. Hopefully, there will be others, however, who see the potential benefits of academics following lines of enquiry that establish hospitality as a robust academic discipline. Bringing together academics from both the hospitality management field and the broader social sciences represents an important step towards establishing a theoretical framework for the study of hospitality in all its domains.

References

Beardsworth, A. and Keil, T. (1997) *Sociology on the Menu.* London, Routledge.

Burgess, J. (1982) Perspectives on gift and exchange in hospitable behaviour. *International Journal of Hospitality Management*, **1**, No. 1, 49–59.

Carper, J. (1992) Strategies for winning guests in competitive times. *Hotels,* March, No. 52, pp.76–9.

Cassee, E.T. (1984) *The Management of Hospitality.* Oxford, Pergamon Press.

Corrigan, P. (1997) *The Sociology of Consumption.* London, Sage.

Gannon, J. (1997) Sophie's World of Hospitality: in search of the concept, unpublished chapter to the Hospitality Research Group, University of Strathclyde.

Guerrier, Y. (1997) Of Guests, Customers and Consumers: images of hotels and restaurants, unpublished chapter to the Hospitality Research Group, University of Strathclyde.

Heal, F. (1990) *Hospitality in Early Modern England.* Oxford, Clarendon Press.

Hepple, J., Kipps, M. and Thomson, J. (1990) The concept of hospitality and an evaluation of the applicability to hospital patients. *International Journal of Hospitality Management,* **9**, No. 4, 305–18.

Higher Education Funding Council – England (1998) *Review of Hospitality Management.* London, Higher Education Funding Council – England.

Joint Hospitality Industry Congress (1996) *Hospitality into the 21st Century: a vision for the future.* London, Joint Hospitality Industry Congress.

Leach, P. (1995) The importance of positive customer service to Ansell's. *Managing Service Quality, 5,* No. 4, 31–4.

Lucas, R. (1997) Hospitality: some conceptual and theoretical considerations, unpublished chapter to the Hospitality Research Group, University of Strathclyde.

Mennel, S., Murcott, A. and van Otterloo, A.H. (1992) *The Sociology of Food: eating, diet and culture.* London, Sage.

Morrison, A. (1997) Hospitality – the Humpty Dumpty Syndrome, unpublished chapter to the Hospitality Research Group, University of Strathclyde.

Telfer, E. (1996) *Food for Thought: Philosophy and Food.* London, Routledge.

Visser, M. (1991) *The Rituals of Dinner.* Toronto, HarperCollins.

Wood, R.C. (1995) *The Sociology of the Meal.* Edinburgh, Edinburgh University Press.

Wood, R.C. (1997) Hospitality and Hospitality Management: no more false dawns?, unpublished chapter to the Hospitality Research Group, University of Strathclyde.

An anthropology of hospitality

Tom Selwyn
The Business School, University of North London

Key themes

- Structures and functions of hospitality
- Hospitality and moral obligations
- Virtues and pleasures
- Hospitality and its symbolic materials

This chapter offers a social anthropological view of hospitality. An opening section briefly considers the purpose and social function of hospitality and then offers some comparative historical and ethnographic material on the subject. Some preliminary comments are made about the social, ritual and cognitive structures within which acts of hospitality are carried out. A second section considers the importance to the practice of hospitality of food. This is illustrated and developed mainly from one ethnographic example, and the chapter ends by returning to more general themes of hospitality's structural organization.

Structures and functions of hospitality

The basic function of hospitality is to establish a relationship or to promote an already established relationship. Acts of hospitality achieve this in the course of exchanges of goods and services, both material and symbolic, between those who give hospitality (hosts) and those who receive it (guests). Since relationships necessarily evolve within moral frameworks, one of the principal functions of any act of hospitality is either (in the case of an existing relationship) to consolidate the recognition that hosts and guests already share the same moral universe or (in the case of a new relationship) to enable the construction of a moral universe to which both host and guest agree to belong.

Acts of hospitality thus either consolidate structures of relations by symbolically affirming them, or (in the case of the establishment of a new framework of relations) are structurally transformative. In the latter case givers and/or receivers of hospitality are (in each other's eyes at any rate) not the same after the event as they were before. Hospitality converts: strangers into familiars, enemies into friends, friends into better friends, outsiders into insiders, non-kin into kin. These principles find expression in ethnographic descriptions of a wide variety of social systems.

Ethnographers of hunting and gathering societies (Woodburn, 1968; Tanaka, 1980, for example), make much of the fluidity and flexibility of the bands which make up the social structure. People customarily leave one group and join another more or less as they please. But, relatively unmarked as it is in comparison with other societies, the business of joining a group is normally accompanied by a small symbolic 'announcement', if it may be described as such, consisting of the newcomer establishing his/her right to share a part of the food of an existing band member, a slight but significant act of hospitality signifying the acceptance by the band of a new member.

By comparison the much more elaborate systems of feasting amongst societies as far apart as the New Guinea Highlands and the Amazon forest (Strathern, 1984; Chagnon, 1992, for example) serve comparable functions. In these cases feasting, and the hospitality it signifies, consolidates and/or establishes links between groups of kin, and is an integral part of the processes of drawing and re-drawing the parameters of alliances between such groups.

The practices of hospitality in such societies as these, however, reveal another of its general features, namely a close kinship with its opposite. In both the Highlands and the Amazon, hospitality is found at one pole of a continuum at the other end of which is warfare. Feasts can sometimes turn into fights. Acceptance and incorporation may rapidly become transformed into hostility, rejection, and even expulsion. However, as Brown (1980) has argued in the case of feasting and warfare in New Guinea, such apparent contradiction should not surprise us, for, to put it simply, both hospitality and hostility imply the possibility of the other. None the less (we may add, *en passant*) this contradiction itself reveals a continuity, for hospitality and hostility have in common the fact that both are expressions of the existence, rather than the negation, of a relationship.

The associations of hospitality with hostility have long been noticed by ethnographers of pastoralist societies. Authors such as Evans-Pritchard (1940) or Peters (1990), for example, writing of pastoralist societies in north and north-east Africa, where feuding is idiomatic, located hospitality at the heart of systems of social order in societies lacking hierarchical systems of authority. Thus the 'peace in the feud' which Gluckman (1973) famously discovered amongst pastoralists is achieved, precisely, through the currency of hospitality and the networks of supportive relations to which an act of hospitality gives rise.

Work in the Mediterranean by authors such as Boissevain and Mitchell (1973) or Gellner and Waterbury (1977) have shown how hospitality articulates networks of kin and friends in social structures organized around such networks. In such settings, as in the kind of local politics described in central India by Mayer (1960), hospitality serves to create and/or consolidate patterns of allegiances and alliances in political structures built upon patron–client relations. This last is arguably one of the functions of hospitality which is most familiar to those inhabiting the circles of twentieth century professional and bourgeois Europe – from within whose embrace Max Beerbohm (1920; quoted in Pritchard, 1981) observed that:

In every human being one or the other of these two instincts is predominant: the active or positive instinct to offer hospitality and the negative or passive instinct to accept it. And either of these instincts is so significant of character that one might well say that mankind is divisible into two great classes: hosts and guests.

The particular case of English hospitality has been examined by Heal (1990) who has traced the career of hospitality in that country from the early modern period to the present. She observes that in seventeenth century England the virtues of hospitality were highly regarded. It was a popular subject in the sermons and writings of priests, scholars and others in the chattering classes. Its origins not only in the Bible but in classical Greece and Rome, where it occupied a central place in social life, were rehearsed.

In contemporary Britain, by contrast, the importance accorded to hospitality has waned considerably – except, of course, in the commercial sphere. Nevertheless, Heal argues that five under-lying principles have governed English hospitality during the period. These are: (i) that the relationship between host and guest is a 'natural' one (i.e. that it is grounded in the nature of social life); (ii) that an intrinsic part of being a host is having regard for the sacred nature of the guest (which refers, broadly, to the honour and status which a guest may bring to the host); (iii) that hospitality is noble; (iv) that altruistic giving is an established and expected part of English social life; and (v) that hospitality and the social relationships and exchanges it engenders are at least as important as those formed in the market place (p.22). We may see for ourselves how some of these ideas have been expressed.

Hospitality as moral obligation

From (at least) the seventeenth century, exploration of the origins of hospitality in the Judeo-Christian tradition was a favoured subject of sermons. Henry Cornwallis (1694), for example, wrote a sermon entitled Set on the Great Pot: A sermon upon hospitality which took its title from the passage in 2 Kings 4: 38 'And he said to his servant, set on the great pot, and feed pottage for the sons of the prophets'. He begins by half apologizing for the apparent 'light and airy' nature of this chosen subject (his address was directed to some distinguished Justices of the Peace as well as the Deputy Lieutenant of Suffolk) but draws their attention to the fact that the prophet Elijah himself was famous for the hospitality afforded to his guests. Since 'They were sons of prophets', he asks, 'will you disdain what they accepted'?

Hospitality, Leisure & Tourism Series

For Cornwallis hospitality was a duty 'injoined on all Christians ... from the laws of nature, from the scripture, and from examples of good men' (p.8). As to its roots in nature, Cornwallis observed that 'the antients called our kindess to strangers ... humanity ... and banished inhospitable men for the society of mankind, and ranked them among the wolves and tygers' (p.10). He identified one of the scriptural origins in the Book of Exodus (22: 21): 'Thou shalt do no injury to strangers', an injunction which he explained in relation to the slavery of the ancient Hebrews in the land of Egypt. This was an experience, he added, which gave rise to Jewish attachment to the value of hospitality, as they would not do to others what was done to themselves. Cornwallis listed a number of famously hospitable persons, including Abraham and Lot (Genesis 18 and 19) and Publius (Acts 28) who entertained Paul for three days, in return for which Paul cured his host's father-in-law of a fever (15). Spicing his argument with reference to the substantial reciprocity to which hospitality gives rise, Cornwallis concluded by bending the ears of his rich and powerful audience with the following aphorism: 'He that giveth to the poor lendeth to the Lord, who gives double interest for the money, and rewards us with temporal and eternal blessings' (p.19).

In 1674 'A Lover of Hospitality' published a sermon on 'The Charitable Christian'. The writer took the theme from Psalms 41: 1–3: 'Blessed is he that considereth the poor. The Lord will deliver him in the time of trouble. The Lord will preserve him and keep him alive, and he shall be blessed upon the earth. The Lord will strengthen him upon the bed of languishing, and will make his bed in his sickness.' The theme of the inbuilt reciprocity within any act of hospitality is emphasized: 'Cast thy bread upon the waters, and after many days thou shalt find it'. Such a reward is contrasted with the fate of the unmerciful man whose character is 'cruel and unnatural' (p.5).

We can find these themes in sermons of the eighteenth century. In 1740, for example, the Welsh priest John Nichol read a sermon at Christ Church, Newgate Street, London, entitled Ancient British Hospitality. Taking inspiration from Verse 13 of Romans Chapter 12 in which the Romans are exhorted by Paul to distribute to the necessity of saints and be given to hospitality, Nichol made the crucial distinction between the Christian value of charity ('discourses on which abound in this city') and that of hospitality, which means charity towards strangers (p.5). He also claimed that the English compound *hospitality* derived not only from the Latin but also from the ancient British practice of giving *house-room* to strangers and by 'entertaining them in a bountiful manner, by making merry with them and being glad' (p.9).

Over a hundred years later hospitality was still being discussed in terms of the spiritual benefits to be derived from providing hospitality to others. In 1869, for example, Madeline Leslie's *The Pearl of Diligence* contained a short story entitled 'Hospitality'. One day Tommy rushed into the kitchen and asked his mother whether they should set the dog on an old woman sitting on a log outside the house on the grounds that she might be a thief. Esther, Tommy's sister, admonished her brother for such a shameful thought and, encouraged by her mother, went out and gave the old woman a glass of cold water. In return the old woman said 'I will tell you what the Lord once said about a cup of cold water – whosoever shall give to one of his people a cup of cold water only, in the name of a disciple, he shall in no wise lose his reward' (p.63). Esther felt happy with this response 'for the blessing of the poor fell upon her'.

Similar sentiments were recorded in Christian Burke's (1896) story 'Given to Hospitality' in which the relationship between the heroine, a Mrs Moore, and her neighbour, Maria Speke, was explored. The pair lived in the East End of London, but while the former and her husband, through small but daily acts of Christian charity 'went their friendly way, and slowly but surely gain(ed) an influence and a power for good in their little neighbourhood, Maria Speke remained at her window, grim and disapproving – yet with a tiny warm corner thawing in her sad, frozen, heart'. Eventually (of course) Maria comes across the biblical passage 'I was an hungred, and ye gave me meat, I was thirsty and ye gave me drink, I was a stranger and ye took me in' whereupon (of course) a 'light flashed' and Maria changed her ways. Later the parish priest describes Mrs Moore to his daughter as 'Given to hospitality' and observes that when he visits her he comes away convinced that his parish is full of angels.

Virtues and pleasures

Cornelius Walford, a scholarly but clearly congenial barrister/ historian and member of the Sette of Odd Volumes read an opuscula he had written, entitled The Rights, Duties, Obligations, and Advantages of Hospitality, to his companion members at the Freemasons' Tavern one February evening in 1885. Prefacing his talk with Horace's dictum *Dulce est desipere in loco* ('how delightful it is to play the fool when we're out of school'), Walford began in fairly sober fashion by laying before his audience some of the background of the practice of hospitality. He began by reminding the company that in the Homeric period, a stranger was given a warm foot bath, with food and wine, and that it was not until the dessert was being offered that the question of his name, country and business were broached. He then pointed up the Biblical references to hospitality (in the books of Genesis, Exodus, Judges, Job, and the New Testament books of Acts and Romans), asserting that such English institutions as the Hospitals of Noble Poverty, medieval soup kitchens, and the medieval guilds themselves, looking after as they did the poor, sick and old, were amongst 'the great social institutions of the Middle-Ages' (p.30). Walford also drew his audience's attention to the etymology of the term hospitality and some of the terms associated with it. Host, for example, derived from the Latin *hostis* (enemy) and hospital from the Latin *hospes*, guest. A hospital was originally a house of entertainment for pilgrims, and the duty of hospitallers such as the Knights Hospitallers (later the Knights of Malta), for example, was to provide pilgrims with *hospitium* (lodging and entertainment).

As the evening in the Freemasons' Tavern wore on, however, Walford introduced the idea of hospitality having sides and aspects to it which went, so to speak, beyond virtue, being associated as they were with the pleasing characteristics of excess, variety and pleasure. He introduced his audience to the Lord of Misrule or the Abbot of Unreason, as the Scots named him – the Master of Ceremonies responsible for the management of feasts at court in the Middle Ages. To give this role, and the atmosphere surrounding it, a nineteenth century resonance he came up with a report that, in a recent examination in Woolwich, students had been asked the question: 'Give the meanings of abiit, excessit, erupit, evasit'. One student had come up with the answer that the meanings were as follows: abiit – he went out to dine, excessit – he took more than was good for him, erupit – it violently disagreed with him, evasit – he put it down to the salmon. Walford then flourished some frothy descriptions, from a selection from 'old chroniclers' of Norman and Saxon banquets in the baronial halls of the time. These were splendid affairs for:

> All sorts of people there were seen together.
> All sorts of characters, all sorts of dresses:
> The fool, the fox's tail and peacock's feather;
> Pilgrims and penitents, and grave burgesses;
> The country people, with their coats of leather;
> Vinters and victuallers, with cans and messes;
> Grooms, archers, varlets, falconers, and yeomen;
> Damsels, and waiting-maids, and waiting women

And what did this company consume?

> Hogsheads of honey, kilderkins of mustard,
> Muttons and fatted beeves and bacon swine,
> Herons and bitterns, peacocks, swans and bustards,
> Teal, mallard, pigeon, widgeon, and, in fine,
> Plum-puddings, pancakes, apple-pies, and custards;
> And withal they drank old Gascon wine.

All this was done with due deference to hierarchy and social status, for 'The rich man sat at the top, and the poor man at the bottom; rank asserted itself by remaining above the salt-cellar and allowing poverty to eat and drink below it'.

But Walford was ultimately no romantic, for he also observed that such sumptuous living as these passages imply was only one side of the picture in a country which was also subject to famine, periods of great scarcity, warfare, domestic feuds, and resultant modes of hospitality which were shaped and straightened by circumstances such as these.

Nevertheless hospitality seems often to be associated not only with benevolence and good works but also with the pleasures, both of the table and the post-prandial night-time activities which followed:

> When the hours of rest approached, I was conducted by my kind host and hostess into a back apartment, where was an ancient but excellent bed. A ceremony now took place which exhibits in the strongest light the hospitality and innocent simplicity of the Icelandic character. Having wished me a good night's rest my hosts departed, leaving their eldest daughter to assist me in pulling off my pantalons and stockings . . . When I got into bed she brought a long board, which she placed before me to prevent my falling out, and, depositing a basin of new milk close to my side bade me good night.
> (Quoted in Langley and Moore (1933), p.195)

As might have been expected, the experience of the Great Depression in the USA focused concerned minds on the more prosaic needs of the poor and needy. A movement grew up in the 1930s around a campaigning paper called *The Catholic Worker* (taking its name from *The Communist Daily Worker*). The aim of the campaign was to revive the medieval idea of the House of Hospitality and actually to provide and organize such houses where food could be dispensed to the unemployed. The chronicler of the movement recalls some of the underlying precepts of the movement as they appeared in the form of maxims by Peter, its founder, and as slogans in poetic form in *The Catholic Worker* itself:

> Modern Society calls the beggar bum and panhandler
> and gives him the bum's rush,
> But the Greeks used to say that people in need
> are the ambassadors of the gods.
> Mahometan teachers tell us that God commanded
> hospitality
> And hospitality is still practised in Mahometan
> countries,
> But the duty of hospitality is neither taught nor prac-
> tised in Christian countries.

To which observation Peter offered the following stirring response:

> Catholic scholars have taken the dynamite of the
> church;
> They have wrapped it up in nice phraseology,
> Have placed it in an hermetically sealed container
> And sat on the lid.
> It is about time to take the lid off,
> And to make the Catholic dynamite dynamic.
>   (Quoted in Day, 1939)

Where have we got to so far? Acts of hospitality serve as one means of articulating social structures. They provide the symbolic means to enable people to leave and join social groups and for hierarchical structures to be at once celebrated and legitimated. As we said early on, one of the main functions of hospitality is to make friends and familiars out of strangers and enemies. Mention of this serves to draw hospitality's 'twin sister', hostility, out of the shadows. But an initial surprise that these two should so closely be related is lessened by the realization that both are alternative means of asserting a relationship with another. In this view the 'opposite' of giving hospitality is not so much making war but choosing simply to ignore the other's existence.

But hospitality is associated with some further rather surprising looking couplings. While undoubtedly the outcome of moral obligations (which are defined and underwritten by doctrinal and ethical injunctions), there is a sense that just around the corner from any act of hospitality there await various kinds of pleasures, including those of transgression and excess, which go well beyond the call of duty. Furthermore, while the essence of hospitality lies in sharing (food, lodging, entertainment), the very process of sharing may involve dominating too: the expression 'below the salt' has not yet entirely dropped out of the barbed lexicon of those in contemporary bourgeois society wishing to undermine a person's social standing. Finally, as Heal (1990) has so effectively emphasized, hospitality is, by definition, concerned with such values as honour and status, the quasi-sacred character of both guest and host, and the embeddedness of this relation in the nature of things. It is thus, also by definition, to be found in a realm which is quite distinct from that other sphere in which social relations are reduced to the level of the market place.

Hospitality and its symbolic materials

Hospitality proceeds by giving and receiving. What, we may now consider, is it that is exchanged and where do the exchanges take place? To answer this we may take the two staple ingredients of hospitality, food and honour. To start with food, the best known and most popular treatment by an anthropologist of the symbolic functions of food is Mary Douglas' (1970) analysis of the Jewish food laws as these are listed and explained in the Old Testament book of Leviticus. Ostensibly, neither this book, nor Douglas' analysis of it, are concerned directly with hospitality. But, insofar as they have to do with what may be eaten and with whom, both are full of implications for the understanding of hospitality.

The ancient Hebrews were not only forbidden to eat certain species of animal but also, as are contemporary Jews, enjoined to prepare food, serve and receive it, in particular ways. The laws are thus central to the proper conduct of any family meal and the relation between the familial host and the guests who share the family meal. Douglas' famous argument is that those creatures which the Hebrews were forbidden to eat (pigs, shellfish, and so forth) were in some definable ways not 'complete' or 'whole' members of their species or class. Fish should be proper fish (creatures who swim in the water), birds proper birds (creatures who fly in the air), ruminants proper ruminants (i.e. cud chewing beasts which also have cloven hooves) and so on. A hard-backed creature which scuttles sideways along beaches and mudflats, for example, can hardly be called a proper fish.

The defining characteristic of food fit for eating and sharing, Douglas argues, is that it should be a complete member of its class: hybrids are not acceptable. The point is that the wholeness and completeness of the creature eaten signifies the wholeness and completeness of those doing the eating: the eating of proper food demonstrates complete membership of the group. The more general point for us here is that the mutual acceptance at a Jewish table by host and guest of a culturally authorized commensal code serves to affirm a common identity. This is what is achieved when the head of the family serves an appropriately prepared meal of appropriate food to familial guests. The moral framework established by proper obedience to the food laws serves to bind the members of a family to each other and the family to the wider community whose members share the code. It also separates both from others who do not share the code. We may emphasize at this point that the food laws do not necessarily exclude anyone from accepting hospitality from a Jewish host on grounds that they do not themselves belong to the Jewish community. Guests of any religious or cultural affiliation may thus be made welcome provided they are prepared to follow the food rules. Thus although non-Jewish guests would not normally be expected to bring gifts of food to the meal (as Jewish guests may be asked to do), there is no barrier to them being invited as guests to the meal itself. What really matters is the symbolic acceptance by guests of the moral authority of the host on that particular occasion.

Douglas' treatment of the Jewish food laws is mirrored in her analysis (1975) of the eating habits of contemporary Western and Christian Europe. She suggests, for example, that all types of meals, from quick snacks at work to more formal Sunday meals *en famille*, need to be understood as part of the annual commensal cycle at the centre of which is the Christmas family feast and, ultimately, the sharing of the paschal lamb at the Christian Eucharist. In this light, the sharing by the guest of a family meal of a Christian household on Sunday, and even more particularly of a Christmas meal, amounts to an affirmation of kinship and community not only with the familial hosts but, through their mediation, with the Holy family itself. These examples introduce us to the idea of food as a symbolic means of defining identity. In order more fully to explore this relationship and, at the same time, to provide some ethnographic groundwork which will later allow a discussion on the relationship between hospitality and honour, we may now turn to the case of hospitality in an Indian village. The ethnography is taken from work carried out in the central Indian village of Singhara by the present author (Selwyn, 1980).

Hospitality in an Indian village: the case of an inter-caste feast

One occasion at which the rules and practices of Hindu hospitality in a rural setting are most manifest is on an occasion marking an important occasion in the life of a family (such as a marriage or thanksgiving) or of a village (such as the establishment of a temple). At such a time, a patron of means (which does not necessarily imply one of high caste) may organize an inter-caste feast to which representatives of all castes, from the highest to the lowest, may be invited. For reasons which will shortly become clear, however, for invitations to such occasions to be accepted by all, including the highest castes, the actual cooks at the feast need to be Brahmans. In order to appreciate the subtlety of the symbolic processes on an occasion such as this, we need, first of all, to explore a little of the social and commensal architecture.

In Singhara village there are people who claim membership in some 21 different castes. Each of these castes (*jatis*) is thought (approximately) be placed within the four-fold hierarchically organized division consisting of the classical *Varnas* (literally 'colours') or caste categories. These consist of *Brahmans* (priests), *Kshatryas* (warriors/rulers), *Vaishyas* (business castes) and *Sudras* (servant castes). For the purposes of the present example, I propose to name these caste categories blocks I, II, III and IV.

Just as the population of the village is divided up hierarchically into these four blocks of castes, so food itself is also divided into various categories. In the context of the sort of inter-caste feast we are about to describe, these food categories are also thought of hierarchically in terms of the degree to which each category is thought to absorb, and thus transmit either the purity and auspiciousness, or the impurities and inauspiciousness, of those handling the food at any stage of its preparation and/or transfer from one person to another. For the sake of this case study, we may distinguish six types of food. 'Raw food' (raw and untreated grain and/or vegetables) is thought to be almost impermeable to the impurities of those who handle items in this category. 'Dry food' (betel nut and cigarettes, for example) is slightly more permeable. 'Wet food' (such as water, tea and *pan*, betel nut and lime chewed in the mouth) is thought to be more permeable still, while fried food (such as fried vegetables, *puris*, and/or *chapatis* fried in *ghi*, clarified butter) is only one category short of the most permeable category of cooked food, namely boiled food (boiled rice). Beyond these categories of raw and cooked food there are two further categories of substances whose importance to the symbolism of a feast will become clear below. *Jutha*, the left-overs given at the end of a feast, is, not unnaturally, thought even more permeable than boiled food while faeces (which, if we look at it from a certain point view is simply food 'transformed' by being eaten, digested, and evacuated) is the most permeable substance of all.

It should be made clear that an inter-caste feast is governed by a more general and inclusive set of rules about transfer of types of food from one person to another. There are many day-to-day contexts in which food is given and received. For example, people customarily keep a piece of betel nut and *saronta* (betel nut cutter) in their pocket and, if meeting a friend by chance while out walking, will as a matter of course cut some flakes and place them in the friend's open palm. They will do the same with *bidis* or cigarettes. People buy each other tea in the market place, or welcome a passer by to the house with *pan*. On all occasions of family celebration, meals will be served. But the point for us here is that each food transaction takes place within a framework of rules about who should give what kind of food to whom.

The rules, a few of which will become apparent as the description of the feast unfolds below, are numerous and complex. Very broadly speaking, one of the overall principles is that low castes accept 'cooked' food from high ones, while high castes accept only dry or raw food from lower ones. But this general rule is just one amongst many smaller ones. The point for us is that each transfer of food in whatever context (however apparently incidental) is known to be a part of a much more comprehensive system of rules, the purpose of which is symbolically to articulate, on each occasion, the caste structure of the village. Thus, by knowing which type of food I can give (and receive) from you, we both know (exactly) our respective places in the hierarchy of castes. But, to return to the feast. The person hosting it was a wealthy trader from the *Sonar*, or goldsmith, caste. This is a caste normally thought to be one of the *Vaishya* castes (i.e. in the lower part of block II). It was held on the veranda and the courtyard of his house in the centre of the village. The particular occasion was the recovery of the host's mother from a serious illness. About 300 persons were invited, from every caste in the village.

The process of preparation and consumption of the feast went as follows. Both paddy and wheat for the *chapatis* came from the fields of the host's family and had been harvested by their daily labourers, some of whom were from block IV castes. On the actual day of the feast, servants were hired to prepare the feast.

The first set of these were from block III castes and they were required to carry out tasks which included taking the wheat grains to the mill to be ground into flour, cleaning the rice (i.e. removing the small stones and other rubbish from it), bringing other ingredients (vegetables, spices, betel nut, and so forth) from shops, and arranging them. All this was done just outside the walls of the Sonar's house and, because of that house's location near the market place, these tasks provided something of a spectacle for passers by. I was told quite specifically and unequivocally that this was the first stage of preparation and that the next stage would have to be carried out by castes of block II, because persons from block III cannot cut vegetables.

Thus, when all the ingredients were ready for them, block II servants began the next stage of the preparation. They had been hired to peel, scrape, cut and wash the potatoes, onions and radishes. They did these in the courtyard of the house, just inside the walls, arranging the food in piles on *thalis* (trays). They also prepared pan, mixing the betel nut which had previously been cut by the block III servants, with the lime and other ingredients, and fixing them on wooden sticks.

The final stage, the actual cooking, was carried out by Brahmans (i.e. block I) in the cooking area in the central part of the house. The seating of the guests took a customary form, with *Brahmans* in the centre of a very large broken and layered semi-circle of people, sitting in rows, each of which consisted of fellow caste members. Guests from the higher castes sat nearer the centre than those from lower ones: guests from block IV castes constituted the edge of the semi-circle, while across the road ('beyond the edge', so to speak) sat two members of the sweeper caste, whose status was thought to be the lowest in the village.

The *Brahman* cooks also served the meal to the guests. Fried food was served to fellow members of block I as well as high block II castes. Boiled food was served to lower block II and all those in block III and IV castes. The *jutha*, left-overs, from the plates of *Brahmans* was later handed to the sweepers – whose traditional role in Indian village society is to take away human excrement from the households of rich and high status villagers. Recalling that, from the time that the raw grain was cut in the fields by servants in block IV castes, and that each of the preparatory tasks for the feast were carried out by persons in progressively higher castes (i.e. that those from block IV harvest, from block III grind (wheat into flour), clean (rice) and cut dry food (such as betel nut), from block II wash and cut moist food (such as vegetables) and prepare tea, while only those from block I actually 'cook' the ingredients over the fire, we are in a position to identify the structure of food transformations at a feast such as this – and from this to go on to draw out what this tells about the nature of this particular kind of hospitality. Food that started off completely raw was progressively transformed by progressively higher castes until being fully cooked over the fire by members of the highest caste. In this state it then came down the hierarchy of guests with progressively more transformed, and thus permeable, categories of food (i.e. from fried to boiled to left-overs) being served as the *Brahman* servers descended the hierarchy of guests. In the particular sense that the role of the sweeper is associated not only with the left-overs on *Brahmans'* plates but

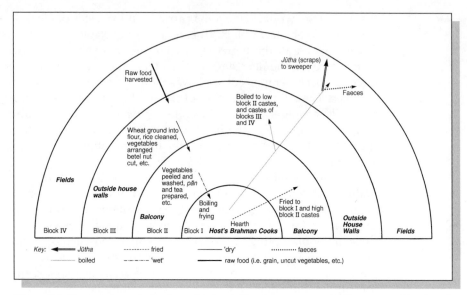

Figure 2.1 The commensal structure of a feast. The figure represents the career of food as it is prepared, cooked, served and eaten at a rural Indian intercaste feast (*bhoj*). It shows how food is transformed by members of castes from progressively higher blocks before being finally cooked and served by Brahman cooks and eaten by the guests.

also (in the way explained above) with the removal of their faeces, the symbolic message of the feast becomes clear.

The whole cycle of food preparation and consumption – from its raw state to it being cooked, digested and evacuated – has involved the entire community of castes in the village, each playing the particular roles which their place in the caste hierarchy dictates. In this sense the feast appears as an elaborate legitimization of the entire social structure of the village and even of wider caste society itself. This is further reinforced by the spatial progression of the food. We have seen how raw food came from fields outside the village to a flour mill just within its boundaries to an area outside the house of the host to that house's courtyard inside its walls to (finally) the very centre of the feast's operations, the hearth on the veranda – from whence it went out once again. The passage of the feast's preparation and consumption also appears to conjoin culture and nature in the following way. All food is clearly 'life-giving' in and of itself. But the message of a feast such as this makes it seem that it gains its life-giving properties as much, if not more, from all the cultural processes which transform it, than it does from its own natural properties. It is this kind of symbolic logic (see Figure 2.1) in which our goldsmith host, through his organization of the feast, has invested.

Conclusions

There is a bridge over the river just outside Sarajevo (the *kozja cuprija*) which traders and visitors from the east need to cross before entering the city. Beside the bridge there is a lodging house which has traditionally offered hospitality to such visitors. Apart from anything else these are customarily offered coffee, of which there are three types. The vernacular name for the first type of coffee is *docekusa*, 'welcome coffee'. Following this the guest, if he has not yet left for the town, is offered *razqa vorusa*, 'talking coffee'. If he has still not departed for the town having taken some cups of this second variety, the guest is served a third type which is known as *sikterusa*, which my informant translated wittily and pointedly as 'fuck off coffee'.[1]

There is a passage in *The Upanishads* which tells us that the feet of a Brahman guest need to be washed immediately he appears on the doorstep. Such a guest, of course, brings honour to the household he visits, but we are told that if this is not done in time all the bad *karma* (pre-ordained fate) of the guest will be transferred to the host and all the good *karma* of the host transferred to the guest.[2]

Which brings us neatly to some concluding remarks. In several passages above, attention has been drawn to the fact that hospitality belongs to the same lineage as hostility, that guests are often former or potential enemies of their hosts, and (as the *Upanishads* reference reveals), that there are times when a guest is a potential source of danger. But from what we have learnt about the nature of hospitality, cross-culturally, it seems clear that what is dangerous is not any innate malevolence in the character of the *Brahman* or the merchant arriving at the inn on the bridge – or any other potential guest for that matter. The danger lies, precisely, in the possibility that the opportunity and promise of a relationship will simply not be taken up, that the stranger remains a stranger, and that the transformative processes which acts of hospitality put in motion will simply wither away before they have been given a chance to take root.

Second, as is clear from the Indian food laws and Douglas' interpretation of our own contemporary eating practices, small acts of giving and receiving food (from the shared packet of crisps in the pub to the exchange of betel nut in the village) are replications at a microcosmic level of much larger occasions, such as meals on Christmas day, baronial banquets, or village thanksgiving feasts. In this sense the rules and practices of hospitality reach far down into the more intimate and incidental occasions of day-to-day social life.

Third, there is a sense in which, unlike some forms of charity, hospitality is neither voluntary nor altruistic, but, in a particular sense, both necessary and compulsory. The crucial point about hospitality is that it is the means, above all others, of forming or consolidating relationships with strangers. In this light it appears as one of the means (as important in this respect as marriage itself) by which societies change, grow, renew and reproduce themselves.

Fourth, as the cry from *The Catholic Worker* implied, the principles of hospitality are, at their best, fundamentally socially 'inclusive', binding the poor as they do to the rest of society. Jews, Christians, Muslims and Hindus alike are enjoined to place the poor amongst the first ranks of those to be given hospitality. Moreover, in many formulations, as Esther felt when she gave the cup of water to the old woman on the log, it is precisely through the poor and needy (as 'ambassadors of the gods') that the host makes a link with the divine.

Fifth, for all its associations with benevolent good work, hospitality seems almost universally also to be associated with the possibilities of pleasures and excesses beyond its own boundaries. In this sense it appears poised between morality and transgression, duty and pleasure, a not entirely playful inter-course between religious injunctions of various kinds, on the one hand, and altogether more Bacchanalian tendencies, on the other.

Sixth, the honour bestowed on a guest by his host derives in large part from the honour the guest brings to his host. This is a principle of exchange well known from studies on traditional kingship (Hocart, 1969; Bloch, 1977). It reminds us that, as in the relationship between king and subjects, so at the heart of each act of hospitality is an exchange of honour between host and guest. What this implies is that in responding to an invitation to an occasion in which hospitality is offered, a guest signals his acceptance of the moral authority of the host.

But this inevitably leads, via (yet again) the sense of danger inherent in any act of hospitality, directly on to a seventh point, bringing our attention back to the Lords of Misrule and Abbots of Unreason. Like carnivals, feasts and grand gestures of hospitality in hierarchical societies always have the possibility of getting out of hand. It is desirable, of course, that the 'poverty below the salt' accept their station and, in accepting it, consolidate the honour and status of the noble host. Yet the possibility of rebellion, betrayal, upset and sudden reversals of status are, by definition, always present.

Thus the lineage of classic films about the mafia, from *Some Like it Hot* to *The Godfather* have given birth to an enduring story line of almost mythical proportions concerned with the fact that it is in the nature of the hospitality given to his subordinate colleagues by a mafia boss that they may seek to depose him. This only reinforces the fact that the honour of hosts is ultimately dependent on the will of guests, and that, inter alia, the status of guest is fundamentally ambivalent – a friend who brings honour and to whom honour is accorded but who, in the end, might turn out to be, or turn into, a deadly foe. That is the meaning of the unwashed feet of the *Brahman* guest left on the threshold too long as well as the guests at the mafia dinner who explode out of a birthday cake in order to spray their hosts with machine gun fire. And it does make sense of Chaucer's (1374) reference in *Troylus and Criseyde* to the announcement that 'there is right now y-come in to towne a geste, a Greek espie' (quoted in *The Oxford English Dictionary* under 'guest') and the passage in *Romeo and Juliet* in which Friar Lawrence asks Romeo where he has been and Romeo replies: 'I'll tell thee, ere thou ask it me again, I have been feasting with my enemy, Where on a sudden one hath wounded me, That's by me wounded.'[3]

An eighth point follows from the universal use of food as the main ingredient of hospitality. The business of preparing, cooking and serving food is, after all, an act of culturally transforming natural substances. The effect of this is to cultivate the impression that the structures of cultural authority which the guests find at the feast and beyond are supported and legitimated not only (perhaps, as we have seen above, through the presence of the poor) by god but by nature as well.

Finally, to return to a point raised by Heal. It is quite clear from the evidence from all the data presented – from the classical and Biblical references to the structures of an inter-caste feast in village India – that the rules and principles of hospitality stand at one remove from the principles and procedures of the market place. There is a relation, of course, and our goldsmith host (also a moneylender and local politician of considerable power) knew that well. Anthropologists know it too, but, following Mauss and Malinowski (both of whom warned against interpreting the meaning of gift exchange in terms of trade) onwards, would strive to maintain an analytical separation between the types of hospitality we have been concerned with here, and commercial hospitality. There would be many, not exclusively anthropologists either, who would feel a sense of anxiety if ever these two were to lose their separate identity. Perhaps this is partly why some would be concerned that the vast majority of post-1975 books in the British Library's catalogue under the keyword 'hospitality' are devoted to the hospitality industry.

Notes

1 Thanks to Aida Daidic (personal communication) for this information.
2 Thanks to Tuvia Gelblum (personal communication) for this information.
3 A passage used as the preface to Rosman and Rubel's (1971) examination of hospitality, rank and exchange amongst North American north-west coast societies.

References

A Lover of Hospitality (1674) *The Charitable Christian*. Holborn, John Hose.

Beerbohm, M. (1920) *Hosts and Guests*. London, Heinemann.

Bloch, M.E.F. (1977) The Disconnection between Rank and Power as a Process. *European Journal of Sociology*, **18**.

Boissevain, J. and Mitchell, C. (eds) (1973) *Network Analysis: Studies in human interaction*. The Hague, Mouton.

Brown, D.J.J. (1980) The Structuring of Polopa Feasting and Warfare. *Man*, **14**, 4.

Chagnon, N. (1992) *Yanomamo: The last days of Eden*. San Diego, Harcourt Brace Jovanovich.

Chaucer, G. (1990, originally 1374) *Troylus and Criseyde*, London, Folio.

Cornwallis, H. (1694) *Set on the Great Pot: A sermon on hospitality*. London, The Sons of the Prophets.

Day, D. (1939) *House of Hospitality*. New York, Sheen and Ward.

Douglas, M. (1970) *Purity and Danger*. Harmondsworth, Penguin.

Douglas, M. (1975) *Implicit Meanings*. London, Routledge and Kegan Paul.

Evans-Pritchard, E.E. (1940) *The Nuer*. Oxford, Clarendon Press.

Gellner, E. and Waterbury, J. (eds) (1977) *Patrons and Clients in Mediterranean Societies*. London, Duckworth.

Gluckman, M. (1973) *Custom and Conflict in Africa*. Oxford, Basil Blackwell.

Heal, F. (1990) *Hospitality in Early Modern England*. Oxford, Oxford University Press.

Hocart, A.M. (1969) *Kingship*. Oxford, Oxford University Press.

Langley, J. and Moore, D. (1933) *The Pleasure of Your Company*. London, Gerald Howe.

Lee, T. B. and Devore, I. (eds) (1968) *Man the Hunter*. Chicago, Aldine.

Leslie, Madeline (1869) *The Pearl of Diligence*. Edinburgh, Alexander Hislop.

Mayer, A.C. (1960) *Caste and Kinship in Central India*. London, Routledge and Kegan Paul.

Nichol, J. (1740) *Ancient British Hospitality*, London, T. Astley in St Paul's Churchyard.

Peters, E. (1990) *The Bedouin of Cyrenaica: Studies in personal and corporate power* (J. Goody and E. Marx, eds). Cambridge, Cambridge University Press.

Prichard, M. (1981) *Guests and Hosts*. Oxford, Oxford University Press.

Rosman, A. and Rubel, P. (1971) *Feasting with Mine Enemy*. Illinois, Waveland Press.

Selwyn, T. (1980) The Order of Men and the Order of Things: An examination of food transactions in an Indian village. *International Journal of the Sociology of Law*, **8**.

Shakespeare, W. (1972, originally 1599) *The Tragedy of Romeo and Juliet* (N. Coghill, ed.). London, Pan Books.

Strathern, A. (1971) *The Rope of Moka*. Cambridge, Cambridge University Press.

Strathern, A. (1984) *A Line of Power*. London, Tavistock.

Tanaka, J. (1980) *The San: Hunter Gatherers of the Kalahari*. Tokyo, Tokyo University Press.

Walford, C. (1885) *The Rights, Duties, Obligations and Advantages of Hospitality*. London, Privately printed opuscula for the members of the Sette of Odd Volumes.

Woodburn, J. C. (1968) Stability and flexibility in Hadza Residential Groupings. In: *Man the Hunter* (R. B. Lee and I. Devore, eds). Chicago, Aldine.

Hospitality, Leisure & Tourism Series

CHAPTER 3

The philosophy of hospitableness

Elizabeth Telfer

Department of Philosophy, University of Glasgow

Key themes

- On being hospitable
- The good host
- Kinds of guest
- Hospitableness as a moral virtue

Hospitableness is the name of the trait possessed by hospitable people. It is clearly something to do with hospitality, so I shall begin with that. We can define hospitality, in its basic meaning, as follows: it is the giving of food, drink and sometimes accommodation to people who are not regular members of a household. Typically givers, or hosts, provide these things in their own homes, and the point is that they are sharing their own sustenance with their guests. This notion may be stretched in various directions: for example, a firm is said to provide hospitality if it gives food and drink to visitors. But the central idea of the concept remains that of sharing one's own home and provision with others.

In doing so, a host accepts responsibility for the overall welfare of his or her guests. As the eighteenth-century gourmet and food writer Jean-Anthelme Brillat-Savarin says: 'To entertain a guest is to make yourself responsible for his happiness so long as he is beneath your roof' (Brillat-Savarin, 1970, p.14). If this is a host's task, it is concerned with more than food, drink and shelter: it means that a host must try to cheer up a miserable guest, divert a bored one, care for a sick one. Traditionally the most important responsibility of all was for the guest's safety – hospitality was a kind of sanctuary, and the host was thought of as having undertaken a solemn obligation to make sure no harm came to his guest while under his roof. This idea is enshrined in many legends. In Wagner's opera *The Valkyrie*, for example, Hunding the jealous husband cannot kill his enemy Siegmund while Siegmund is his guest – he has to wait until Siegmund leaves and then pursue him.

The nature and importance of hospitality has varied very much in different times and places. But this variation does not mean that there is no trait of hospitableness to discuss. Any trait will manifest itself in ways which differ according to prevailing conditions and conventions. For example, in a society with an institution of duelling, people can be courageous in ways impossible in a society with no such institution. In this discussion of hospitableness I hope to unearth basic concepts which underlie differences such as these.

Brillat-Savarin's translator uses the phrase 'entertain a guest' – does this mean the same as 'provide hospitality'? There are contexts in which it is natural to speak of hospitality rather than entertaining, and giving a meal to a stranded traveller is hospitality but not entertaining, but giving smart dinner-parties seems like entertaining rather than hospitality. Where there is a difference, then, hospitality is associated with the meeting of need, entertaining with the giving of pleasure. But this difference is only a matter of nuance. Often the two words are equivalent, and I shall use 'entertaining' to mean the same as 'providing hospitality'.

So far I have spoken of hospitality as a private affair, based on a private home and given, not sold, to chosen guests. From this perspective the idea of commercial hospitality seems like a contradiction in terms: the location of it is not a home, the hospitality is not given, the guests are not chosen. 'The American usage "hospitality industry" suggests an immediate paradox between generosity and the exploitation of the marketplace' (Heal, 1990, p.1). But I shall argue that this contrast between true private hospitality and a false commercial imitation is too simplistic: for example, we shall see that the private host can be self-interested, the commercial one motivated by concern for his guests' welfare. We should not forget that an important forerunner of the modern hotel was monastic hospitality, which had features of both private and commercial hospitality: the hospitality was given for disinterested reasons, but the guests were unchosen and the host was a religious institution, not a private person. In what follows I shall start from the basis of private hospitality, but try to show as I proceed that commercial hospitality at its best shares many features of private hospitality and that commercial hosts may possess the virtue of hospitableness.

The good host

How do we get from hospitality to hospitableness? A possible link might be the notion of a good host. But what is a good host? One might say (starting with the private host) that a good host is one who fulfils all the tasks of a host, and give a list of these tasks: he or she refills empty glasses, makes sure that guests are offered second helpings, and so on. However, any such list cannot describe the *essence* of a good host, since it applies only to the conventions of a particular time and place. Perhaps we can derive a more general formula from the observation of Brillat-Savarin already quoted. If entertaining guests is making yourself responsible for their happiness so long as they are beneath your roof, a good host is one who does make his guests happy – or as happy as a host's efforts and ministrations can make them – while they are in his care.

Being a good host involves skills as well as effort. Some of these skills, like the tasks of a host, are clichés: for example, a good host can prevent a heated argument from becoming a quarrel. If we want a general formula for these skills, it must be this: what good hosts are good at is making their guests happy. In other words, they know what will please them and are able to bring this about.

Is being a good host equivalent to being hospitable? If we say after a party that the host was very hospitable, we may only mean that he or she was a good host – skilful and attentive. But being a good host is not really enough for being hospitable. For we would say that a host was not genuinely being hospitable if we discovered that he or she had an ulterior motive for being so attentive, one that had nothing to do with any desire to please the guests or any belief in an obligation to do so.

Genuinely hospitable behaviour, then, requires an appropriate motive. However, whether someone should be described as a hospitable *person* depends not only on his or her motive but also on how often hospitable behaviour occurs. One can say, 'She's very hospitable when she entertains, but she almost never does'; such a person is scarcely a hospitable person. A hospitable person, I suggest, is someone who entertains often, attentively and out of motives appropriate to hospitality. (I shall discuss appropriate motives in the next section.)

Being a good host is not even necessary for being hospitable, since we can say, 'He is a very hospitable person, but not really a good host'. At first this seems paradoxical: one might think that the motives which prompt genuinely hospitable people to entertain would also prompt them to look after their guests properly. But the paradox disappears when we recall that a good host has to be skilful as well as attentive. Hospitable people are attentive, but they are not necessarily skilful and therefore may not be good hosts.

To sum up – and I am still talking about private hosts – a good host is not behaving hospitably unless he or she also has an appropriate motive. A person who regularly behaves hospitably is said to be a hospitable person; he or she will also be a good host, so far as attentiveness is concerned, but may lack the skill which would make him or her a good host without qualification.

How do these ideas apply to the commercial sector? The first question is: what *is* a host in the commercial sector? A firm that runs a chain of hotels might describe itself as in the hospitality business, and perhaps even as being hosts – certainly as 'hosting' events. But the professional people who are most nearly parallel to the private host are those who are directly in charge of the welfare of the guests: namely, the owners or managers of hotels or restaurants. These after all are the people who, if they seem to stamp their personality on what goes on, tend to be referred to, affectionately or otherwise, as 'mine host'.

Good commercial hosts of this kind, like their private counterparts, are good at securing their guests' welfare – 'guests' in the commercial context, of course, being people who have paid for

Hospitality, Leisure & Tourism Series

their services, not people they have invited. What counts as welfare in this case will largely depend on what the customer is paying for, and may differ in some ways from what makes a private guest happy. For example, in a smart hotel customers may want and reckon they have paid for sophistication and elegance and/or privacy and discretion, whereas in a seaside family hotel guests may want informality and conviviality. Like his private counterpart, the commercial host will need to be attentive and skilful, but the skills required in elegant establishments may be beyond most amateur hosts (not all).

It should be noted that being a good host in the commercial sector is not the same thing as being a good hotelier or restaurateur. Quality as a host concerns only those aspects of the business which directly affect the guests, but the good hotelier or restaurateur has to be good at (or delegate to, and keep control of, those who are good at) all aspects of the business, including handling staff, managing the finances and the business's relationship with the wider community.

Can a commercial host be hospitable? On a superficial view this seems to be ruled out, on the ground that he or she always has an ulterior motive, namely the profit motive. But in the next section I hope to show that such a conclusion is too hasty.

Hospitable motives

I have said that if behaviour is to count as genuinely hospitable, it must have an 'appropriate' motive. What is appropriate? As an approach to this question, I shall begin with a list (which I do not claim is exhaustive) of possible motives for offering hospitality, beginning as before with private hospitality.

Firstly, there is a group of other-regarding motives. These include the desire to please others, stemming from general friendliness and benevolence or from affection for particular people; concern or compassion, the desire to meet another's need; and allegiance to what one sees as duties of hospitality, such as a general duty to be hospitable, a duty to entertain one's friends or a duty to help those in trouble. The first two types of motive in this group seem to embody the spirit of hospitality: someone who entertains from one of these motives is thought of as hospitable. However, there might be doubt about duty as a motive for genuine hospitableness, because it seems to be at odds with the idea of *warmth* contained in hospitality. If people entertain out of a sense of duty, are they being hospitable or merely dutiful? I suggest that they are being hospitable provided that what I called the spirit of the hospitality is generous. Suppose I am tired of entertaining, but out of a sense of duty invite new neighbours to dinner. If when they come I enter into the spirit of the occasion and want to please them, I am surely being hospitable. But if I continue to feel resentful, I am only being dutiful (though if the neighbours cannot tell the difference, perhaps I am still doing the right thing!).

A second group of motives may be called reciprocal motives. Examples of these are a desire to have company or to make friends, and the desire for the pleasures of entertaining – what we may call the wish to entertain as a pastime. I call these 'reciprocal' because they are not so purely 'other-regarding' as the first group, but they need not be purely self-regarding either. Someone who entertains to have company or to make friends is at the same time offering company or friendship to the guests. Similarly, hosts who entertain because they enjoy entertaining will normally bring pleasure to the guests as well as enjoying themselves, and one source of the host's pleasure will normally be the pleasure of their guests.

The latter kind of entertaining is also reciprocal in a stronger sense: not only are hosts both giving and getting pleasure or company, they also entertain in the hope that the hospitality will be returned. This does not destroy the hospitable, other-regarding nature of such entertaining, because both parties have a kind of tacit agreement that they are jointly doing something of mutual benefit. The balance is delicate: if one party does all the entertaining, they are permitted to feel that their hospitality is being abused and they are being imposed upon, but if they are too calculating about an exact return they are thought to be self-interested rather than hospitable.

There can be purely self-regarding versions of these reciprocal motives. For example, there are hosts who entertain for pleasure and who are essentially indifferent to the pleasure of the guests, since what they enjoy about entertaining – for example, cooking elaborate dishes – does not depend on whether guests enjoy themselves. Such hosts are not genuinely hospitable – though if their guests do enjoy themselves, they may either not see this or not think it matters. Similarly a lonely person might invite people for the sake of their company and be indifferent to their welfare; for example, he spends so much time telling them his troubles that they have to go before he gets round to feeding them. Such a person is not hospitable. However if he invites people purely to relieve his own loneliness but is genuinely solicitous of their welfare once they come, we surely think of him as hospitable.

What matters in assessing motives for hospitality, then, is not only the initial reason for inviting people, but also what we may call the spirit in which they are entertained: what moves the host when the guests are there. A host can redeem a self-regarding motive for an invitation by being concerned for the guests once they arrive.

A third group of motives for hospitality are not reciprocal because they spring from a desire to benefit the host rather than the guests. A common, fairly harmless motive of this kind is vanity: a desire to show off something, such as one's culinary skills or smart house. If hosts are moved only by vanity we think they are not being genuinely hospitable; hospitableness must have some regard for the guests. But in practice, of course, motives tend to be mixed. For example, a host may serve a particular dish out of vanity – that is, because she wants to impress the guests rather than because the she thinks they will like it – but otherwise be mainly influenced by a desire to please guests. We would still count the person as hospitable if the dominant consideration is the guests' pleasure, but the more the host is dominated by the desire to show off her skill or sophistication the less hospitable she is.

Some self-interested motivations for offering hospitality (seduction, for example, and other forms of manipulating people through the pleasures of hospitality) are less harmless. Paradoxically they tend to be dependent on actually pleasing the guest: unless the guest is pleased the manipulation does not succeed. But the host's motivation is ultimately self-interested. He is pleasing the guest for his sake, not theirs, and the situation is neither an other-regarding gift nor a reciprocal and equal exchange of benefit. Needless to say, such a person is not genuinely hospitable.

In the private sphere, then, hospitable motives are those in which concern for the guests' pleasure and welfare, for its own sake, is predominant, or where hosts and guests freely exchange hospitality for mutual enjoyment and benefit. And hospitable people, those who possess the trait of hospitableness, are those who often entertain from one or more of these motives, or from mixed motives in which one of these motives is predominant.

How do the motives of commercial hosts compare with these, and do they allow us to speak of them as acting hospitably? The first point to note here is that commercial hosts are not in a position to choose how often to entertain or to choose the guests, so we cannot speak of their motives in making these choices. However, we can ask about their motives in choosing this occupation in the first place, and in performing their various actions concerning the guests. It is natural to assume at first that both sets of motives must be self-interested: people choose to go into 'the hospitality industry' to earn a living, and the individual actions which constitute doing the job are motivated by the desire to keep the job, or to keep the business going if it is their own. But this is surely far too simple. People may take a job rather than be idle because they want a decent living, but they may choose this kind of job for motives resembling those of the hospitable private host: they enjoy making people happy by entertaining them. Again, they may duly perform their tasks because they want to keep their job, but if they try to perform them well, or do more than the job strictly requires, this can be because they genuinely want to please the guests or they have some notion of values of hospitality to which they aspire.

What about the profit motive? It is true that the need to make ends meet financially is a constraint within which commercial hosts work, but maximizing profit need not be the main motive of those who sell commercial hospitality. (Of course it may be so in some cases, and so may other self-regarding motives, such as vanity in the case of the flamboyant restaurateur/chef, but one is not tempted to think that such hosts are hospitable.)

I conclude that if a commercial host looks after his guests well out of a genuine concern for their happiness and charges them reasonably, rather than extortionately, for what he does, his activities can be called hospitable. Admittedly, his guests are paying for what they get, but if we recall that there can be reciprocal motives for hospitality we can see this kind of hospitable behaviour as an extension of that idea. This kind of host gives generous, not minimal, service, because he wishes to please the guests; the guests pay, not by hospitality in their turn, but by a sum of money which they see as low enough to be a good bargain and a foundation for friendly relations between host and guest. To say that a commercial host cannot be said to behave hospitably simply on the ground that he is paid for his work is like saying that doctors cannot be said to behave compassionately because they are paid for what they do.

The comparison with the doctor suggests another question: do we want to say that the commercial host who behaves hospitably in the context of his job is a hospitable *person*, possessing the trait of hospitableness? I think we would say that a host who was hospitable *only* in that context could not be called a truly hospitable person, any more than the doctor who shows compassion only at work is a truly compassionate person. But both may be fully possessed of the trait in question if they show it in private as well as professional life, and both may have chosen their particular profession precisely because they possess that trait.

Kinds of guest

We can classify types of hospitality not only by motivation but also by kinds of guest. As we shall see, there is a correspondence between the two classifications, but it is by no means exact. I shall distinguish three kinds of guest: those in a relationship to the host which is not simply that of guest to host, those in need, and friends proper. Again I shall start with non-commercial hospitality.

Where guest and host stand in a relationship, it can be either an official relationship which involves a duty of hospitality (for example, that between students in a university hostel and a warden who is expected to entertain them) or an unofficial connection, such as that between colleagues, neighbours, fellow parishioners, parents whose children are friends, or of course relations – those whom people call their circle. I do not include, in the term 'one's circle', people with whom the only relationship is one of friendship.

I shall not discuss official hospitality at length. A person could not have a trait of hospitableness based only on fulfilling official duties of hospitality, since these duties come and go with a particular post, whereas traits are a long-term disposition. However, officials can carry out official duties of hospitality in the same friendly spirit in which they might entertain those in their circle, and when they are thought of as hospitable it is because they do this. I shall therefore assume that hospitable officials can be regarded as extending their circle to include those they have an official duty to entertain, and not discuss them separately.

Possible motives for entertaining one's circle are enormously varied. One such motive – or ingredient in motivation, for motives can be mixed, as we said – is a sense of duty. In more formal societies, people have strict obligations to entertain, according to their status, others in their circle; these obligations are governed by rules, and are no less binding than the warden's obligation in our own society to entertain the students in her hostel. In our own society such rules are largely gone, but we are still apt to feel that entertaining one's circle is a good idea and perhaps a duty. This sense of duty does not only apply when a host has an official duty to entertain particular guests. People feel that they ought to entertain new neighbours or colleagues, or relations whom they have not seen for a while, on the looser ground that they think that they ought to express solidarity, or strengthen the bonds of family and community, and they see entertaining as a particularly good way of doing this.

Another kind of motive for entertaining one's circle, one which is hard to characterize, is something like the wish to be friendly, to offer some degree of personal relationship. Entertaining is a good way to be friendly because it involves the offer of a degree of intimacy, a share in the host's home life. This motive, as well as duty, can lead people to entertain those with whom their connection is essentially official; it is as if they were saying, 'Let's not be merely business partners, we are human beings as well'. Similarly, the warden might entertain his students 'to show that he is human'.

Where someone frequently entertains his or her circle from one of the hospitable motives I distinguished earlier, he or she is one sort of hospitable person and has one sort of hospitableness. Entertaining one's circle cannot be sharply distinguished either from entertaining those in need or from entertaining one's friends. But there are some points to make about each of these other categories of guest which justify taking them separately.

A second kind of guest is the person in need of hospitality – either a need for food, drink or accommodation as such, or a psychological need of a kind which can be met particularly well by hospitality, such as loneliness or the need to feel valued as an individual. I shall give the name 'Good Samaritan hospitality' to the activity of entertaining people because they seem to have such a need. Good Samaritan hospitality can be shown to anyone, whether connected to the host or not. But the clearest cases of it are those where the guest is a stranger and the only possible reason for offering it is the perception of the guest's need. This kind of hospitality is perhaps the most fundamental kind of all. As I said earlier, in simple communities all travellers are strangers in need of food and shelter simply in virtue of being away from their own home, and there is usually felt to be a corresponding obligation of hospitality. Strangers who need hospitality in a modern urban setting, with its hotels and restaurants, do not need it simply because they are strangers. But there is still room for Good Samaritan hospitality, as is shown by the true story of a couple who invited a complete stranger to come for Christmas because they had heard her on the radio talking about her dread of a lonely Christmas after a recent bereavement.

There are many kinds of motivation for Good Samaritan hospitality, including consciously religious motivation, sense of duty, and loving-kindness. In a particular case it may often not be clear, either to the hosts or others, whether they are acting out of duty or loving-kindness; phrases like 'We felt we had to do something' sound like duty, but may instead express the strength of a compassionate feeling. A person who, from any of these motives, regularly entertains others because they need it is a hospitable person – though the word 'hospitable' is too weak for especially saintly hosts.

The third group of guests are friends, by which I mean friends proper or intimates, rather than simply one's circle. People entertain their friends because liking and affection are inherent in friendship (Telfer, 1971, pp.224–7); the liking produces a wish for the friends' company (as distinct from company in general), the affection a desire to please them. Liking and affection of course express themselves in other ways as well, but there is a special link between friendship and hospitality, one which I have already mentioned in connection with entertaining one's circle. Because it involves the host's home, hospitality (provided it is not too formal) is an invitation to intimacy, an offer of a share in the host's private life. When given to friends, who are already intimates, it has the effect of maintaining or reinforcing the intimacy.

However, there is a kind of paradox about entertaining the same people too often. If they reach a stage when they can 'drop in' and 'take pot luck', they scarcely count as guests and become 'almost part of the family'. Is turning friends into family the essence of this kind of hospitality, or does it go beyond hospitality? I think one might choose to say either. The important point is that there are two ways, each of which may have its place, in which I may try to please my guests. I can either make a special fuss of them, or deliberately avoid a special fuss and make them feel at home.

As always, attributing the trait of hospitableness to a person describes them as going beyond the average. Friends are not thought of as hospitable merely because they entertain each other, since this is to be expected. To count as hospitable in this sphere, hosts must be unusually ready to entertain their friends and unusually devoted to pleasing them. The same considerations as before apply about ulterior motives: if someone is always inviting his friends in to dinner simply to show off his cooking, he is not a hospitable person – but the friends may not mind, as long as the cooking is good.

Do we have a duty to entertain our friends? A hospitable friend is not normally acting *out of* a sense of duty. But it does not follow that there is no such duty; on the contrary, there are two reasons why we might assert that there is such a duty.

First, friends sometimes need hospitality. This reason is not based only on need, as with Good Samaritan hospitality, since I may have a duty to entertain a friend in circumstances where I would not be obliged to do the same for a stranger. But we think of ourselves as having, even as having *undertaken*, special obligations towards our friends which we do not have towards strangers. We may also have a sense of an informal system of protection whereby everyone is looked after in this way by his or her friends.

Second, friends gain positive psychological benefits from hospitality. For example, if we share a meal with friends or have them to stay, we include them in an informal ritual of fellowship; we strengthen their self-esteem by our readiness to share our own lives with them; and we rest and refresh them by waiting on them and by providing a pleasant atmosphere. In short, by our hospitality we can further our friends' psychological and physical wellbeing, and this is something that we have a duty to do. It is not such a pressing duty as meeting their needs. But it may be just as important, because prevention of loneliness, self-hatred and depression is better than cure.

As I have already said, we are not normally acting *out* of duty when entertaining friends. Sometimes, however, affection is not enough to motivate us: for example, we may be too wrapped up in our own troubles to feel affectionate. But we can still 'make an effort', as they say, and entertain friends out of duty. I argued earlier that entertaining can count as hospitable when its motive is duty, provided the spirit in which it is carried out is generous. However, there is a special problem about entertaining *friends* out of duty, in that it might be thought hypocritical: we are acting as though we have the usual motive for hospitality to friends when in fact we do not. Perhaps we can reply that if these are actions which we would not do for just anyone they are the actions *of a friend*, and so they need not be seen as hypocritical even if they lack the spontaneity which normally goes with friendship.

How does this classification of types of guest apply to commercial hospitality? In the first instance it applies insofar as private hosts use commercial hospitality instead of their own homes to entertain private guests of all three kinds. So far I have written as though private hospitality is always in a private home, but that is not always the case. To the degree that the nature and the benefits of hospitality of all three kinds depend on the host's sharing his home life with his guests, such hybrid hospitality will lack some value. But in many situations it is perfectly appropriate to entertain guests away from home: the eponymous Good Samaritan looked after his beneficiary by taking him to an inn and paying for his accommodation there. One might even raise someone's morale more by entertaining him in a grand restaurant rather than at home, if what he needed was not intimacy but luxury.

In the second place, the relationship between guests paying for themselves and their commercial hosts falls into one of three patterns which correspond roughly to the kinds of private guest I have distinguished. The first pattern corresponds to the official kind of entertaining inherent in some roles, but here the roles are the ordinary business ones of customer and provider. But as I have said earlier, it is possible for a commercial host to carry out his or her role more or less hospitably. The second pattern arises in the situation where customers have special needs which they are hoping to meet through commercial hospitality: for example they are escaping from chaotic troubles for a while in a quiet country hotel or looking for a confidant in the host of a pub. Although hosts in these situations are selling hospitality rather than giving it, they can still show or fail to show concern and compassion in meeting the guests' special needs and can still approach or fail to approach Good Samaritan hospitality. The third relationship is that between commercial hosts and guests who are also their friends, as when regulars at a pub become friends of the landlord. Here the problem is that a commercial host who is attentive to his friends in a way at all resembling the private entertainment of friends is likely to neglect his other customers; perhaps a commercial host cannot be hospitable in a really friendlike, as distinct from friendly, way in his commercial setting.

So far I have written as though commercial hospitality is a kind of pale imitation of private hospitality, private hospitality necessarily being far superior. But this is by no means obvious. Here for example is Dr Johnson:

> There is no private house in which people can enjoy themselves so well as at a capital tavern. Let there be ever so great plenty of good things, ever so much grandeur, ever so much elegance, ever so much desire that everybody should be easy, in the nature of things it cannot be: there must always be some degree of care and anxiety. The master of the house is anxious to entertain his guests – the guests are anxious to be agreeable to him; and no man, but a very impudent dog indeed, can as freely command what is in another man's house, as if it were his own. Whereas, at a tavern, there is a general freedom from anxiety. You are sure of a welcome; and the more noise you make, the more trouble you give, the more good things you call for, the welcomer you are. No, Sir, there is nothing which has yet been contrived by man, by which so much happiness is produced as by a good tavern or inn.
>
> (Boswell, 1934, p.451)

It is easy to feel some sympathy for this view. If we want to defend private hospitality against this attack we might point out that the mention of plenty, grandeur and elegance suggests that the host Johnson is thinking of is trying chiefly to impress the guests rather than please them. As we saw, this kind of hospitality is not really hospitable: genuinely hospitable hosts, aiming to please their guests, will not cause them this kind of anxiety. But Johnson might well reply that those genuinely hospitable but inept hosts who embarrass their guests by being over-solicitous about their welfare may be just as bad.

It might also be said that Johnson leaves out of account the role of what I called Good Samaritan hospitality: going to the inn and calling for good things is enjoyable, but does not do much to relieve loneliness and friendlessness. However, a good commercial host, as we have seen, will try to befriend lonely customers, and can fulfil this kind of role for misfits who do not have friends. It is true that an important benefit of the hospitality of friends, as we saw, is that it makes its recipient feel wanted as an individual, and that being welcome as a good customer is not the same thing. But for someone who has no proper friends a genuinely friendly landlord, one who does not see him *only* as a customer, is a valuable substitute. Indeed, people sometimes feel in need of this kind of company precisely because it does not involve the demands of personal relationships.

This last point links with another criticism which might be made of Johnson in that he fails to grasp that the pleasure of being privately entertained is not simply that of having agreeable food and drink, which might be better at the pub, but a complex pleasure which depends to a great extent on the fact that one is *in someone's home*. It is true that there can be a certain intensity about private entertaining which stems from this intimacy and heightens the experience. But a defender of Johnson can say that we do not always want this. For a relaxing evening which makes no demands, commercial hospitality, if it is hospitable in its own way, comes into its own.

Hospitableness as a moral virtue

I turn finally to the question of whether hospitableness is a moral virtue. As before, I shall first examine private hospitableness and then consider whether, if this is a virtue, the commercial host can also be said to have this virtue, or a similar one. To do this I need to start by considering what a moral virtue is in general, and here I shall make use of the account of moral virtues given by Philippa Foot in her paper 'Virtues and Vices' (Foot, 1978, pp.1–18).

Foot claims that moral virtues possess three features. First, moral virtues are qualities which 'a human being needs to have, for his own sake and that of his fellows'. Second, they are qualities of will, rather than of intellect, situation or physique. Third, they are corrections of some common human tendency to either excess or deficiency of motivation. I shall consider the three types of hospitableness (hospitableness towards one's circle, Good Samaritan hospitableness and hospitableness to friends) in the light of these criteria.

Foot suggests that whereas courage, temperance and wisdom benefit both their possessor and others, justice and charity chiefly benefit others, sometimes at their possessor's expense: '. . . communities where justice and charity are lacking are apt to be wretched places to live . . .' (Foot, 1978, pp.2–3). Hospitableness resembles charity in that it benefits others rather than oneself. But would we say that a community without hospitableness is a wretched place to live, and that human beings therefore need to have this quality? It would be more plausible to say that the corresponding fault is one which human beings need to avoid. For example, if people are inhospitable to their circle, and do not entertain family, colleagues or new neighbours even when they really ought to do so, society is the poorer – even more so if people fail in Good Samaritan hospitality, and do not look after those in need in an emergency: for example, motorists whose cars are stuck in a snowdrift near one's house.

But there seems to be a gap between avoiding the fault of inhospitableness and being positively hospitable, doing more in this sphere than the average person. The trait of hospitableness seems to be only one way among others of being useful: a person can be just as generous, public-spirited, compassionate or affectionate whether or not he is positively hospitable. And whereas we might think that everyone ought to cultivate the broader qualities of generosity and compassion, it seems to be optional whether they show these qualities through hospitableness or in other ways. One cannot try to be every kind of good person.

I think that this optional feature applies even to hospitableness to friends. Admittedly I argued earlier that there is a natural connection between friendship and hospitality which makes it likely that a good friend will also be a hospitable one. But as before we can distinguish between being inhospitable and not being positively hospitable. Failure to meet a friend's need for hospitality clearly makes someone inhospitable. But the obligation to benefit our friends in the kind of way hospitality benefits them seems to leave some room for choice: perhaps we can give our friends such benefits in other ways instead.

It might be objected at this point that, since anyone without friends is excluded from a network based on friendship, the trait of hospitableness to friends is not of general benefit. Admittedly it is not of universal benefit, but a society where people are hospitable to their friends is presumably better on balance than one where they are not. However, what is of more general benefit than hospitableness to friends is a less exclusive kind of hospitableness, springing from other broad traits as well as affection, and extended to friends proper, those in one's wider circle and those in need. Hospitableness which is confined to friends is a useful trait, but because of its narrowness a less useful one than the kind of hospitableness – probably what most people mean by the word – which embraces others too.

If hospitableness is an optional way of realizing broader virtues, why would a person choose this rather than other ways of doing good? One reason might be enjoyment: a person who enjoys entertaining has a disposition which will make it easy to be genuinely hospitable. Another possible reason is talent. Hospitableness is not fundamentally a matter of talent, as we saw, but people may be moved to seek it by the thought that they possess talents, interests or gifts of temperament that would enable them to be particularly useful in this way. A third reason is the possession of relevant gifts of fortune: for example, the owner of a large or beautiful house, or of a fine orchard or vegetable garden, has something special to offer, and perhaps special obligations too. But probably the most important reason why people choose to pursue the trait of hospitableness is that they are attracted by an *ideal* of hospitality, founded on a sense of the emotional importance of the home and of entertaining and of the special benefits which sharing them can bring.

Foot's second criterion of a moral virtue is that it is a quality of will; she uses 'will' in a wide sense, to cover what is wanted and cared about as well as what is chosen. The purpose of this criterion is to distinguish moral virtues from physical and intellectual gifts and talents. My account of hospitableness meets this requirement in that it distinguishes hospitableness from being a good host, and depicts hospitableness as depending on devotion and a spirit of generosity rather than on skill.

It might seem that if moral virtues depend on wants and choices rather than talents they can be acquired by anyone who chooses. This is however not obvious; it may not always be possible to mould one's wants in the appropriate way. In the case of hospitableness it might also be claimed that circumstances, rather than temperament, can prevent someone from becoming hospitable, because not everyone has the resources with which to entertain. (I have heard hospitableness called a middle-class virtue, presumably on these grounds.) But it is an over-simpification to say that people may not have the resources to entertain. Not everyone can provide lavish hospitality, or even conventional middle-class dinner parties, and admittedly home-less people cannot share their homes. But even a beggar can be hospitable by sharing food with a newcomer; hospitality includes the sharing of one's own provisions, and the more needy a person is, the more generous and truly hospitable the sharing is.

The third feature of moral virtues, according to Foot, is that they help people to do what is difficult by correcting some excess or deficiency of motivation to which human beings in general are prone. All the kinds of hospitableness which we are considering pass this test, in that they counteract a common lack of motivation. Many of us do not entertain very much, not because we have chosen to pursue other ways of exercising virtues, but because we are too mean, lacking in compassion or coldhearted.

Conclusions

In this discussion of hospitableness as a virtue I have examined various kinds of private hospitableness – hospitableness to one's circle, Good Samaritan hospitableness and hospitableness to one's friends – in terms of Foot's three criteria for moral virtues. I suggested that whereas hospitableness conformed to the criteria of being a quality of will and of counteracting a common deficiency of motivation, it does not seem to fit the idea of being necessary for tolerable human life: what is needed for that is only avoidance of inhospitableness. I suggested that hospitableness can be seen as one way among others in which someone may choose to exercise various different more general virtues: benevolence, public-spiritedness, compassion, affectionateness. We might call it an optional virtue: we all ought to try to be compassionate, benevolent and affectionate, but we do not all need to try to be hospitable.

At this point we might ask whether hospitableness has the degree of unity that calling it an optional virtue suggests. It seems impossible to practise all kinds of hospitality: I may have to choose not only whether to try to be a hospitable person but also what sort of hospitable person to try to be. Thus I cannot entertain my friends if my house is always full of alcoholics 'drying out', and I cannot offer my home as a refuge for alcoholics if I am always occupied with my friends. There is even a potential conflict between friends and one's wider circle, in that if one always sees friends in a wider context, this seems to involve a dilution of friendship (but we did observe earlier that the kind of hospitableness which includes both groups is better than the kind which was confined to friends).

Given these difficulties, someone attracted by the ideal of hospitableness has a choice: they may decide to aim at one kind of hospitableness and not the others, or they might strive to be all-round hospitable people, balancing the claims of different kinds of hospitality. Two factors make this balancing easier. First, there can be claims of need among one's own circle of the kind that a Good Samaritan would acknowledge in any case. Second, the friends of hospitable Good Samaritans, if they are true friends, will sympathize with their Good Samaritan activities and perhaps help with them. A potentially alienating activity can thus become part of the friendship.

How does this account of hospitableness as an optional virtue apply to the commercial host? We have seen that he or she can be said to have the trait of hospitableness provided he or she is not hospitable only when on duty. If hospitableness is an aspect of various moral virtues, it can also be so in the commercial host. But there is a sense in which hospitableness is not an optional virtue for commercial hosts. In choosing that kind of job they have in effect chosen hospitableness as one way in which they will try to show generosity, kindness and so on, since so much of their life is spent in contexts where hospitableness is called for.

References

Boswell, James (1934) *Life of Johnson* (George Birkbeck Hill, ed.; L.F. Powell, rev.), Vol. II. Oxford, Oxford University Press.

Brillat-Savarin, Jean-Anthelme (1970) *La Physiologie du Gout* (trans. Anne Drayton as 'The Philosopher in the Kitchen'). Harmondsworth, Penguin Books.

Foot, Philippa (1978) Virtues and vices. In: *Virtues and Vices* (Philippa Foot, ed.). Oxford, Basil Blackwell.

Heal, F. (1990) *Hospitality in Early Modern England*. Oxford, Clarendon Press.

Telfer, Elizabeth (1971) Friendship. *Proceedings of the Aristotelian Society*, Vol. LXXI, 223–41.

CHAPTER 4

The hospitality trades: a social history

John K. Walton

*Department of Historical and Critical Studies,
University of Central Lancashire*

Key themes

- Growing trade and travel
- Dissent and control
- Regulation of excess
- Eating and travelling for leisure

Commercial hospitality has its roots in supplying to travellers, through the market, the basic human needs of food, drink, shelter and rest. This core of services has been embellished in various ways in different settings, through the provision of (for example) medical, sexual and entertainment options for customers; and all these aspects of hospitality go back a long way and have ebbed and flowed over time as well as varying between places. This chapter examines the rise of commercial hospitality in a British setting, while taking due note of the export and import of ideas and practices in response to international flows of travel and investment. It pursues the key themes through from medieval times, while taking note of enduring continuities alongside the changes and resisting the temptation to view history as progress towards an ideal state which usually approximates disturbingly to current circumstances.

Accommodating travellers

The hospitality trades are as old as commerce, migration and pilgrimage, and there is evidence of specialized premises providing refreshment and accommodation in Roman times and again from the eighth century. Such services usually involved the supply of alcohol, although there were also hostels which simply provided accommodation. Potential threats to public order and temptations to adulteration or false measures led authorities at local and national level to take an interest in regulating the trades even before taxation gave them a more immediate motive for inspection. The City of London had pretensions to licensing alehouses by the late twelfth century, and in 1266 the Assize of Bread and Ale sought to impose fair prices on alesellers nationally. A hierarchy of commercial outlets, from inns which provided stabling, through taverns which sold wine as well as ale, to humble cottage alehouses, was emerging in recognition of the differing needs of comfortably-off merchants and other travellers, urban refreshment-seekers and rural communities. Its development accelerated after the Black Death of the fourteenth century boosted living standards for the survivors by creating labour shortages. From the mid-sixteenth century onwards, accelerating population growth (with a hiatus in the later seventeenth century), expanding internal trade, intensifying state interest in the maintenance of order and the productivity of labour, together with religious concern to regulate the morality of public behaviour, combined to make the hospitality trades increasingly important and visible (Clark, 1983).

The decline of older forms of hospitality to travellers also boosted this trend, while the post-Reformation disappearance of pilgrimage was more than balanced by the rise of secular forms of travel for enjoyment, interest and the pursuit of physical health, although the traffic flows changed, with Bath becoming more attractive than Canterbury. The church-ale, which raised money for parish purposes, also declined at about this time, as did the church as social centre for parish gatherings. The duty of hospitality which had been assumed by the proprietors of substantial estates and country houses, which had fallen upon the wife as part of an extensive array of social obligations, was falling into decline in the later sixteenth century, while the dissolution of the monasteries removed another source of non-commercial catering for travellers (Heal, 1990). Informal 'open house' cottage hospitality to kin and even passers-by persisted at the wakes and feasts of northern England into the second half of the nineteenth century, but by that time those who commented on it saw it as anachronistic (Walton and Poole, 1982). Corporate bodies began to employ professional caterers, as in the case of Hull Corporation, where Isabel Langcaster, who died in 1637, 'left her late husband's servant all the spits and racks which she kept at the mayor's house' (Laurence, 1994, p.150). Courts, guilds and colleges worked in similar ways. But above all the ever-growing mercantile traffic on the roads and waterways of England, supplemented by nobility and gentry heading for London on legal business or shopping missions or to the spas to take a cure, was supplied with food, shelter and entertainment on a commercial basis. Substantial inns proliferated along all the main roads out of London, supplementing a much smaller number of medieval foundations, while alehouses became ubiquitous and increasingly attracted the suspicious attention of those in authority (Clark, 1983).

We know more about alehouses from the mid-sixteenth century because of the growing concern to license and control them, in their guise as harbourers of vagrants and encouragers of unruly amusements, gambling, sexual frolics, criminal conspiracies, Sabbath-breaking, distractions from church services and from work, defiance of authority, and noisy, violent disorder. In 1495 justices of the peace were empowered to close alehouses and to require keepers to provide sureties for good behaviour; but more effective legislation came in 1552, when an alehouse licensing system was formally vested in local justices, and holding an alehouse licence became a discretionary privilege rather than a legal right. Further legislation in 1563 and 1570 limited the number of taverns to be permitted in specific towns, and in the early seventeenth century successive attempts were made to tighten up the control of alehouses and of 'tippling' or sustained drinking for more than an hour at a time. A census of the drink trade in England and Wales in 1577 (with taxation in mind) found up to 24,000 establishments, as well as over 2000 inns and 400 taverns. This was a ratio of perhaps one licensed premises to every 30 households, a good indication of the extent to which commercial hospitality had penetrated economic arrangements and everyday life by the middle of Elizabeth I's reign (Monckton, 1969; Clark, 1983, pp.41–3). At the local level provision was sometimes even more lavish towards the mid-seventeenth century: 25 Essex townships had 107 known alehouses (52 unlicensed) in 1644, while in Lancashire 30 townships had 226 alehouses, as many as 143 being unlicensed. This was a ratio of one alehouse for every 20 households in the Essex villages, and one for every 12 in Lancashire; and it marked the sudden relaxation, in the Civil War period, of a long campaign to restrict the numbers of these meeting places, which were often very small and informal (Wrightson, 1982, p.168).

Alehouses were too important to be suppressed wholesale, and in the absence of effective local enforcement systems any attempt to do so would have been defied. Their roles in victualling, providing cooking facilities (customers often brought their own food), supplying a convivial pipe of tobacco from the early seventeenth century, offering lodgings to legitimate travellers and providing work for the old, the infirm and single women, thereby relieving potential distress without recourse to charity or the emergent parish poor-rate local taxation system, gave them powerful rhetorical and practical defences against their detractors. The focus of the campaigns of the early seventeenth century, backed up by the central government's Books of Orders which tried to suppress superfluous alehouses to preserve the barley supply in the frequent times of dearth which haunted these economically transitional years, was directed against the humbler alehouses where the village poor gathered, and which were thought capable of drawing others into debauchery and poverty.

Attacks came from the more literate and 'godly' of the villagers, an elite which was distancing itself from the more relaxed common culture of 'good neighbourliness', which tolerated occasional drunken silliness. It was often associated with Puritanism, a broadly-defined tendency within the Church of England which combined introspective conscience-searching with the fear that the sins of others would provoke divine displeasure against the wider community, and which was in the ascendant in many places, culminating in the Interregnum between 1649 and 1660 after the execution of Charles I. In the county town of Dorchester, for example, such groups saw 'a large proportion' of the population as 'in great need of reformation and discipline', especially the young, who might slip free from household discipline and follow dissipated paths, drinking, singing, engaging in idle chatter, being drawn into promiscuous sex which might beget bastards to be a charge on the community, disrupting church services when they went at all, and neglecting their work (Underdown, 1992, pp.79–84). Drink damaged families and plunged them into deeper poverty. But efforts to suppress it proved unsustainable, driving it underground rather than preventing it altogether, and dividing communities, bringing gossip and ridicule to the doors of the reformers. Keith Wrightson has argued that, '... At the level of the local community, the struggle over the alehouses was one of the most significant social dramas of the age'; and in the long run it was the bottom level of the emergent hospitality industry, among whom perhaps a quarter of the traders were women, which won out against its enemies (Wrightson, 1982, p.167).

Higher up the scale of provision, inns were growing impressively in scale and numbers during the century after the restoration of the monarchy in 1660. This was part of a wider pattern, as the middle ranks of commerce and the professions proliferated and prospered, and what Peter Borsay has called an 'urban renaissance' brought classical architecture (or at least frontages), luxury trades, public walks, dancing and display to provincial towns which were becoming centres of polite society. The rise of the 'coaching inn' was part of this process. Borsay describes the 'great inns' of the 'elite of the innkeeping fraternity' as 'among the most spectacular examples of tradesmen's wealth'. A small town like Penrith, on the main road to Carlisle and Scotland, might have three or four such buildings, 'about three or four storeys high and of hewn stone', by 1731; at about the same time the George at Northampton 'looks more like a palace than an inn', and the Bull at Stamford, on the Great North Road, 'would pass in Italy for a palace'. Borsay lists several other prime examples as 'the true palazzi of the English Augustan town' (Borsay, 1989, pp.210–11). Such inns had extensive stabling as well as accommodation for guests and their servants, and dining facilities on the grand scale. Henry Fletcher of the Royal Oak in Kendal, a smallish north-western market town, had a Red Room, a Green Room, a 'coffy house', a 'billyard room' and three parlours in 1743, when metropolitan houses had been following this path for a generation. As early as 1686 this northern market and manufacturing town was capable of supplying 279 guest-beds and 439 places for horses, although some of these would have been provided by 'small tavern and alehouse keepers who combined other trades with the sale of liquor and the furnishing of modest accommodation for travelling traders and country people'.

Tiny market towns of 1000 people or so, such as Kirkby Lonsdale and Appleby, could find beds and stabling for well over a hundred visitors on this basis (Marshall, 1975, pp.4–8). Inns also developed a trading role, as merchants met in private rooms and took the larger transactions away from the public eye of the market place; and the innkeepers acquired prosperity and prestige among the leading citizens of their towns (Everitt, 1973). As the Royal Oak evidence hints in its relatively small way, the larger inns were offering sophisticated entertainments to their guests: as Borsay says, their association with the affluent made it 'natural that they should adapt to service the growth in polite leisure', providing theatres, music clubs, book clubs, assemblies for dancing, and even (in the case of the Angel at Yeovil) a museum of antiquarian curiosities. The spa resorts, especially Bath, began to offer up-market lodging-houses as well as inns to accommodate their affluent visitors, and the development of a seasonal accommodation industry using purpose-built as well as adapted premises began at the seaside, with Brighton, Margate and Scarborough leading the way. The growth of urbane polite society, with its demand for news, political information and conversation, fuelled the parallel growth of the up-market coffee-house, which spread across the provinces from origins in Oxford, London and Bristol in the mid-seventeenth century (Borsay, 1989, pp.144–6).

By the mid-eighteenth century the great inns, which provided stabling, horse and carriage hire and relatively sophisticated catering, were a cut above the generality of what had come to be called 'public houses', which had become common terminology for licensed premises. The term 'alehouse' was still used legally for all premises licensed by the justices of the peace to sell alcoholic drinks, but 'in everyday speech . . . it was now reserved for the smallest local drinking places, and often used more or less pejoratively alongside "pot-house"' (Jennings, 1995, p. 19). There were also unlicensed drinking-dens, known in Bradford as 'whisht' or hush-shops because their existence, although often tacitly tolerated by the authorities, was supposed to remain a secret. As the untrammelled urban growth of the late eighteenth and early nineteenth century took hold, such places began to revive and increase in numbers, although they were also on the increase in the wilder areas of poverty-stricken rural counties like Sussex, where (it was alleged) poachers and thieves shared out their proceeds (Wells, in Emsley and Walvin, 1985).

Regulating excess

These developments on the lower rungs of the hospitality ladder worried the authorities just as had the proliferation of alehouses in an earlier period of population growth and economic turbulence. The century after 1660 had seen alehouses become more respectable, as the smaller and less salubrious ones were gradually squeezed out, the alehouse was no longer needed as an informal instrument of poor relief, and the larger places benefited from the increased purchasing power of prosperous times to approach the status of the inns. But gin shops proliferated, especially in London, to alarm moralists and reformers from the early eighteenth century, and in the later eighteenth century unlicensed alehouses also revived, although the number of inns and public houses failed to expand in step with population, and in many counties a renewed round of campaigns by local authorities from the 1780s saw the suppression of many of the smaller local pubs in back streets and isolated places. Magistrates feared sedition as well as crime and immorality: strangers from a higher class would be easily recognized in this setting, and radical politics, illegal trade union activity and machine-breaking schemes could be pursued undisturbed when these became issues from the turn of the eighteenth and nineteenth centuries. But when legislation came, it favoured the developing fashion for free trade in all things rather than responding to authoritarian fears of subversion. The 'Beerhouse Act' of 1830 sought to buy support for a beleaguered Tory government by making the poor man's beer (this was a gendered rhetoric) cheaper and more accessible, boosting beer consumption at the expense of more damaging spirit drinking, and benefiting growers of barley and hops. It allowed any householder to retail beer on payment of a two-guinea (£2.10) excise licence, subject to (among other things) 10pm closing and maintaining order. This liberated beerselling from the control of the magistrates, and made it easier for political radicals to meet without fear of direct consequences. Four years later the cost of an on-licence was increased to three guineas (£3.15), but closing time was extended to 11pm, and not until 1869 did the magistrates recover their licensing powers. This was an important freeing-up and expansion of the lowest levels of the legitimate hospitality trades (Clark, 1983, Chapters 8, 11, 14; Harrison, 1971; Jennings, 1995, pp.79–81).

Beerhouse numbers grew very rapidly, offering a competitive challenge to established public houses. Within six months over 24,000 excise licences had been issued, although the take-up rate varied widely, with ports like Liverpool well to the fore; and towns where pubs had been in short supply soon saw beerhouses in the majority of their licensed houses. Proprietors were drawn mainly from the ranks of skilled labour, and amenities varied widely. Many premises were small cottages knocked together, but others were purpose-built. Bradford's Red Lion was unusually well-appointed, with 'yew tree and Windsor chairs, longseating, ale tables and bar fittings ... plus bagatelle board and cottage pianoforte and various engravings, including Christ blessing little children and The stolen kiss'. Games played included dominoes, draughts, skittles, cards, shove-halfpenny and 'puff and dart', most of which were already available in the eighteenth century, although landlords had to be careful not to be caught permitting gambling. Basic food (bread and cheese or bacon and eggs) and lodging were often provided, and a significant minority of beerhouses were haunts of prostitutes, some of whom (as in Blackburn where this was said to be the norm) were ostensibly employed as servants. Beerhouses might also play host to popular blood sports (pugilism, dog- and cock-fighting, rat-, badger- and fox-baiting) or offer singing-rooms, *poses plastiques* (strip-shows thinly disguised) or exhibitions, as in the Liverpool show which put customers under the influence of laughing-gas and invited the audience to laugh at the obscenities they uttered. They provided a safe haven for Chartist meetings and an accessible venue for friendly societies, which offered cheap mutual insurance. They became, in short, central to the social life of many working people, women as well as men, especially in the teeming early- and mid-Victorian industrial towns (Jennings, 1995; Walton and Wilcox, 1991).

The lowest class of beerhouses, run by labourers in cottage parlours, overlapped with the cheap brothels and common lodging houses which had long been a feature of every urban centre from the market town upwards, and often of those 'open villages' without a resident landlord which housed rural labour forces for a wide area. Sleaford, a Lincolnshire market town with about 4000 inhabitants at mid-century, had two cottage brothels in Back Lane behind the church, which were identifiable as such in the 1851 census, and other 'disorderly houses' elsewhere. Two of the prostitutes were witty enough to give 'free trader' as an occupation, responding ironically to the contemporary exaltation of untrammelled commerce in (almost) everything (Ellis, 1981, pp.17–18). Nearby Horncastle, of similar size but with an important river navigation running through it, had perhaps 15 brothels in the 1830s and a maximum of 20 in the next decade, before a police campaign reduced their numbers: such establishments were not the sole prerogative of London or Liverpool. They were squalid, noisy and violent, attracting frequent intervention from police and neighbours, and we hear less of the quieter, more up-market 'accommodation houses' which serviced middle-class men (Davey, 1983, p.32). The common lodging house, offering a share of fire and mattress for a rock-bottom price, seems to have had its origins in the early eighteenth century; but it became the focus of a full-scale early Victorian moral panic, and remained a magnet for social investigators (whether reformers, sensation-seeking journalists or, in effect, well-connected tourists shown the sights by police patrols, like the French academic Hippolyte Taine in Manchester) throughout the nineteenth century and beyond. It was recognized to be the last resort of the impoverished before the ultimate humiliation of the workhouse, and part of its frisson was the idea that the honest and unfortunate poor would rub shoulders very closely, in the fetid and crowded sleeping accommodation, with thieves and prostitutes. But there was a parallel discourse, harking back to the 'low' sixteenth-century alehouse, which highlighted the irresponsible fun of being a member of the 'underworld', caring nothing for morals, cleanliness or appearances, and enjoying huge fry-ups in front of the communal fire while sharing stories of past escapes and depredations. Sanitary and police regulations at mid-century made life more difficult for lodging house proprietors, but they met such an obvious need that there could be no question of suppressing them (Taine, 1958; Davey, 1983; Thompson and Yeo, 1971).

The established public houses had to respond to the new competition from the beerhouses, over and above their existing problems with specialist outlets for the sale of spirits (the famous 'gin palaces' which spread from London in the 1820s), with the 'chop houses' and other primitive restaurants (heirs to the earlier cookshops) which competed for another aspect of their trade, and with coffee stalls which began to attract working-class custom from the 1820s and 1830s. The pubs reacted partly by changing appearance and ground plan, looking less like ordinary houses displaying signs, and introducing plate glass, gas lighting (sometimes with spectacular effects) and more opulent internal decor (with extensive use of mirrors), as well as (by the 1850s and 1860s) adopting distinctive architectural flourishes on their corner sites, with turrets, arches and eclectic embellishments. Luxurious-looking surroundings became available to the poor for the price of a drink. Bars were opened out to accommodate greater crowds, and barmaid service from behind a counter, with overtones of glamour, replaced scurrying potboys and further enhanced efficiency, while the cooking of working men's food was rapidly abandoned. These changes were pioneered in London, but soon spread to the provinces (Harrison, 1971; Girouard, 1984).

Additional competition for existing businesses came from the magistrates' increased willingness to license new pubs, which were at least under their control, to reduce the scope for beerhouses to spread; but much of this development took place in the spreading suburbs of the larger towns (Girouard, 1984). The 1830s and 1840s also saw the beginning of important changes in all of the 'three major roles' played by the pub in nineteenth-century Britain: 'transport centre, recreation centre and meeting place' (Harrison, in Dyos, 1977, p.162). The railways brought the demise of the coaching inn, which survived only at the limits of the system by 1860 (in the Lake District, for example, where tourists wanted to explore beyond railheads). Faster travel meant less demand for refreshments en route, although the great refreshment rooms at Rugby or Swindon struggled to serve trainloads of people at ten-minute refreshment stops before the advent of on-train catering on long-distance services, and railway food acquired its enduringly awful image, helped by Dickens's description of Mugby Junction. Quicker journeys also entailed fewer overnight stays, and these were increasingly channelled into a distinctive new building type, the railway hotel, which sprang up at termini and at tourist destinations from the 1840s onwards, reaching its apotheosis in the Gormenghast spires of the Midland Railway's St Pancras (Simmons, 1986). Commercial travellers became railborne, drovers and their charges left the green roads, and wayside inns lost their passing trade. Canal-side pubs which had catered for bargees also suffered. On the other hand, pubs flourished around railway terminals and along the new routes for horse omnibuses and later trams which radiated from city centres, although as fewer (and poorer) people walked to work along these routes the trade of houses between stops might be damaged.

The pub as recreation centre flourished, as enterprising speculators tapped into rising demand and sought to lure customers away from cheaper back-street rivals. Hence the gaudiness; but some of the larger pubs also developed enter-tainments on a grand scale. The Eagle off London's City Road, rebuilt in 1839–40, 'set a new standard of splendour for public houses which was not to be equalled for many years', with its pleasure gardens (and garden orchestra), statues, fountains, cosmoramas, rope-dancers, ballet and much more. Suburban pubs offered huge dancing platforms and leafy promenading areas for families. The music hall emerged from such ventures, which were pioneered in Lancashire as well as London, as Bolton's Star offered assorted musical and comic turns and a museum by mid-century (Girouard, 1984, p.35; Poole, 1982). At the more obviously disreputable end of the scale, the pub as masculine republic might be associated with pugilism or popular blood sports, or salacious mock trials full of double (and indeed single) entendres; but from the 1870s it also acted as one of the midwives of football as spectator sport, which proved altogether more respectable. The pub as meeting-place, meanwhile, continued to flourish, meeting the needs of a popular associational culture (friendly societies, political groups, trade unions, debating societies, botanists, enthusiasts for birds and animals) which usually had no alternative to the landlord's large room and payment of a 'wet rent' through consumption of his wares. The pub helped migrants to build a social life in strange surroundings and put workers in touch with employment opportunities. It was, however, in most cases a rival rather than a complement to the family, in terms of expenditure as well as sociability; and as such it remained a target for reformers' wrath (Harrison, 1971).

The heyday of the urban pub came between the 1850s and the 1890s, when a range of speculators, from Birmingham jewellery manufacturers to London clergymen, sought to take advantage of increasing working-class spending power, especially in city centre locations. Specialized pub architects used pictorial effects in glass and tiling and extravaganzas in carved wood and patent ceiling surfaces to create enticing environments. The pub resisted the threats and competition of the temperance movement (whose coffee palaces were financial failures, but helped to stimulate more commercial and less 'improving' ventures like Lockhart's Cocoa Rooms), and survived the casualties inflicted by magistrates and builders on popular suburban pleasure venues; and increasingly it diversified its offerings into snacks, soft drinks, Bovril and coffee, with ginger beer on draught. A frenetic burst of speculative building at the end of the century was followed by a rush of bankruptcies, and the peak of per capita alcohol consumption had already been scaled in the mid–1870s. By the Edwardian years the long decline of the pub had begun (Thorne et al., 1986; Girouard, 1984).

In some ways it had been foreshadowed by the withdrawal of the solid middle classes in the early Victorian years. The pubs of the second half of the century multiplied status gradations through small bars which segregated labour aristocrats or tradesmen from their poorer neighbours, and provided protected spaces for women to drink, making it easier for working-class women to visit the pub without necessarily compromising their respectability by late Victorian times. But they no longer accommodated the professionals or substantial employers who had still frequented the higher-class ones (though not the beerhouses or dram-shops) into the 1840s and perhaps the 1850s. At the top end of the scale the rise of the gentleman's club creamed off the most affluent. These establishments proliferated in and around London's Pall Mall from the 1810s and 1820s onwards, pioneering new styles in classical architecture and making statements about power and wealth through their self-confident bulk, while boasting the most fashionable French chefs. They catered for men of particular tastes and opinions: the Reform for Whigs, the Carlton for Tories, the Athenaeum for artists and literary men, the Travellers', the United Service, the Oxford and Cambridge, and (for gamblers) Crockford's, among many others. They offered a masculine environment, with membership controlled by vote as well as subscription level, and their imposing libraries, smoking rooms, morning rooms and dining accommodation offered privileged enclaves for like-minded people, enabling aristocrats and affluent professional men to escape from their families as well as their social inferiors. Gentlemen could dine and stay overnight at their clubs, and unless they had raffish tastes and sought plebeian company, usually in a 'sporting' and betting context, there was no need to go further. The big provincial centres followed suit, although some early examples, like the autocratically-run John Shaw's punch club for Manchester merchants, were rather rough-and-ready; but in its highest and most intimidating form this was a metropolitan phenomenon (Pevsner, 1957, pp.537–41, 568–71, 584; Stancliffe, 1938).

Eating and travelling as leisure activities

The Victorian years also saw the rise of the hotel, the restaurant and the sophisticated large-scale caterer. Inns and the larger public houses traded up to assume the more prestigious title 'hotel', which connoted a high standard of accommodation and catering and suggested a select clientele. Originally hotels lacked public dining-rooms, the food being served to guests privately, to order, in their suites; and from the 1820s some of London's best chefs were working on this principle (Mennell, 1985, p.155). This definition was soon outmoded, however, and purpose-built premises in central London began by catering for those affluent families who no longer kept up a London house, and extended their range to London tourists, especially Americans, while the later nineteenth century saw a broader middle-class market catered for in extensive multi-storeyed buildings with smaller rooms.

Alongside the railway hotels, the mid-Victorian years were the golden age of the grand hotel, at the seaside or in the Highlands, promoted speculatively by a limited company, as at Scarborough. Here, Cuthbert Brodrick's 'wondrous' eleven-storey Grand, completed in 1867, offered 'the advantages of a Boarding House with the luxury of complete appointments, good cuisine, prompt attendance, and strict selectness of a first-class Family Hotel. There is no good reason why Englishmen patriotic enough to patronise

English watering-places should be deprived of the advantages enjoyed by those who go abroad'. This advertising leaflet makes clear that the hotel concept was a continental import, desirable but also exotic, which needed to be domesticated. Characteristically, the manager was M. Fricour, from the Hotel Mirabeau in Paris. Technology was called in to reassure (central heating, electric bells, steam kitchen lifts, 'hydraulic ascending room'), and when the *table d'hôte* was opened out to non-residents they were carefully vetted and their local address was checked (Pevsner, 1966, p.331; Scarborough Pamphlet No. 229). This was an up-market provincial example of a widespread set of developments, with troops of servants in hierarchical array, including imported chefs to provide sophisticated cuisine, some of whom went on to open pioneering restaurants wherever the market looked promising. The most opulent hotels took care of the reputation of their own restaurants: when the Savoy Hotel opened in the Strand, close to London's clubland, in 1890 the chef was the legendary Georges Auguste Escoffier (Mennell, 1985, p.158). This was one example among many of the practice and personnel of leading continental hotels being brought to England. When affluent families required large-scale catering for special occasions closer to home, meanwhile, specialist firms like Spiers and Pond were emerging to provide it.

Comfortably-off bourgeois society, like its aristocratic 'betters', increasingly preferred to eat at home, when the husband was not at his club; and the rituals of exchanging hospitality became increasingly demanding. Mrs Beeton's has become the classic advice manual, first published in 1861, but it was one of many competitors in a brisk Victorian market. Good servants, especially cooks, were at a premium, but domestic entertaining could also be sustained by hiring a chef, waiters and even place settings and table decorations, if the regular establishment of domestic servants and the supply of plate and cutlery were insufficiently impressive. This preference for the private and domestic over the public and unpredictable, except on great occasions, was a characteristic of the Victorian middle-class family which inhibited the growth of a restaurant and cafe culture on the European model (Mars, 1997). On the other hand it boosted the grocer's licence for selling wine to be consumed at home, a Gladstonian innovation which was taken up most readily on the fringes of middle-class residential areas with few pubs, and which helped the emergence of a pattern whereby 'by the 1860s, the respectable classes were drinking at home, or not drinking at all' (Harrison, in Dyos, 1977, p.166).

As ladies began to sally forth to the new shopping streets and department stores which opened in London's West End and in favoured streets of provincial towns from the 1850s and 1860s onwards, however, some kind of respectable catering provision for them became necessary. So female safe havens developed, enabling ladies to refresh themselves without the embarrassment of being taken for prostitutes or pursued by strangers, in the form of department store cafes, confectioners', and tea rooms like those of Miss Cranston in Glasgow. Chains of refreshment houses also developed, aiming at a 'respectable' lower middle-class clientele of both sexes, as the 'white-blouse revolution' brought women into a widening range of city-centre employments. The Lyons corner houses, founded in 1894, quickly became famous as the reliable, cheap chain which most effectively met this need (Girouard, 1984, p.206).

Other kinds of popular catering outlet, at a straightforwardly working-class level, were beginning to spread from the later nineteenth century, often complementing the pub rather than offering alternatives to it. The fish and chip shop, originating around 1870 (although fried fish and chipped or baked potatoes had been hawked around urban streets since at least the 1840s), spread rapidly through working-class areas, first as an after-the-pub snack, then as a provider of mid-day meals for factory workers and labour-saving fill-ups for families, with around 25,000 outlets in 1913 and an inter-war peak of nearer 35,000. These were almost all small-scale single-family enterprises, with only a few small chains (despite contemporary fears) and a handful of larger and more up-market restaurants, one of which (Harry Ramsden's of White Cross, Guiseley, in industrial Yorkshire, which opened in 1931) formed the basis for eventual multiplication of branches and stock market flotation in the 1990s. The problem was always the replication of standards and quality control (Walton, 1992; Mosey and Ramsden, 1989; Berry, 1991). Tripe and other offal also formed the basis of cheap restaurants, with a longer pedigree. Lancashire was a particular stronghold, and there were attempts to go up-market in the early twentieth century, as at Vose and Son's Tripe de Luxe Restaurant and Tea Room, which opened in Wigan in 1917 and featured panelled walls, furniture 'of the Early English style', and a Ladies' Orchestra (Houlihan, 1988, p.6). Soon afterwards this trend was pursued by combines with chains of restaurants, most famously Parry Scragg and United Cattle Products, which survived into the 1970s. But most corner-shop tripe purveyors and fish friers were drawn from the skilled working class, and in industrial and seaside Scotland and Wales, especially, the trade became a haven for Italian immigrants from the turn of the century, in tandem with ice cream and alongside the distinctive cafes which became popular meeting places, generating some controversy in early twentieth-century Scotland because they brought young people of both sexes into contact in a relaxed setting, as well as providing gaming machines.

London's Italian community, centred on Soho, also joined French and other migrant groups to provide distinctive restaurants which were at the core of metropolitan bohemian society, but also set fashions which spread elsewhere (Sponza, 1988, pp. 94–115; Colpi, 1991). Italians were also quick to move into the craze for milk bars which provided another alternative to the pub in the 1930s (Forte, 1986). At an opposite extreme of cosy Englishness was the spread of the tea room, often trying to re-create an imagined rustic cottage past, which became a feature of suburbs and market towns, and especially of the country roadsides and picturesque villages which became tourist and excursionist destinations for the cars and charabancs of the inter-war years. As we saw above, similar idioms could be introduced into tripe restaurants, and a thorough study of the tea room vogue would be needed to tease out the varieties of context and ambience. J.B. Priestley, making his 'English journey' in 1933, met an ineffectual dabbler in various businesses who described his own venture into this field:

> I tried it once. The wife was keen. In Kent. Good position, too, on a main road. We'd everything very nice . . . We called it the Chaucer Pilgrims – you know, Chaucer. Old style – Tudor, you know – black beams and everything. Couldn't make it pay . . . If you ask me what let us down, I'd say the slump in America. It was on the road to Canterbury – you see, Chaucer Pilgrims – but we weren't getting the American tourists. I wouldn't touch a tea room again, not if you gave me one.
>
> (Priestley, 1934, p.6)

These small catering businesses had a high mortality rate, and survival usually required a second source of income in the family. Few fortunes were made: it was more a matter of hanging on and scraping a living. The tea room as business venture attracted speculators of a more middle-class background than the fish and chip trade, with a very different ruling aesthetic and set of social pretensions (except where fish and chips acquired the pretensions of a restaurant). The pub, with its extensive hierarchy from back street to ostentatious drinking palace, drew in a wider cross-section, although the rapid spread of the tied house system and the decline of the home-brew pub in the late nineteenth century altered the balance between independent businesses, tenants and managers. The new inter-war roadhouses on by-passes and arterial roads, built in 'Brewer's Tudor' and catering for the motor trade, added a new dimension, catering for modern needs in mock-medieval surroundings (Girouard, 1984; Thorne *et al.*, 1986).

The other sector of the hospitality trades which showed rapid expansion from mid-Victorian times to the 1930s was tourism, especially in the seaside resort, a distinctive kind of town which was prominent among the fastest-growing urban centres of the period. As the working-class seaside holiday originated in late Victorian Lancashire, with Blackpool the main beneficiary, and then developed a generation later in the West Riding and West Midland industrial districts, and as London's armies of white-collar workers and small traders found their way to the coast, so a new tier of cheap accommodation developed to service their needs during a short summer season. The established hotel and boarding-house trade, which catered especially for solid middle-class families for up to a month at a time, was augmented by cottage and terraced accommodation for working-class visitors who might stay for a few days or a week. Where 'respectable' landladies with capital and servants, usually spinsters or widows with annuities or investments to eke out, offered full board and sitting-rooms, their new counterparts were often working class, augmenting a family income, working round the clock for the summer and pressing their children into service too, and offering crowded, minimum accommodation with services (and therefore costs) cut to the bone for visitors who could only just afford the trip. Whether the visitors were Lancashire cotton workers, Yorkshire miners or, in the south west, Swindon railway workers with a week's holiday and a privilege rail ticket, this added a new down-market dimension to the hospitality trades; and where demand was high, as at Blackpool, new purpose-built 'company-houses', ordinary terraces with extra bedrooms, mushroomed around the railway stations. Thus was a precarious but lively new hospitality industry born, with its own folklore surrounding the rules by which landladies protected themselves and the extra charges they tried to levy for hot water or use of cruet (Walton, 1978, 1983 and 1994).

This was not the only model for popular holidaymaking in the heyday of the British seaside. There were various forms of self-catering, including the 'bungalow towns' of converted tramcars and railway carriages which colonized makeshift landscapes from the turn of the century, and the rise of the caravan from the inter-war years; and there was the holiday camp, which also had turn-of-the-century origins but was being organized on a commercial basis, and also by trade unions, local authorities and the Co-operative movement, to supply cheap chalet accommodation and collective enjoyment to a clientele which was dominated, in the first instance, by white-collar workers. The almost-eponymous Billy Butlin arrived on the scene in 1936, and the camps enjoyed a post-war heyday in which some commentators were impressed by their vigour and cheerfulness, others horrified by what looked like exploitative regimentation (Walton, 1994; Ward and Hardy, 1986; Hardy and Ward, 1984). At their peak, however, they only accounted for around 5 per cent of domestic holiday 'bednights', compared with (in 1967) nearly 28 per cent spent 'staying with friends', a telling reminder of the continuing, unobtrusive importance of uncommercial hospitality in people's daily lives (Bramley, n.d., Table 5).

Another 1967 statistic found that just over 15 per cent of 'bednights' were spent in licensed hotels; and the holiday hotel trade kept a resilient, conservative middle-class market, which resisted the swelling siren songs of 'abroad'. There had been little inter-war investment in seaside hotels, and hardly any in the post-war generation; but the desiderata of that generation which was moving into middle age in the post-war years were probably summed up by the popular travel writer S.P.B. Mais, writing about the Cawdor Hotel at Tenby in 1949. It was 'the ideal hotel', unpretentious, courteous, quietly efficient, with plenty of space at mealtimes, generous and 'exquisitely cooked' portions, and:

> The virtues of the Cawdor are legion. The stairs do not creak; the water is always hot; the lavatories are reading-rooms in little. There are no draughts; there are verandas on two floors; the doors stay shut; the windows open easily; there is a full-sized billiard room; there is a piano in the lounge; tea is not a pernickety drawing-room affair, but a solid sit-down business in the dining-room; the house is not old enough to be ghost or spider-ridden, not modern enough for chromium plate or fumed oak. Its smell is the smell of the Exmoor farmhouse in which I spent my heavenly childhood.
>
> (Mais, 1949, pp.11–12)

This was an ideal whose time would soon pass; and some of these virtues would not have looked like good business to a keen proprietor. Chloe Stallybrass and Julian Demetriadi have chronicled the decline of the seaside hotel during the third quarter of the nineteenth century, although the census statistics are particularly fallible at the lower end of the market, where there were also many conversions from boarding-houses to holiday flats and apartments. The problems posed by government policies, especially selective employment tax, VAT and necessary but costly fire precautions in the early 1970s, played their part; but the wider context must also be considered, especially the rise of the Mediterranean (and then the longer-haul) package tour and the revolution it wrought in expectations about accommodation standards, which were difficult to meet in Victorian premises with complicated plumbing (Stallibrass, 1978 in Shaw and Williams, 1997).

The decline of the seaside resort is one of several post-war British themes which need serious research. Others include the transformation of the pub, the rise of the wine bar, and the revolution in eating out, which includes the movement of Chinese, Greek Cypriots and Turks into the fish and chip trade as well as the rise of Chinese, Indian, Italian and other ethnic restaurants, the opening out of new tastes in food, wine and beer, and the proliferation of new kinds of fast food, with particular attention to the American chains like McDonald's, Burger King and KFC. But such phenomena as Pierre Victoire also need to be set in historical context. The development of themed hotel chains, and purpose-built resorts like Center-Parcs, also offers enticing research possibilities for those who are prepared to look behind the present, which anyone who wants to investigate present problems has of necessity to do. A particularly important theme, which has been touched on glancingly in this chapter, is the conditions of work in the hospitality industries, which have been examined critically not only for Burger King but also for smaller businesses and indeed their proprietors (Reiter, 1991; Gabriel, 1988). And when a whole (and compelling) academic thesis has been constructed around the 'McDonaldization of society', while contemporary work on tourism and hospitality floods into print, the need to add a serious time dimension, with all the comparative elements that entails, becomes paramount (Ritzer, 1998; Alfino *et al.*, 1998). I hope this introduction to the history of hospitality will prove fecund in themes for others to follow.

Conclusions

The modern hospitality trades represent both a continuation and break with traditions that extend through millennia. The caring treatment of travellers together with mutual obligations between guest and host were widely recorded through the early centuries of Roman Britain. Despite periods of expansion and decline there was a steady growth of trade between communities and consequently a growth in the number of people travelling. Initially, traditional values relating to the hospitable treatment of strangers enabled travellers to be accommodated in private dwellings. As the volumes of travellers grew, specialist inns emerged as places where travellers were accommodated, and the nature of the hospitality relationship began to change.

As Selwyn shows in Chapter 2, the eighteenth century witnessed an increased concern to reaffirm the moral obligations of hospitality. Some of these comments are contemporary with Samuel Johnson's declaration about the benefits of a good inn quoted in Chapter 3. Certainly, there has been an ongoing concern with the 'morality' of hospitality that has at times reflected the need to maintain the obligations of guests and hosts, and at other times has attempted to regulate the context of hospitality provision in the conduct of alehouses and the places where alcoholic drinks were provided for the poor.

Growing affluence and increased transport encouraged more travel and leisure eating for increasing numbers throughout the last couple of centuries, as people could eat more than they needed and could spend increasing amounts of leisure time on travel and eating away from home. Hotels, guest houses and bed breakfast accommodation, together with restaurants and cafes as we know them today, emerged to meet these needs.

References

Alfino, M. *et al.* (1998) *McDonaldization Revisited*. New York, Greenwood.

Berry, Arthur (1991) *The Little Gold-mine*. Liverpool, Bullfinch.

Borsay, P. (1989) *The English Urban Renaissance*. Oxford, Clarendon.

Bramley, Glen (n.d.) Tourism in Britain and Some Local Economic Effects (typescript in Lancaster University Library).

Clark, Peter (1983) *The English Alehouse: A Social History 1200–1830*. Leicester, Leicester University Press.

Colpi, Terri (1991) *The Italian Factor*. Edinburgh, Mainstream.

Davey, B.J. (1983) *Lawless and Immoral*. Leicester, Leicester University Press.

Dyos, H.J. and Wolff, M. (eds) (1977) *The Victorian City*, pbk edn, Vol. 1. London, Routledge.

Ellis, Charles (1981) *Mid-Victorian Sleaford*. Lincoln, Lincolnshire Library Service.

Emsley, C. and Walvin, J. (eds) (1985) *Artisans, Peasants and Proletarians*. London, Croom Helm.

Everitt, Alan (1973) The English urban inn. In A. Everitt (ed) *Perspectives in English Urban History*. London, Macmillan.

Forte, Charles (1986) *Forte: The Autobiography of Charles Forte*. London, Sidgwick and Jackson.

Gabriel, Yiannis (1988) *Working Lives in Catering*. London, Routledge.

Girouard, Mark (1984) *Victorian Pubs*. New Haven, Yale University Press.

Hardy, Dennis and Colin Ward (1984) *Arcadia for All: The Legacy of a Makeshift Landscape*. London, Mansell.

Harrison, B. (1971) *Drink and the Victorians*. London, Faber and Faber.

Heal, F. (1990) *Hospitality in Early Modern England*. Oxford, Clarendon Press.

Houlihan, M. (1988) *A Most Excellent Dish: Tales of the Lancashire Tripe Trade*. Swinton, Neil Richardson.

Jennings, Paul (1995) *The Public House in Bradford, 1770–1970*. Keele, Keele University Press.

Laurence, Anne (1994) *Women in England 1500–1760*. London, Weidenfeld.

Mais, S. P. B. (1949) *I Return to Wales*. London, Christopher Johnson.

Mars, Valerie (1997) Ordering dinner, PhD thesis. University of Leicester.

Marshall, J.D. (1975) *Kendal 1661–1801*. Kendal, Titus Wilson.

Mennell, S. (1985) *All Manners of Food*. Oxford, Basil Blackwell.

Monckton, H.A. (1969) *A History of the English Public House*. London, Bodley Head.

Mosey, Don and Harry Ramsden Jnr (1989) *Harry Ramsden: The Uncrowned King of Fish and Chips*. Clapham via Lancaster, Dalesman.

Pevsner, N. (1957) *The Buildings of England: City of London and Westminster*. London, Penguin.

Pevsner, N. (1966) *The Buildings of England: Yorkshire: the North Riding*. London, Penguin.

Poole, Robert (1982) *Popular Leisure and Music-hall in Nineteenth-century Bolton*. Lancaster, Centre for North-West Regional Studies.

Priestley, J.B. (1934) *English Journey*. London, Heinemann.

Reiter, E. (1991) *Making Fast Food*. Montreal, McGill-Queen's University Press.

Ritzer, G. (1998) *The McDonaldization Thesis: Explorations and Extensions*. New York, Sage.

Shaw, Gareth and Allan, Williams (eds) (1997) *The Rise and Fall of British Coastal Resorts*. London, Mansell.

Simmons, Jack (1986) *The Railway in Town and Country 1830–1914*. Newton Abbot, David and Charles.

Sponza, L. (1988) *Italian Immigrants in Nineteenth-century Britain*. Leicester, Leicester University Press.

Stallibrass, C. (1978) The holiday accommodation industry: a case study of Scarborough (PhD thesis, University of London, 1978).

Stancliffe, F.S. (1938) *John Shaw's Manchester*. Sherratt and Hughes.

Taine, Hippolyte (1958) *Notes on England*. London, Thames and Hudson.

Thompson, E.P. and Yeo, Eileen (eds) (1971) *The Unknown Mayhew*. Harmondsworth, Penguin.

Thorne, Robert, *et al.* (1986) *Birmingham Pubs 1880–1939*. Gloucester, Alan Sutton.

Underdown, David (1992) *Fire from Heaven*. London, HarperCollins.

Walton, J.K. (1978) *The Blackpool Landlady: A Social History*. Manchester, Manchester University Press.

Walton, J.K. (1983) *The English Seaside Resort: A Social History 1750–1914*. Leicester, Leicester University Press.

Walton, J.K. (1992) *Fish and Chips and the British Working Class*. Leicester, Leicester University Press.

Walton, J.K. (1994) The Blackpool landlady revisited. *Manchester Region History Review*, 8, pp. 23–31.

Walton, J. K. and Poole, R. (1982) The Lancashire wakes in the nineteenth century. In R. Storch (ed) *Popular Culture and Custom in Nineteenth-century England*. Beckenham, Croom Helm, pp. 100–124.

Walton, J. K. and Wilcox, A. (1991) *Low Life and Moral Improvement in Mid-Victorian England: Liverpool Through the Journalism of Hugh Shimmin*. Leicester, Leicester University Press.

Ward, Colin and Hardy, Dennis (1986) *Goodnight Campers!* London, Mansell.

Wrightson, K. (1982) *English Society 1580–1680*. London, Hutchinson.

CHAPTER 5

Putting up?
Gender, hospitality
and performance

Jane Darke

School of Planning, Oxford Brookes University

Craig Gurney

*Centre for Housing Management and
Development, University of Wales*

Key themes

- Hospitality in the home as performance
- Gender roles and hospitality
- Taboos and etiquette in the visit
- Tensions and taboos in the guest and host relationship
- Differences between commercial and home-based hospitality

The absence of a broad feminist perspective on hospitality seems a curious oversight given that many host–guest relationships are overlain by social relations of gender (Aitchison, 1999). Sociologists have long since established that our words give us away; thus expressions such as land*lady*, bell-*boy* or house*wife* assume a crucial significance when considering the importance of gender in accounting for hospitality roles and expectations. Hospitality is, thus, deeply implicated in any analysis of patriarchy.

Our starting point in this chapter is that the term 'hospitality' has been *selectively appropriated* to denote a large-scale service industry providing overnight accommodation and/or drink and/or food on a commercial basis. It represents, in essence, the commodification of domestic labour. To use the term in this way involves an extended metaphor, implying that good practice in commercial hospitality is a simulation of a visit to the home of an ideal host, attentive to the guest's every need. Yet this ideal is hard to attain. The interaction between host and guest takes place within a context of social expectations which may be discrepant. Specifically, norms relating to the 'performance' (Goffman, 1959) of the host and of the guest should be observed. The home, normally a private 'back region', is exposed to scrutiny and its occupants, particularly the woman presumed to be managing its presentation, are likely to be judged on the result. Seen in this way, hospitality can be understood as a particularly fragile experience for the guest whilst the host carries a heavy burden of risk, ideological conformity and impression management. These experiences and burdens are highly gendered, tending to reproduce existing patterns of inequality and difference.

The context for this account is previous writing by the authors and others (Darke, 1994, 1996; Gurney, 1990, 1996, 1997; Lawrence 1987; Madigan and Munro, 1991; Rybczynski, 1986; Cooper Marcus, 1995) on the personal significance of the home for women and men, the presentation of the home as a facet of the presentation of self, and the way feelings about the home are mediated by gender and tenure. Much of this literature – which straddles housing sociology, cultural/feminist geography, anthropology and environmental psychology – shares an intellectual commitment to anti-positivism and to a narrative style. For some (Darke, 1994; Cooper Marcus, 1995), this is evident in self-disclosure, biography and 'stories' whilst for others (Gurney, 1997, 1999a; Anthony, 1997) it is apparent in ethnographic or life-history data from small, purposive samples. We make no apology for our continued use of these techniques in this chapter but would direct the sceptical reader to recent contributions on feminist epistemology within sociology (Ramazanoglu, 1992) and the role of 'narrative identity' in geography (Gutting, 1996).

Chapter 10 by Botterill in this volume also includes a discussion of these issues in relation to hospitality research in general. Despite the fact that the authors were born into different generations, social classes and genders we share a belief that these techniques are neither anti-intellectual nor anecdotal but, rather, that they provide possibilities to reflect upon established trends and debates and offer opportunities to point up directions for further research.

Our aim is to foreground gender in an analysis of hospitality. Our use of the extant hospitality literature is necessarily selective and we make no attempt to rehearse debates reviewed elsewhere in this volume. Instead we focus on one aspect of hospitality: overnight visits to the home as a gendered performance. In this chapter we concentrate on overnight stays, with only passing references to guests who are given food and drink but do not sleep in the house.

There are many types of event covered in the stay of a guest in the home of a host. We suggest that there is a continuum from the informal 'putting-up' to the formal visit, and begin by discussing their respective characteristics. The visit requires 'impression management', and there are many ways in which the host or the home may be found wanting. The hospitality industry is imitating the idealized visit rather than 'putting up'. The distinction between the put-up and the visit is similar to that made in conjunction with meals by people interviewed by Martens and Warde (1998), who did not regard meals taken regularly with family and close friends as 'proper entertaining'.

It is difficult to demarcate our area of interest, the overnight stay where the 'housewife' is manager of the process, from related variants such as the country house party or the 'paying guest' or lodger. The former depended on a small army of servants, the latter represents the interface between the commercial hospitality sector and the visit to someone's home. Indeed Chapter 6 by Lynch and MacWhannell and Chapter 7 by Randall explore this interface in this volume. It is clear that among the aristocracy and gentry, visits to others' homes have long been a common pattern: cases are described in ancient sagas. In the early nineteenth century, Jane Austen's plots would be impossible without them. However, many of our informants from middle and working class families recall few such visits taking place during their childhood and suggest that overnight visiting was rare until a generation ago. Less formal family visiting was common, where a family spent time staying with grandparents or other kin, often substituting for a paid holiday.

Our discussion does not therefore claim validity over a timeless and placeless social world. It is specific to the middle class (the group most likely to be making and receiving visits without paid staff to do part of the work), to the late twentieth century, and to Britain. The impulse to offer hospitality may be less 'natural' and universal than some writers have implied (Lashley, Chapter 1, this volume; Heal, 1990; Telfer, 1996). The host's orientation to the home may, on the one hand, positively require the presence of guests as admiring audience to an accomplished home-making performance. At the other extreme, the host may preclude any outsiders visiting because they create extra work and destroy a hard-won sense of the home as haven, or guests potentially threaten to expose the host's incompetence at presenting home and self. The expectations for hosts and guests vary not only by gender but according to whether the home is perceived primarily as a symbol of economic success, the embodiment of the discerning taste of the occupier, or the site of family life, and so on. The hospitality event may vary too by age or generation and social class. The meanings associated with the home are complex: most, but not all, will be congruent with the wish to welcome guests.

Hospitality as performance

In this part of the chapter we develop a theoretical framework influenced by ideas contained in Goffman's *The Presentation of Self in Everyday Life* (1959), using this framework to demonstrate the fragility of hospitality as a highly skilled and socially constructed 'performance'.

Goffman explains his use of the metaphor of a theatrical performance as follows.

> I have been using the term performance to refer to all the activity of an individual which occurs during a period marked by his (sic) continuous presence before a particular set of observers. It will be convenient to label as *front* that part of the individual's performance which regularly functions in a general and fixed fashion to define the situation for those who observe the performance.
>
> (Goffman, 1959, p.32).

The place in which observations of an individual or 'team' performance take place and the relationship to the observer are crucial in this argument. Thus, Goffman argues that the *setting* (or stage) within which the performance takes place and the *appearance* and *manner* of the performer(s) are key determinants of the 'front' of everyday life. These three determinants are analogous in his dramaturgical framework to the stage and props, costume and characterization. These factors are crucial in sustaining what Goffman calls the 'impression management' of a performance to avoid 'letting the side down', 'gaffs' or 'causing a scene' (Goffman, 1959, pp.203–30). Anyone familiar with the fly-on-the-wall docu-drama filmed at the Adelphi in Liverpool will appreciate the distinction between the back region of the kitchen and the front of the reception desk. Thinking about hospitality as a performance opens up a number of theoretical possibilities which we develop in this chapter. These centre around three propositions which we state below.

Classifying hospitality as performance

There is an immense variety in the types of performance needed to accomplish certain hospitality tasks. At home, the guest who overstays their welcome might notice the gloss of the host's impression management fade away. In a bed and breakfast setting the host would not be expected to offer the performance standards associated with a five-star hotel. In a top hotel the guest should reasonably be expected access to 'home' comforts and, in many cases much more. To illustrate this Table 5.1 demonstrates how staging arrangements and performance expectations for domestic hospitality differ according to their place on a continuum of invited residential through to uninvited non-residential.

Rules, resources and obligations

Expectations, rules and resources exist for both host and guest in the performing roles of the 'good host' and the 'good guest'. Whilst the performance expectations placed by a honeymoon couple upon the staff at a five-star hotel might differ from those of a young male visiting his parents, there remains a set of taken for granted assumptions which mediate (un)reasonable requests, behaviour or service. At the heart of this dynamic is the idea of hospitable obligations. Hoteliers may be contractually obligated to guests whilst home-hosts might be obligated by kin, duty or loyalty. Heal (1990), for instance, has discussed the pervasive obligation to offer hospitality in its historical context, whilst Douglas (1975, 1990), Mauss (1990) and Carsten and Hugh-Jones (1995) have all stressed the importance of understanding customs and expectations connected with hospitality in the context of the culture as a whole. Mauss argues that hospitality always implies

Table 5.1 A four-fold classification of domestic hospitality as performance

Performance for	Staging implications and performance expectations
(a) Invited residential guests	A sustained performance of hospitality which incorporates *decorum*, *politeness* and *impression management* to sustain tidiness and order may be required for days on end. It may prove difficult to defend a back-region from the intrusion of guests or for hosts to easily move back-stage as the boundaries between insiders and outsiders will increasingly blur in proportion to the length of the visit. Tensions between guests and hosts may emerge as a result the former's judgements of the latter's domestic styles or between hosts (if multiple) if one has a more propinquital relationship to the guests than the other. These tensions may have profound consequences for an individual or team performance and a deleterious effect upon privacy during or after the visit.
(b) Invited non-residential guests	A temporally specific performance of hospitality which is easier to maintain and plan than in (a) above. Examples might include guests 'coming round for a drink', a meal or a party. For the host the staging might include the selection of appropriate music, the preparation and presentation of food and drinks. For events like a children's party or a formal dinner party these staging activities will be considerable and may also involve the rigid confinement of the performance in a front region. As in (a) above tensions and inconsistencies may emerge within the performance team with profound consequences for sustaining individual privacy. Indeed given the bounded nature of the performance, a performance team may cram or over-act and thus increase the risk of *faux pas* (Mike Leigh's film *Abigail's Party* provides a good example of this).
(c) Un-invited residential guests	There may be an obligation of kin, loyalty or reciprocal felicitousness for a host to be hospitable to such a guest. An unannounced guest might reasonably be expected to receive short shrift when seeking a bed for the night, but the normal rules of the good host/guest are liable to change during periods of emergency. Those affected by bereavement, violence, burglary, etc. are likely to be accommodated but may be too preoccupied to notice a less than perfect display of hospitality. Children evacuated and billeted and adults 'bombed out' during the 1939–45 war speak of the way in which strangers rallied round to offer the kind of hospitality at short notice which would normally only be offered to close kin members.
(d) Un-invited non-residential guests	The staging implications of delivering an unexpected performance for friends and family who 'just pop round' are massive. By extending Goffman's framework this is analogous to a quick scene-change. Mess and disorder may have to be quickly hidden out of sight in the front region (under cushions, behind furniture etc.) and moved into a back region. At the very least mess must be managed (by moving mess off a sofa to offer a sitting-space), performers might have to get dressed or curtail inappropriate behaviour as part of the scene change. When aspects of identity which may, in normal circumstances, be celebrated in decor or books, are present, decisions about their removal to a back region may have to be quickly made. This might include, for example 'de-dyking the house' (Johnson and Valentine, 1995) when a landlord, parent or even 'gas-man' calls.

Source: *Based on Gurney (1998)*

reciprocal obligations, so that the guest owes a debt of honour to the host. The expectation is that hospitality should be reciprocated in kind, although this does not always happen, especially within families (Finch and Mason, 1993). As with any social norm, departures from the ideal are the subject of anecdotes and cautionary tales which serve to socialize the hearer or to reaffirm that the teller and the hearer (if not the subject of the anecdote) share the same understanding of social norms. Martens and Warde (1998) describe their interviewees as talking at length about occasions where there was uneven reciprocity of hospitality in the home.

'Doing' hospitality: the hostess with the mostest?

The performance of hospitality is fragile and precarious necessitating careful and continual impression management. Whilst 'letting the side down' always carries the risk of sanctions either material (deduction of wages, fine, loss of performance bonus) or moral (shame, ostracism, embarrassment) the risks of failing to meet required standards of hospitality are particularly grave. The appropriation of the ideal host's standards of hospitality across the commercial sector (discussed above) raises expectations for standards of domestic hospitality. Whilst a number of broadly feminist researchers have sought to problematize the simplistic relationship between women, domestic interiors and the meaning of home (Darke 1994, 1996; Gurney 1997, 1999b; Watson, 1991; McDowell, 1999, pp.71–95), it remains the case that women's identity is much more closely tied up with the home than men's and, thus, that judgements on housekeeping standards are at the hub of a complex set of patriarchal social relations. This has led us to postulate a relationship between discourses of women's roles in families and those of the hostess. In effect what we are arguing is that the hospitality in the commercial sector offers the services of a surrogate mother or wife.

Of course, to argue a relationship between gender, home and home-stay hospitality is by no means new (see, for example, Ireland, 1993; Morgan 1996; Bowlby et al., 1997) but it remains unclear how a feminist perspective might develop within hospitality. For instance, it is an oversimplification to say that women are the producers/hosts and men the consumers/guests but men are much more likely to consume in the sector which is more highly commodified. In the less commodified, less regulated sector (i.e. farm/home stay sector) traditional images of the landlady as either too inviting or too uninviting described by Lynch and MacWhannell (Chapter 6, this volume) and others come to the fore.

The wife-like services do not normally include sex. This topic will be briefly discussed below: here we suggest that this sector of the hospitality industry has been neglected by researchers. A sub-sector has arisen to exploit sex tourism, particularly involving settings and destinations where acts may be practised that are prohibited at home. The 'deviant' search for sexual *frisson* has been normalized in mainstream hotels through pay-to-view television channels offering soft porn in Britain and hard-core material where laws are more permissive. Of course, the chambermaid has long been the subject of male sexual fantasies and the term 'hostess' has acquired sexual connotations that lead us to use the term 'host' for both genders, and host(ess) when we are talking of gendered but non-sexual roles *vis-à-vis* guests in the home.

Taboos and etiquette in the 'put up' and the visit

A 'put-up' is normally initiated by the guest. He or she may need somewhere to stay because they are on a journey or have things to do in the area, or they may just want to see the host. For example, a parent or close friend of a student who has moved from the home area to study may ask to visit. By inviting themselves they have signalled their willingness to accept whatever conditions they may encounter in the host's home, although they may carry hopes that it will conform to norms of cleanliness and tidiness.

Anticipating our discussion of the visit, which is seen as archetypally involving a female host, and an owner occupied home, the person doing the putting up may be male or female, and in any tenure including licensee (for example, in a hostel) or tenant. Obviously the host must be housed. It is not possible to be put up in a night shelter, nor could someone be visited who lives and works in other people's homes as an agency carer. The put-up further contrasts with the visit in being low on expectations. The self-invited guest must take 'pot luck'[1] on what there is to sleep on (from uncarpeted floor or inflatable in the host's one room, to a proper bed in a spare room) sleep in (what type of bedding or none), and whether there is food available.

Even with putting up there is by no means a complete absence of expectations. Depending on the degree of closeness of the relationship, the host is expected to accede to the request to visit or at worst re-negotiate an alternative date (although the would-be guest should also accept a get-out statement that for particular reasons it is really not feasible to put them up). The home should not constitute more than a mild health hazard. Even if no food is available, an offer of tea, coffee or an alcoholic drink is expected.

Where the host is middle aged, middle class and established in a marriage or long-term relationship, there is a greater expectation that the stay should take on some of the characteristics of the visit as discussed later.

The expectations on the guest are perhaps more precise than those on the host. As the guests have initiated the visit they are expected not to complain at discomfort, poor facilities or lack of privacy, or the (deficiencies in) cleanliness and tidiness of home and occupants. This is a particularly delicate path to tread for the mother of young adults who have left the parental home. She may be amusedly shocked at the chaos in the home, especially if it is shared (and her offspring therefore lacks full control over its state), but to be actively censorious puts the relationship at risk. Guests who are put up should observe rules such as, (a) be restrained in consuming household resources (telephone, milk, toilet roll etc.), (b) avoid breaking anything, and (c) avoid leaving any detectable bodily wastes.

The social expectations surrounding the conduct of hosts and guests become much more elaborate when we move from the put-up to the visit. Table 5.2 indicates some of the expectations involved.

Writing for an audience of hospitality specialists, we realize that it is a grave error to fail to differentiate between hotels: at least between the smaller owner-run establishment, the cheaper chains, the upmarket chains and the more aspirational 'country house' hotel. These will of course vary in the lavishness with which they can meet the above minimum standards, and in some cases whether these standards apply at all.

We discuss later some instances where these rules were violated and the discomfort that resulted. Concern and anxiety about possible transgressions are characteristic of the visit. First we discuss how the visit is based on a naturalized perception of particular households and tenures as 'normal'. The ideal visit is premised on the concept of a lady of the house (normally the wife of the male host) whose main occupation is the maintenance of the household. In contrast to the put-up, on a visit the home is expected to be very clean and very tidy, with personalized touches by the 'housewife': cushions,[2] ornaments, a vase of flowers from the garden. There are contradictory expectations. It is expected that the host(ess) has taken particular care to make the home worthy to welcome the visitor, but also that the home is always *almost* as clean and tidy as this and that the visit has not required considerable extra labour.

This type of visit is not impossible in a home lacking a female presence, but this is a part of the 'ideal' experience of hospitality in the home. Men are presumed less capable of adding the

Table 5.2 Expectations of overnight stays

	Hotel	Bed & breakfast	Home
Boundaries	Assumed extensive back region. Part maybe visible, e.g. glimpsed kitchens. Boundaries generally clear.	Back regions exist and boundaries may be unclear and graduated, e.g. host's kitchen and lounge accessible, but bathroom and bedroom not.	Rules not clear. May be negotiable, may vary according to identity of guest.
Presentation	High standard of cleanliness, *a sine qua non*, must appear as routine aspect of performance.	As hotel, but some leeway, e.g. if the establishment is a working farm.	Expected to be moderately clean and tidy, but many contingencies to this – see text.
Bedroom	Clean tidy, not used for any other purpose. Curtains contribute to decorative scheme, cut out light and give privacy.	As hotels, probably more 'individual character' – less branded coherence.	Likely to have other uses, child's room. Variable expectations about decoration. Curtains for privacy and light exclusion.
TV usage	TV in each guest's room or in TV lounge.	TV in rooms or in lounge: may be shared with hosts.	Negotiated with host if TV in house: usage may be class related.
Bed linen	Comfortable standard bed and base with newly laundered linen. Provision of towels of towels for guests – usually more than one.	Bed as hotel, though may be lower quality. Linen may be lower quality – nylon sheets – one towel per guest.	May be mattress on the floor or inflatable. Sheets and towels expected to be clean, but more a sense of making do.
Facilities	Bedside lights and many other lighting points, wardrobe, shelves, drawers, chairs, trouser press, full length mirror, waste paper basket. Guest may complain if some of the basics are absent.	Increasingly similar expectations for hotel bedroom, though some limitations – trouser press, scale of provision lower.	Mirror, wardrobe and draw space, waste paper basket, but any of these may be improvised, e.g. door on hook and chair in place of wardrobe, mirror only in bath room, angle poise lamp.
Personal touches	Standard includes complimentary toiletries, may include bowl of fruit, or flowers. Pictures and ornaments add these personal touches, selected to be tasteful but inoffensive.	Some of the same features as hotels, though there may be added touches from the hostess's personal touch – flowers from the garden.	Depends on the host and whether it is a stopover or visit – see text.

	Hotel	Bed & breakfast	Home
Bathroom	En-suite provision is the standard expectation.	As hotel, but an allowance may be made for 'character'. May share bathroom with other guests – rarely with the hosts.	Typically shares facilities with hosts, though a trend towards separate provision, and may soon become a 'back region'.
Tea/coffee	Many have facilities in the room, in some cases available via room service.	Kettles and tea bags, etc. in the rooms.	Hosts provides this or gives permission for the guests to help themselves in the kitchen.
Alcohol	Hotel bar or mini-bar in the room.	Usually none provided.	Host offers drinks.
Food	Main meals, not usually available outside 'normal meal times'; though snacks at any time. Expectation that dietary needs will be met. Guests waited on – some self service.	Typically breakfast only provided, unless negotiated otherwise. Vegetarian but no other options. Guests waited on – some self service.	Meals to fit the routine or convenience off the hosts. Guests expected to notify when expecting main meals and of any dietary requirements. Breakfast may not be cooked. Guests may help with preparation, clearing up and washing dishes.

personal touches, and the authors' experiences in carrying out interviews in people's homes suggest that this is indeed the case, although not invariably true.[3] The social construction of the home is gender-stereotyped: the husband's role is to achieve career success which carries rewards sufficient for him to provide a home for his wife and children; the wife's is to make creative decisions about the furnishing and arrangement of the home, and to organize its day-to-day management so that it provides the husband with an ordered and fragrant refuge from the public realm.

These gender stereotypes are so naturalized that we are apt to forget that this *beau ideal* was *constructed* by the rising middle class around the time of the industrial revolution (see Davidoff *et al.*, 1976; Davidoff and Hall, 1987; Forty, 1992). It then spread to sections of the working class (whether imposed or willingly embraced is not clear) whose pay claims came to be based on the idea of the 'family wage' (Land, 1980) that permitted a man to support a wife and children. For a wife to be in paid work was considered until recently to reflect badly on the husband's earning capacity. Despite some re-negotiation of who does the domestic labour, it is still assumed to be the woman's responsibility to oversee and to assign tasks to others who may 'help', and to determine the standards to be aspired to. It follows that she is to blame if the presentation of the home and facilities provided for a guest should fall short of the ideal.

Your own home?

The link to owner occupation relates not only pragmatically to the availability of space, but also to the idea of home ownership as an achievement and a sign of success (Gurney, 1996, 1999a, 1999c). At one level, it is simply more difficult to accommodate guests in a rented house. If the home is rented from a local authority or housing association, the tenant will have met criteria based on housing need including having too low an income to buy a house. Typically the property will usually be allocated a home that only just has sufficient bedrooms for the members of the household. A visit is therefore inconvenient, as it requires someone to move from their bedroom or a living room to be temporarily converted. Only close kin and very close friends would be 'worth' such disruption, and the event may have more of the characteristics of a put-up than a visit.

For those in privately rented accommodation this tenure is more likely to be a temporary arrangement, used by those in the early stages of their housing career, those 'between' owner occupied homes or between relationships. In both of these cases the scope for creating an impression by displaying the occupier's taste in furnishings is severely diminished. If the occupier requires housing benefit this will not cover the cost of a spare room, and even for those paying their own rent the tenure is seen as offering poor value for money and few will choose to rent a larger house so that they can accept visits. The occupier's friends are likely to postpone their requests to visit until the situation has been 'normalized' by a move into home ownership, though family members may well be accommodated.

Home ownership is regarded by governments and by most of the population as the 'normal' way of obtaining housing, with renting seen as second best (see Gurney, 1999a, 1999b). Other tenures are seen as requiring to be accounted for, as though they signal some deficit in the occupier (for a discussion on this see Gurney, 1999a). Tenure alone cannot give rise to social exclusion, but if an exclusion index were constructed, rented tenure might be one indicator, in that one means by which social bonds are strengthened and inclusion brought about is through reciprocal services, including visits. Mauss (1990) has argued that reciprocity in hospitality is constitutive of a society.

Darke (1994, 1996) and Gurney (1996, 1997) both argue that the meaning of home is differentiated by gender. Gurney has postulated a five-way but un-gendered typology of ideologies of home ownership – see below. Darke has suggested that for women there are three components in their feelings about the home. It is a work-site, it is a 'performance' subject to judgement by others, and it is a haven or 'back region' where the occupier can relax and escape from the performance requirements of everyday life. These components are in mutual conflict and thus give rise to contradictory feelings towards the home. The presentation of the home is a facet of the presentation of self, and may similarly be a source of anxiety over the adequacy and competence of the performance. This work may also simultaneously be satisfying, conferring a sense of achievement and of having properly discharged one's social obligations to loved ones. Relaxation and escape cannot be total as there is always room for improvement: 'a woman's work is never done'. Although today the actual work may be shared (though rarely equally), it is still the woman who is seen as custodian of the standard of performance. The guest is the person best able to notice any shortcomings.

Gurney (1996) found that women had more elaborated discourses around the meaning of home than did men. For both genders by far the predominant meaning was to do with emotions, but this meaning was *more* dominant for women. Men were more likely to think that *owning* a home made a difference to their feelings about it, and to stress the idea of ownership as a sign of financial achievement. However, among his sample of homebuyers in a inner suburb of Bristol, Gurney (1996) identified five distinct types of ideologies of home ownership, which could also differentiate householders in their attitudes to hospitality and their expectations of guests.

The first group were referred to as *pragmatists*. They are not wedded to the idea of home ownership per se but use it as a rational way of providing a home for themselves and their children, likely to be very important in their lives. Standards of presentation of the home are also likely to be set pragmatically as a balance between the work involved and social norms, with the home seen more as a setting for family life than an opportunity for a creative statement. The home-as-haven is very important.

The pragmatists' motive for inviting guests is simply that they enjoy their company and want to see them. The guests are assumed to reciprocate these feelings and there is no particular obligation to admire the home although they are expected to like and approve of the children. However, the pragmatism over standards of presentation of the home may clash with the expectations of some visitors such as grandparents who themselves have a different ideology of the home. The particular problems of visits from in-laws are discussed below.

Petty tycoons were strong believers in the home as investment and in their own financial acumen. Even where the housing market perversely failed to support this belief, bricks and mortar were seen as a sound prospect in the long run. Petty tycoons expect to have to work hard to achieve their financial goals and this will extend to the presentation of the home, where they will routinely set high standards. The home as haven may be relatively less important as they expect to spend what leisure they have in socializing with associates who can further their business interests.

Guests will often share these values: others may be subjected to a eulogy on property ownership. The role of guests is to recognize the symbols of economic success embodied in the home, and to discuss business prospects including the state of the property market, provided this is not one of collapse.

Conflictual owners are couples for whom the house is a site of battle. The conflicts may be over discrepant expectations over the division of labour and standards to be achieved in the home, or they may originate in another sphere and be carried over into the home. The presentation of the home may depend on whose standards are in the ascendant, but the labour involved in achieving it will be resented. In general the work of running a home is made tolerable through a sense of cherishing and being cherished by others, or of something owed to oneself, and will become oppressive if these are absent. The conflicts in this home mean that it cannot function as a haven.

Some potential guests may choose not to visit this battleground. Others may come out of solidarity with the party seen as wronged. Guests may be manipulated into taking sides or acting as seconds in the conflict. This is certainly not the type of event being simulated by the hospitality industry although it may be seen in *Fawlty Towers*.

For *extrinsic owners* the home is a means of expression on which they have lavished considerable labour, although this is generally a labour of love. Their homes are seen as evidence for their owners' creativity and thus positively require an audience. The labour is a necessary means to the end of having an individualized house. The home may appear a haven with the emphasis on comfort and homeliness but rarely is comfort prioritized over appearance. Extrinsic owners cannot resist the opportunity for further displays.

The role of guest is indispensable as audience for and admirer of these efforts. Extrinsic owners are likely to go to particular trouble over a visit, with the hope that the visitor will return in future for a further bout of admiration. This is the closest to the event being imitated by the commercial hospitality sector, especially the better quality bed-and-breakfast establishments: indeed, it may be the wish to display the home and the confidence that others would enjoy it as much as they, that lead the owners to move into the bed-and-breakfast business. The individualized but carefully contrived look, as seen in home decorating magazines, is also the aim of many small select hotels.

The final type of home owners are referred to by Gurney as *lexic-owners*. These were uncritical believers in home ownership, often using identical conventional phrases to confirm the rightness of their choice. Their narrative repertoire will include the desirability of their neighbourhood and its contrast with other areas seen as rougher. Buying a home is an achievement of which they are proud and the presentation of the home will signal this pride: the work involved is 'no trouble', they may even 'whistle while you work'. The home conspicuously constitutes a haven: it is 'the Englishman's castle' as 'there's no place like home'.

Visitors are made welcome and comfortable: 'make yourself at home', 'it's not a show house, it's *our* house'. Rather than exclaiming at the individuality displayed in the decor, the guest should confirm that the hosts have thoroughly achieved conventional expectations: 'you've made this a little palace'. The competent but unexceptionable presentation will be imitated by the cheaper hotel chains offering a standard product across a continent, although they will be unlikely to match the warmth of welcome offered by the lexic-owner.

Expectations and taboos in domestic hospitality

We have argued that the nature of the hospitality event is variable and that it is related to the meaning the home holds for the hosts. However, these variants occur within the context of social expectations that apply to a large section of British society and which we tentatively outline below. Social norms are transmitted and reinforced through stories told, more often describing transgressions of these norms than their observance. Following Table 5.3 which sets out these social rules, we describe some incidents where the rules were not observed.

Table 5.3 Taboos for hosts and guests in domestic hospitality

Hosts	Guests
Set times for breakfast – but may be unavoidable if all adults work.	Complaining about times for breakfast.
Neglecting guests.	Raiding the fridge except for milk for tea/coffee, ice for drinks, etc.
Asking a guest to leave.	Outstaying one's welcome.
Invasion of privacy, e.g. seen naked.	Ditto, also encroaching on 'back region' of home, for example entering untidy study.
Audible or visible sexual persona.	Ditto.
Revealing awareness of guests' sexual persona.	Revealing awareness of host's sexual persona. Over-promotion of own sexual persona (see text).
Home falls short of expectations outlined above.	Breaking or damaging anything.
Leaving any bodily wastes in bath-room – or (worse still) elsewhere.	Complaining about anything.
Leaving olfactory traces.	Ditto.
Drinking to excess or failing to provide slightly more drinks than guest wants.	Drinking to excess (may be exceptions).
	Getting into the wrong bed. Wetting the bed.
	Treating hosts as servants or hoteliers, e.g. ordering meals, expecting laundry or childcare services, leaving cups or bath dirty after use.

Tensions in the host–guest relationship

Expectations around the cleanliness and tidiness of the host's home will vary along a number of dimensions. Where there are young children it is not reasonable to expect the home to be immaculately tidy although it *is* expected to be sufficiently clean not to constitute a health hazard. Similarly, expectations change if the host is elderly or infirm. As a precaution, higher expectations are projected on to in-laws as guests than one's own family: they must not be given cause to feel that the family joined to their own has lower standards. However, this relationship is structurally prone to tension. This may be manifest when a normally pragmatic household unusually finds itself conflictual at the visit of in-laws. CG found himself offering to pack his partner's mother's suitcase for her during a very long visit during which his parenting and hospitality skills were subject to a constant critical tirade. The situation is now managed by inviting her to keep her daughter company whilst CG is away at conferences.

The generation gap applies both ways. Overnight guests of teenagers are particularly problematic: are they a boy/girl-friend, are they intending to have sex, does the parent wish to prevent this? The liberal parent who makes up the double bed in the spare bedroom, then finds that the guest is not the child's sexual partner, is just as embarrassed as the parent who attempts to prevent any sexual activity under the parental roof. There are further issues to be negotiated. Are all parties expected to have breakfast together? Should the host attempt to engage the guest in conversation, merely say hello, or pretend not to have noticed them? What if the stay extends for several nights? What is said if, on return from work the next day, the house is in unacceptable chaos, items are broken, that night's supper disappeared from the fridge?

Visits in general may give rise to conflicts over 'who does what' to prepare the house, particularly if the guest is closer to one party than the other. This is an issue for guests too. Whilst it is acceptable to help with the preparation or cleaning up after a meal which the guest shares, cleaning the host's home is much more problematic as it implies criticism of the host's standards. Tidying up is worse still as items that are wanted may be thrown away or put in the wrong place. But it is equally unacceptable to create excessive mess, or to fail to offer any help. Recently tensions were raised when CG and partner 'put-up' a visiting researcher for a couple of weeks during which time they were treated as hoteliers and were upset that no offers were made of help with childcare, cooking or washing-up.

The use of television with and by guests appears to be class related. The authors' observations are that television is rarely turned off in working class or lower middle class homes, whereas upper middle class hosts will negotiate viewing with their guests. Exceptions may be made for sports coverage or if it is known that some parties are avid followers of a particular programme, but the message should be that conversing with the guests offers greater satisfaction than anything the TV schedules can offer.

Stories about taboos broken

Stories about broken taboos are not always easy to tell. There is a taboo against stories that show a third party in an excessively poor light, and some taboos may be so strong that the speaker is reluctant to describe his/her own breaches.

A relatively mild taboo is the one about not neglecting guests. A clash of expectations may occur when a family member from an older generation, who themselves used to have guests in the era when few wives went out to work, stays in a household where all adults work. It took JD's parents a long time to realize that it wasn't in fact very convenient for their adult children to have them to stay during the working week. 'Oh, do you have to go to work?' – said to a sister who is a schoolteacher. The degree of inconvenience may vary with the competence of the parent to get their own breakfast, clear up after them, leave and lock the house, complete their pleasure trips or shopping, return and re-enter the house, without endangering themselves or the security of the house.

The taboo about not asking guests to leave was broken on both sides when JD had a problematic guest. Many people can recount stories of having offered a bed on a temporary basis and then finding themselves with a guest who was more difficult to manage and staying for longer than anticipated. This guest was a former colleague who had then worked abroad for a few years. At first it seemed like a round trip to several old friends but these friends later realized he had nowhere else to go. He drank various drinks cupboards dry, and engaged her in long, gloomy discussions during the time she needed to spend in preparation and marking. Taking these tasks into the bedroom (the only zone off-limits for house guests) and doing them far into the night made her ill and she asked him to leave, but felt guilty because he'd been staying for a much shorter time than other friends had managed to tolerate. He moved into a cheap hotel but left with unpaid bills, was re-housed as vulnerable in a council flat and died a couple of years later.

Taboos on bodily products are much stronger. All cultures have rules and prohibitions surrounding bodily emissions. The home is normally the setting where these are managed and disposed of unseen by others. Guests risk discovering shortcomings in the way these back-region functions are dealt with, or the guest's own performance in this respect may be inadequate. Elsewhere, one of the authors has developed more fully ideas about corporeal dirt and taboos associated with coital noise and elimination noise in constructing homes amongst house-sharers (Gurney, 1998, 2000). There is greater potential for embarrassment at overhearing coital noise from family members of a different generation. As sexual activity is now seen as required rather than prohibited (Foucault, 1990) the rules are somewhat ambiguous. CG recalls an episode as a student when his girlfriend invited a friend and her new man to stay – who made sure that it was known at the time, and afterwards, that they were having sex in the bath.

A friend's son, in his twenties, had a problematic encounter when he went back with a girl to her parental home after a party. After visiting the bathroom in the night he was unable to remember which door he'd come from and eventually found himself climbing into bed with her mother. (Anthropologists of course are familiar with the strong taboo and almost universal horror of sexual contact with the mother of a sexual partner.)

The worst breach JD can remember concerning bodily emissions was when a student lodger left a soiled sanitary towel on the side of the bath which was found by an extremely fastidious visiting aunt – who thought it was JD's. This particular aunt regularly breaks the taboo on complaining. She will ask for any of the missing elements of bedside light, mirror or waste paper basket, and prescribes precisely what she likes for breakfast and how it should be cooked. She therefore complained about the (very) offensive article – but JD was too flustered to explain who the culprit was. CG recalls a bed-wetting experience when a friend from his home town visited him as a student and claimed the attic roof had leaked into the bed. Worse still, he was sleeping on a house-mate's inflatable mattress so the responsibility for cleaning it fell to CG.

In some situations humour may be deployed as a way of managing potential tensions, for example by house sharers when one of them has a sexual partner to stay. Nakedness, entertaining female friends or lovers in an all-male shared house ranged in CG's experience from comedy to vulgarity. Coital noise, breakfast table put downs and other lapses recalled from childhood, include a contraceptive wrapper found under the bed (presumably from a previous guest), which caused embarrassing questions to CG's parents when he found it.

The fast-changing norms about facilities in the home are a way of reducing unwanted encounters with others' bodily emissions. Only very recently has it become virtually standard for builders of three bedroom houses to provide two bathrooms, one of them en-suite with the largest bedroom. It appears that householders have traded a spacious bathroom for a cramped shower room with olfactory invasions to the master bedroom but having the benefit of privacy. Clearly this variable is again class linked, but in the middle class it is rapidly becoming the norm to provide a guest bathroom.

Conclusions

We have attempted to demonstrate the risks in the hospitality industry's use of a metaphor based on encounters in the home. The hosts' performance is only occasionally secure, and may be judged inadequate by the guest (or vice versa) due to different expectations of gender roles, of the functions of home and of generation and social class. The home is a container of polluting activities from which a guest cannot always be shielded. It is women who are seen as responsible for standards of performance. If the entry of a guest into the home carries so many perils, is it wise for the hospitality industry to appropriate this metaphor?

'Putting up' is almost exclusively initiated by the guest and the host is frequently providing what Telfer described earlier as 'Good Samaritan' hospitality. In these circumstances, the provision of hospitality represents mixed experiences and tensions for the host, particularly the hostess. Putting up involves more intimate and ongoing relationship between host and guest than is the case when providing hospitality in the form of meals or parties. The resident guest has access to the 'back region' to an extent that would not apply to dinner guests. Furthermore, the precise nature of what both hosts and guests can and cannot do in the eyes of the other become more complex and difficult to manage.

In these circumstances it is perhaps not surprising that 'putting up' represents a form of hospitality fraught with difficulties because of the different expectations of guests and hosts. In the commercial setting these tensions are particularly relevant in guest houses, or situations where 'paying guests' share the private domain with their hosts. Even in the larger hotels, these tensions between guests and host can be compounded by the very anonymity seen by some as a benefit of commercial hospitality provision. Many hotels experience situations where guests use the hotel bedroom – the guest's private space for which they have paid – in a way that is unacceptable. Vandalism of hotel property, unacceptable lapses in personal hygiene and soiling the facilities are experiences that have common cause with putting up in domestic settings.

Notes

1 We recognize that we are here using a metaphor from a related area of hospitality – the arrival of guests at short notice for a meal – where, due to lack of opportunities for the host to pre-plan, the guests must count themselves lucky to be sharing

whatever is in the cooking pot. The expression is also used in North America to denote a meal shared between a group of kin and/or friends in which everybody brings an item of food, the 'luck' arising when all dishes are delicious and between them include an appropriate range of food to correspond to a conventional menu (on which see Douglas, 1975; Visser, 1991).

2 In one episode of the sex war comedy on BBC television 'Men Behaving Badly' the male characters were grumbling about the women's wish, seen as typical of women, to brighten up the living room with scatter cushions.

3 It is not intended to suggest that the man necessarily shares the aspiration to add personal touches of the type described. We are not sure whether the less elaborate presentation often seen in homes with no female occupier is due to ignorance on how to achieve a personalized look, or different aspirations for the presentation of the home.

References

Aitchison, C. (1999) New cultural geographies: the spatiality of leisure, gender and sexuality. *Leisure Studies, 18*, 19–39.

Anthony, K. (1997) Bitter homes and gardens: the meanings of home to families going through divorce. *The Journal of Architectural and Planning Research*, **14**, 1–19.

Bowlby, S., Gregory, S. and McKie, L. (1997) 'Doing home': patriarchy, caring and space. *Women's Studies International Forum*, **20**, 343–50.

Carsten, J. and Hugh-Jones, S. (eds) (1995) *About the House – Levi-Strauss and Beyond*. Cambridge, Cambridge University Press.

Cooper Marcus, C. (1995) *House as a Mirror of Self: Exploring the Deeper Meanings of Home*. Berkeley, Conari.

Darke, J. (1994) Women and the meaning of home. In: *Housing Women* (R. Gilroy and R. Woods, eds), pp.11–30. London, Routledge.

Darke, J. (1996) The Englishwoman's castle, or don't you just love being in control? In: *Changing Places: Women's Lives in the City* (C. Booth, J. Darke and S. Yeandle, eds), pp.61–71. London, Paul Chapman Publishing.

Davidoff, L. and Hall, C. (1987) *Family Fortunes: Men and Women of the English Middle Class 1780–1850*. London, Hutchinson.

Davidoff, L., L'Esperance, J. and Newby, H. (1976) Landscape with figures: home and community in English society. In: *The Rights and Wrongs of Women* (J. Mitchell and A. Oakley, eds). Harmondsworth, Penguin.

Douglas, M. (1975) Deciphering a meal. In: *Implicit Meanings* (M. Douglas, ed.), pp.249–75. London, Routledge and Kegan Paul.

Douglas, M. (1990) Foreword to *The Gift: The Form and Reason for Exchange in Archaic Societies* (M. Mauss, ed.), pp.vii–xviii. London, Routledge.

Finch, J. and Mason, J. (1993) *Negotiating Family Responsibilities*. London, Routledge.

Forty, A. (1992) *Objects of Desire: Design and Society since 1750*. London, Thames and Hudson.

Foucault, M. (1990) *The History of Sexuality*. Harmondsworth, Penguin.

Goffman, E. (1959 [1971 imprint]) *The Presentation of Self in Everyday Life*. Harmondsworth, Penguin.

Gurney, C. (1990) *The Meaning of Home in the Decade of Owner Occupation: Towards an Experiential Research Agenda*. Working paper 88. Bristol, School for Advanced Urban Studies, University of Bristol.

Gurney, C. (1996) Meanings of home and home ownership: myths, histories and experiences. Unpublished PhD thesis, University of Bristol.

Gurney, C. (1997) '. . . Half of me was satisfied': making sense of home through episodic ethnographies. *Women's Studies International Forum*, **20**, 373–386.

Gurney, C. (1998) The neighbours didn't dare complain: some (taboo) thoughts on the regulation of noisy bodies, the myth of the back-region and the disembodied housing imagination. Paper presented to European Network for Housing Research conference: *Housing Futures: Renewal, Sustainability and Innovation*. Cardiff, 7–11 September.

Gurney, C. (1999a) Pride and prejudice: discourses of normalisation in public and private accounts of home ownership. *Housing Studies*, **14**, 163–183.

Gurney, C. (1999b) 'We've got friends who live in council houses': power and resistance in home ownership. In: *Consuming Cultures: Power and Resistance* (J. Hearn and S. Roseneil, eds). Basingstoke, Macmillan.

Gurney, C. (1999c) Lowering the drawbridge: analogy and metaphor in the social construction of home ownership. *Urban Studies*, **36**, No. 10, 1705–1722.

Gurney, C. (2000) Accommodating bodies: the organisation of corporeal dirt in the embodied home. In: *Organising Bodies: Institutions, Policy and Work* (L. McKie and N. Watson, eds). Basingstoke, Macmillan.

Gutting, D. (1996) Narrative identity and residential history. *Area*, **28**, No. 4, 482–90.

Heal, F. (1990) *Hospitality in Early Modern England*. Oxford, Clarendon Press.

Ireland, M. (1993) Gender and class relations in tourism employment. *Annals of Tourism Research*, **20**, 666–84.

Johnson, L. and Valentine, G. (1995) Wherever I lay my girlfriend that's my home: the performance and surveillance of lesbian identities in domestic environments. In *Mapping Desire: Geographies of Sexuality* (D. Bell and G. Valentine, eds), pp.99–113. London, Routledge.

Land, H. (1980) The Family Wage. *Feminist Review, 6*, 55–77.

Lawrence, R. (1987) *Housing, Dwellings and Homes: Design Theory, Research and Practice*. Chichester, John Wiley & Sons.

Madigan, R. and Munro, M. (1991) Gender, house and 'home': social meanings and domestic architecture in Britain. *Journal of Architectural and Planning Research*, **8**, No. 2, 116–31.

Martens, L. and Warde, A. (1998) Dining out domestically: a sociological analysis. Unpublished paper for the International Sociological Association Congress, *New Strategies for Everyday Work, Free Time and Consumption*, Montreal, July/August.

Mauss, M. (1990) *The Gift: The Form and Reason for Exchange in Primitive Societies*. London, Routledge (originally published in 1950 as Essai sur le don).

McDowell, L. (1999) *Gender, Identity and Place: Understanding Feminist Geographies*. Cambridge, Polity Press.

Morgan, D. (1996) 'My house is your house': home, hospitality and nationalism. Unpublished paper presented at British Sociological Association conference *Worlds of the Future: Ethnicity, Nationalism and Globalization*. Reading, 1–4 April.

Ramazanoglu (1992) On feminist methodology: male reason versus female empowerment. *Sociology, 26*, 207–12.

Rybczynski, W. (1986) *Home: A Short History of an Idea*. New York, Viking.

Telfer, E. (1996) *Food for Thought: Philosophy and Food*. London, Routledge.

Visser, M. (1992) *The Rituals of Dinner*. London, Viking.

Watson, S. (1991) The restructuring of work and home: productive and reproductive relations. In: *Housing and Labour Markets: Building the Connections* (J. Allen and C. Hamnett, eds), pp.136–54. London, Unwin-Hyman.

Home and commercialized hospitality

Paul Lynch

*Department of Business and Consumer Studies,
Queen Margaret University College, Edinburgh*

Doreen MacWhannell

*Department of Management and Social Sciences,
Queen Margaret University College, Edinburgh*

Key themes

- The concept of 'home'
- Significance of gender
- Female entrepreneurship
- Host–guest dynamics

The concept of 'home'

> We others who have long lost the more subtle of the
> physical senses, have not even proper terms to express
> an animal's inter-communications with his surroundings,
> living or otherwise, and have only the word 'smell', for
> instance to include the whole range of delicate thrills
> which murmur in the nose of the animal night and day,
> summoning, warning, inciting, repelling.
>
> Home! That was what they meant, those caressing
> appeals, those soft touches wafted through the air, those
> invisible little hands pulling and tugging . . .
> (Grahame, K., 1992, p.45, *The Wind in the Willows*)

For the purpose of this chapter, commercial hospitality within the private home refers to a range of accommodation from private house bed and breakfasts to guest houses, from many small hotels to townhouses, from self-catering cottages to host families. These types of operation share the fact that the physical accommodation is a primary home for the hosts.

Rybczynski (1988, p.40) states that the term 'hotel' referred in the seventeenth century to large individual townhouses where the nobility and richest bourgeois lived which were both grand and luxuriously appointed, i.e. what we would call mansions. Thus, as Riley (1984, in Wood, 1994, p.67) argues: 'because the upper classes constituted the major market for early hotels, many early British establishments sought to reproduce the spatial and cultural aspects of the aristocratic domicile'. It is this very particular concept of the aristocratic domicile, which has been the predominant model for hospitality practices, particularly given the initial customer base. It is this aristocratic model which has served as the benchmark for standards of quality, of service (Riley, 1984), and has come to permeate the thinking processes of hospitality educators in areas such as food service. However, one can distinguish the aristocratic model upon which the hotel is based from the bourgeois model of the home. Whilst it may be argued the bourgeois home seeks to emulate the aristocratic model, it is, nevertheless, a distinct model in itself.

When we refer to the bourgeois home we need to be able to locate the definition in both time and geography. However, it is difficult to point to a moment in history and define categorically what a bourgeois home is; the bourgeois concept of home was and is an evolutionary concept which has come to take on different meanings and significance. Rybczynski (1988) describes how bourgeois (i.e. town dwellers') homes have evolved from quite public dwellings, as substitutes for restaurants, bars and hotels in the medieval period to *a place of comfort* involving convenience, efficiency, leisure, ease, pleasure, domesticity, intimacy and privacy in the twentieth century. In this context he suggests 'discomfort' arises when the balance between isolation and publicness is not met. So, comfort is a key idea and it is noteworthy how contemporary external imposed definitions of comfort through grading schemes may be perceived as based upon assumptions and values about discomfort.

In the hospitality industry, definitions of comfort, which also embrace prevailing codes of behaviour, dress codes, food service rituals, familiarity with different standards of cuisine, are mediated through the grading and classification schemes. This grading scheme might be perceived as a top down aristocratic model. According to Wood (1994, p.68), Carmouche (1980) and Riley (1984) suggest that hotels embrace bourgeois (i.e. middle class) values and that 'overtones of the haute bourgeois values of the early hotel era persist'. Whilst haute bourgeois, aristocratic and bourgeois values are identified as prevalent in hotels, working-class values are not mentioned as a role model, although Carmouche suggests that working-class needs are met by boarding houses, small private hotels, and other forms of tourist accommodation. This might be seen to infer that such forms of accommodation are adopting a working class model of the home. Ryan (1991, in Wood, 1994, p.70) points out that '. . . increasingly hotels no longer offer a style of accommodation that is more comfortable than home'. Wood (1994, p.70) sees this comment as reflecting increased 'domestication' of hotels, and a process of environmental continuity between the hotel and the home. Here, Wood seems to be basing his comments upon a non-aristocratic model of domestication. He also highlights (Wood, 1994, p.77) the link between the hotel and the home model: 'historical analysis suggests that hotels as social institutions have closely followed in development the growth of home-centred values'. Interestingly, Wood (1994, p.78) makes the following points:

> In the United Kingdom, as elsewhere, alternative forms of accommodation (in particular self-catering accommodation) is growing at the expense of the conventional hotel and boarding house sectors. This constitutes on the one hand a rejection of pseudo-domestication of the hotel and on the other the embracing of a substitute that hardly differs at all from the home circumstance. The difference between the two is not that one offers more freedom than the other, but that self-catering offers fewer constraints: the normal social relations of the family unit

within the domestic residence can be transferred with minimum disruption into self-catering.

Wood (1994, p.79) concludes by suggesting that a sociology of hotels illuminates connections between domestic and touristic experiences which as an area of enquiry has been inexplicably ignored. Thus, Wood lends support to the idea of the relevance of understanding the home in order to understand hotels, owing to the latters' borrowing from the former.

However, in discussing the relevance of the home to hospitality, it is perhaps restricting to locate the debate in the context of a class definition of the home, or indeed a physical or service description of the home. Rather, it is the symbolic significance of the home which is important, what the home represents which is drawn upon as much as the external coverings.

Rybczynski (1988) identifies the meaning of home as bringing together the meanings of house and of household, of dwelling and of refuge, of ownership and of affection. 'Home' meant the house, but also everything that was in it and around it, as well as the people, and the sense of satisfaction and contentment that all these conveyed. Thus home has multiple meanings, and operates on different levels both simultaneously and for individuals. Adding commercialized hospitality to the equation further complicates the dimension of the home and its meanings.

'Home' as an idea is not a simple concept but one which has multiple meanings and significance: worksite, memories and associations, place to rear family, a refuge, prison, statement of independence (Sixsmith and Sixsmith, 1991); ideas of security, affection and comfort (Franklin, 1986); a place of self-expression, a cocoon, a place of deep contentment in the innermost temple of the soul (Cooper Marcus, 1995); a relatively recent term of nostalgia (Rybczynski, 1988); associated with comfort, domesticity; a place under feminine control; place of ritual and customs (Telfer, 1995; Rybczynski, 1988); site of patriarchal relations (Whatmore, 1991).

Leroi-Gourhan (1984) suggests that the defining moment of mankind was not the creation of the tool but the domestication of time and space; it is this domestication symbolized by the home which is mankind's defining achievement. Part of the symbolic significance of the home is the idea of freedom which is identified by Wood (1994) as less available in hotels. What has this to do with hospitality? When the early hotels borrowed concepts from the aristocratic home, these concepts were not simply ones of service, and attitudes to food and values, but also the meaning and symbolic significance of the home. Whilst attention to date has focused upon the more tangible elements of the home, and the aristocratic home has provided a benchmark for standards for all types of hospitality accommodation, the intangible elements of what a home signifies, the nature of relations within the home, have been overlooked. The 'small' end of the accommodation sector, where the home is the physical unit of hospitality provision – and this provision is arguably furthest removed from the aristocratic model of hospitality (Carmouche, 1980) – has largely been overlooked for research purposes. A number of reasons have been put forward for this neglect (Lynch, 1996) including practical difficulties of research but also what has been referred to as a hospitality management research myopia. The small end of the accommodation sector brings to mind images of 'poor service', 'family disputes', 'tacky furnishings'. Such negative images, as well as being caricatures of dubious accuracy, act as a deterrent to understanding the reality, and contribute to the significance of home as a concept being overlooked in the hospitality research arena.

The predominance in terms of the number of units of 'home' accommodation is seen in Table 6.1. Even restricting the definition to home accommodation types 1 and 2 described below, and to only include guest houses, farmhouses and bed and breakfasts, 42 per cent of the accommodation units may be classified as offering commercial hospitality within the home setting; this figure is in itself highly problematical, for example, some guest houses may not have hosts living on the premises, and it excludes those hotels which are also a family home. Information on usage and financial importance of the different forms of accommodation units is more difficult to obtain. However, it is apparent that there is significant demand for 'home' type of accommodation units, and there is some evidence to suggest demand is particularly concentrated amongst higher spending tourists (Stringer, 1981; Lynch, 1998). It is possible to distinguish three broad types of 'home' accommodation:

1 Commercialized hospitality within the private home where the owners live on the premises and public space is shared by visitors and the owner's family – this category may be subdivided by the degree of integration of the visitor with the family and their activities, for example, private house bed and breakfasts, host families.
2 Commercialized hospitality where the owner lives on the premises and the unit is also the family home but where public space for the visitor is separated from that of the family, for example, small hotels, town houses, guest houses and some bed and breakfasts.

3 Self-catering where the home owners live off the premises – this category would be further sub-divided into those where the home is usually a second home and those where the accommodation unit is purely a letting unit and home is a created concept (Wood, 1995 refers to this as 'pseudo-domestication').

Wood (1994) identifies other alternative forms of accommodation such as self-catering accommodation growing at the expense of traditional forms such as hotels, motels and boarding houses (a somewhat antiquated term). Some explanation of the popularity of home accommodation is required. Wood (1994) suggests that their appeal in part is due to self-catering offering fewer constraints upon behaviour as well as a rejection of the pseudo-domestication of hotels. In addition, and significantly, he suggests that normal social relations of the family can be transferred without disruption into self-catering. Wood's argument is that social control or the lack of it is a key attraction rather than price. However, it should be emphasized that the freedom is not simply owing to a reduction in social constraints but also at a level of spiritual freedom associated with what the home signifies.

The appeal of self-catering and private home accommodation is also based upon what the home as an accommodation unit represents. A discernible trend amongst property letting companies who are increasing their share of the self-catering accommodation market is the use of personal names for properties, of furnishings with a personal and less-standardized hotel-type feel, more homely. Rybczynski (1988) points out that in the medieval ages homes were personified by being given proper names and that in the twentieth century these were replaced by numbers. Today one sees re-personification occurring in, for example, the Holiday Property Bond company whose members pay a bond to permit usage and 'ownership' of the company's accommodation which converted one property, formerly farm-yard stables, in the Yorkshire countryside into self-catering units and chose resonant names for the units, such as 'Starlings' and 'Curlews'. Similarly, the guest house owner who names their property 'A Haven'. In this way the provider is appealing to a nostalgic sense of the home, personalized, of comfort, of security, of an image of homeliness.

Owing to the interest of the authors, it is proposed to focus upon hospitality offered within the private home on a commercial basis. The term 'commercial' is used very exactly to convey a sense of an activity 'viewed with regard to profit' (Longman, 1992, p.322). The introduction of commercial motivations to the provision of hospitality within an environment which is also a

	Wales[1]	Scotland	Northern Ireland	England	Total
Hotels	1,758	2,466	137	6,922	11,283
Guest houses	3,502	1,360	160	8,813	13,835
Farmhouses	1,262	–	–	2,699	3,961
Bed and breakfasts[2]	–	5,482	942	11,854	18,278
Self-catering accommodation[3]					
Cottage	1,492	2,983	–	50,000[4]	54,475
Houses/bungalows	1,295	2,397	–	–	3,692
Farmhouses	341	-	–	–	341
Flats/flatlets	3,205	2,309	–	14,800	20,314
Chalets	3,913	1,517	–	–	5,430
Other	–	1,681	–	–	1,681
Total self-catering	10,246	10,887	432	64,800	86,365

Sources: Adapted from: Beioley, S. (1990), BTA/ETB Research Services (1997), Northern Ireland Tourist Board (1998), Scottish Tourist Board (1998), Wales Tourist Board (1998)

Notes
1 Information dates back to 1991.
2 The Welsh Tourist Board has not identified bed and breakfasts as a distinct category for the collection of data.
3 Figures for Wales exclude properties let through letting agencies.
4 Includes houses, cottages, chalets, villages and bungalows.

Table 6.1 Numbers of accommodation units in the United Kingdom registered with National Tourist Boards

refuge, a locus of genuineness where one can be oneself, which is also an arena for patriarchal relations, is particularly fascinating, and raises important questions about the nature of hospitality.

The significance of gender

Without wishing to reinforce gender differences, it does seem that the providers of commercialized hospitality within the private home are overwhelmingly female (see for example, Walton, 1978; Stringer; 1981, Whatmore, 1991 or Lynch, 1998) with increasing male representation as establishments become larger, for example, small hotels. Hosting in the home is generally perceived as a gendered occupation. Explanation for this is partly structural associated with women's place in the labour market and partly embedded in patriarchal relations within the home (Whatmore, 1991). Rybczynski (1988, p.160–1) points to gender differences in the idea of the home: the masculine idea of the home is primarily sedentary, that is, the home as a retreat from the cares of the world, a place to be at ease; the feminine idea is dynamic, to do with ease, but also with work, and so over time the focus shifted 'from the drawing room to the kitchen'. Tannen (1991) identified gender differences in preferred home location with females preferring locations closer to city centres than male partners owing to more restricted mobility. Gurstein (1989 in Cooper Marcus, 1995, p.184) confirms previous studies where women are working at home in order to be closer to their children, to maintain family responsibilities, and to have more control over their work; unfortunately then finding that work life can take precedence over home life both spatially and temporally.

Recent studies have pointed to women with children being less spatially mobile resulting in more limited employment opportunities (Hanson and Pratt, 1995). Thus, making use of the home, an existing worksite from a gendered perspective, is a logical solution. Studies have previously identified that women are at a disadvantage compared to men in raising financial resources for business start up (Watkins and Watkins, 1984). It is entirely logical that in the face of such financial, spatial and structural difficulties, that the home, already a worksite, should be made use of as a business resource.

So the concept of the 'bed and breakfast' for example, must hold a particular fascination for those interested in feminist and gender debates. Within feminist perspectives the traditional, family unit, as contained within the 'home', has been viewed as a site of patriarchal relations. The public/private debate, with regard to the social relations of women and men and the worlds of 'work', allows us to focus on that very concept of unpaid/paid work or domestic labour which is a main contributor to a household.

It is perhaps useful therefore to briefly consider some second-wave feminist debates. These focused on the concept of 'work' per se challenging the view that only paid work, outside the home, was indeed the only valid form of 'work'. This brought debates regarding sex differences into both the public and private worlds of work (Novarra, 1981). Of interest here, in a debate concerning the 'home', is Oakley's classic research (Oakley, 1980; Oakley, 1985). She not only raised issues regarding the role of the 'housewife', but fully explored the work of that private domain, commonly classed as 'housework'.

Other feminist debates considered concepts of caring and motherhood in relation to housework (Cowan, 1983), the exploration and challenging of the notion of the 'working mother' (Apter, 1985), and continued to explore how domestic life was organized within the context of economic change (Morris, 1990). More recently Walby (1997) and Pascall (1997) have continued to contribute to debates on continuing sexual divisions of labour within the labour market, recognizing the role of both social and public policy, class and ethnicity, in addition to gendered work relations. In consideration of the work which contributes to that of the bed and breakfast, the aforementioned discussion creates an interesting situation. Especially if '[W]omen whose whole work is in the home ... know that they are not considered to "work"' (Pascall, 1997, p.37).

For the work carried out in providing a 'bed and breakfast' establishment is traditionally seen as 'women's work'. It could be said that such work epitomizes the female, domestic environment: the unpaid work of the traditional 'housewife'. This would include, for example, shopping; the preparation and cooking of food, including the attractive presentation of the meals; washing bed linen, changing, making beds; cleaning of toilets and bathrooms; the organizing and cleaning of a household, in order to maintain attractive, clean and hygienic conditions, but also in creating a 'home', an atmosphere which is ordered, welcoming and safe.

The analogy can perhaps be taken further extending into other areas, albeit drawing on stereotypical qualities which again have normally been attributed to women. For the notion of a 'home' creates further notions of 'homeliness', where caring, caretaking and the creation of a homely atmosphere are required. With the focus again on a female figure 'running' a bed and breakfast, the term managing is still rarely used, even further extensions may be made into traditional roles of women in the home. The guests can be considered perhaps as part of an extended family, while living in the home, the key provider being seen almost as a 'mother' figure. Guests will have 'the run of the house', with a house key, but some rules will exist to maintain order; the times of meals is one example. Meals will normally be shared. Formality is, however, kept to a minimum, first name terms are commonplace, unlike a hotel or guest house environment. The concept of the 'landlady', seems rather too formal for most bed and breakfasts, for the key objective of the bed and breakfast is surely to create homeliness and informality. A 'home from home' in fact.

Stringer (1981, p.363) refers to the provision of this homely atmosphere emphasizing however the financial exchange for the service provided. He notes, in relation to his research, the relationship between the host and guest that '[T]he contract between the two parties was seen to go beyond the obvious service referred to in the title "bed and breakfast"' further noting that '... a social relationship is constructed which is probably quite rare in such simple economic transactions, and which at the same time can be of surprising depth' (Stringer, 1981, p.364). The concept of 'home' as a social construction, can also be seen to encompass, particularly in Western cultures, 'ideas of security, affection and comfort' (Madigan and Munro, 1991). Perhaps even more interesting to the discussion here are their views that women and men not only 'experience housing differently' but the provocative statement that 'there are good grounds for believing that the home occupies a greater centrality in the lives of women as compared to men, as a result of women's domestic role' (Madigan and Munro, 1991, p.117). This issue is unable to be explored fully here but reasons given, notwithstanding changes in divisions of labour, are women still taking responsibility for the majority of domestic work and childcare.

Issues therefore of the feminine, including stereotypical, notions of femininity and the concept of paid and unpaid work in sociological terms, are implicit within discussions of the 'bed and breakfast' as a site of hospitality. The work entailed in managing such a household is no different from the private, domestic household of the family. Except there is a financial reward. So perhaps the bed and breakfast could be seen as overturning a patriarchal site of traditional exploitation and oppression of women. It in fact challenges this very notion, turning it on its head. A wise move surely to be paid for what has previously been unpaid, and to create a small business out of housework.

Recent research however on female mini-entrepreneurs and their microenterprises, argues that such enterprises are still 'largely home-based operations based on work women are already doing as part of their gender-specific role' (Ehlers and Main, 1998, p.424). In other words the bed and breakfast. The issue of female entrepreneurship will now be discussed adding further complexity to the debate.

Female entrepreneurship

Within hospitality research, entrepreneurship has received relatively little attention. Studies undertaken in the hospitality sector have tended to mirror the approach of much of the broader research on entrepreneurship and only focused on formally established organizations. Further, neglect of accommodation workers has been identified (Lennon and Wood, 1989), and a failure to relate findings to wider macro-social and economic factors. Overall, the level of knowledge regarding the hospitality entrepreneur remains low, and this is particularly so regarding small businesses which predominate in the industry (Quinn, Larmour and McQuillan, 1992). Providers of hospitality within the home on a commercial basis suffer from a perceived lack of

Hospitality, Leisure & Tourism Series

seriousness, as if what is being offered is not true hospitality, and are often ascribed motivations of 'only for pin money' or 'just a lifestyle entrepreneur'. Arguably, such ascriptions rather than shedding light on the activities and understanding of such people achieve the reverse effect. In part, this may be an ethnocentric reflection of a perceived low importance of the small accommodation unit within the hospitality accommodation structure of the United Kingdom. By contrast, in Eire where the small accommodation unit is identified as having a key role in the hospitality accommodation structure, tourist board policy and infrastructure for small accommodation providers is more supportive. Similarly, in developing countries, petty entrepreneurs are identified as key components towards a developing tourism economy (Dahles, 1997).

Attempts have been made to understand female entrepreneurs, for example, Goffee and Scase (1985) proposed a typology of female entrepreneurs. They identified four types of female entrepreneurs: conventional, innovative, radical and domestic trader. The conventional and domestic trader are of interest here. Conventional are those who try to counteract labour market subordination, and the example of guest house owners is cited; domestic traders are those who challenge in a limited way the primacy of the domestic role, for example, host families (Lynch, 1998). What is important to note here is that the categories are not static, that whilst one may start as a domestic trader, the process of entrepreneurship may change one to different patterns of behaviour and thus one may become a different type of entrepreneur in the Goffee and Scase typology, for example, a conventional entrepreneur. In addition, the categories are themselves simplifications and may hide different sub-categories (Lynch, 1998).

The motivations for receiving guests into the home on a commercial basis are complex. Lynch (1998) identifies how women working at home may experience social isolation. Thus, inviting strangers into the home is a means of reducing such loneliness whilst meeting socially constructed obligations of childcare, housework, etc. Financial motivations and those associated with achieving independence are significant as well as motivations of self-fulfilment associated with the nature of the home itself: a desire to reflect social status and to practice creative and social skills. Understanding such motivations is important as they are brought by the host into any interaction with the guest (Stringer, 1981).

The nature of such entrepreneurship can be best understood in the context of a conventional family life course. Family life course refers to the 'phases' of a conjugal household which focuses upon

Jo Coleman

Information Update Service

Butterworth-Heinemann

FREEPOST SCE 5435

Oxford

Oxon

OX2 8BR

UK

Keep up-to-date with the latest books in your field.

Visit our website and register now for our FREE e-mail update service, or join our mailing list and enter our monthly prize draw to win £100 worth of books. Just complete the form below and return it to us now! (FREEPOST if you are based in the UK)

www.bh.com

Please Complete In Block Capitals

Title of book you have purchased:..

....

Subject area of interest:..

Name:..

Job title:..

Business sector (if relevant):...

Street:..

Town:.. County:...

Country:.. Postcode:....................................

Email:..

Telephone:...

How would you prefer to be contacted: Post ☐   e-mail ☐   Both ☐

Signature:.. Date:..

☐ Please arrange for me to be kept informed of other books and information services on this and related subjects (✔ box if not required). This information is being collected on behalf of Reed Elsevier plc group and may be used to supply information about products by companies within the group.

FOR OFFICE USE ONLY

Butterworth-Heinemann,
a division of Reed Educational
& Professional Publishing Limited.
Registered office: 25 Victoria Street,
London SW1H 0EX.
Registered in England 3099304.
VAT number GB: 663 3472 30.

BUTTERWORTH HEINEMANN

A member of the Reed Elsevier plc group

a monogamous, heterosexual couple. This is described as follows in the context of farming families:

> Marsden (1979: 118) identifies five phases . . . 'marriage and the setting up of a conjugal household; an expansion phase associated with the birth of children; a dispersion phase, when children leave home; an independent phase, when the conjugal couple live alone following the departure of children; and a replacement phase when the farm is taken over by the children and the older couple retire off the farm. Within this framework, it is the specific form of patriarchal gender relations, between men and women in the socially constructed roles of husband and wife, which becomes the focus of analysis . . . Patriarchal gender relations constitute an active social process by which women are subordinated to men through a range of social processes and institutions.'
>
> (Whatmore, 1991, p.42)

Whilst Marsden applies the family life course to the farm, with little adaptation it could be adapted to different forms of hospitality units using the home. The family life course is a useful conceptual tool to locate entrepreneurs and to understand the dimensions of socially constructed gender roles. For instance, in the study of small hoteliers, it may prove particularly valuable as a means of understanding how gendered roles can underpin the interactions with guests and with staff. Similarly, understanding small hotels as both a business worksite as well as a family home, albeit business and home space may be separated geographically, can only deepen our understanding and facilitate the devising of appropriate support policies. Thus, one might wish to rethink traditional business strategy concepts when analysing and devising policies for small accommodation enterprises in order to reflect the importance of home and its influence on business strategies. For instance, using home as a key concept, the importance of personal relationships in forming and developing business networks, for example, for recruitment or with customers, is much more readily understandable.

Host–guest dynamics

Gender as an issue permeates the host–guest relationship. Cooper Marcus (1995) draws attention to how the home environment can be a reflection of the relationships taking place within. In this respect, the symbolic significance of the home for the dwellers is important. A home can be used symbolically in different ways: status object, expression of aesthetic taste, cosy refuge, place for expression of order and beauty. Therefore, it may be useful and informative to explore guests' desire and need for such symbolic meanings.

Cooper Marcus (1995) identifies the home and its contents as representing symbols of our ego-selves. She identifies role conflict arising when one or both members of a couple work and live in the same space. Two elements are in conflict for the person working at home as one adopts a work role where one is expected to be efficient, professional, asexual and sexually guarded and a home role where one is expected to be more casual, relaxed, and nurturing, especially the woman. This raises questions in the context of receiving guests attracted to the idea of the home with its particular connotations and where the home is being used for a work role by the host and its connotations. Studies such as Stringer (1981) and Pearce (1990), have identified the insights into the realities of family life as a key attraction of guests, particularly from overseas. Thus, home accommodation can serve as a cultural icon.

A further tension relates to the universal perception of home as a refuge, i.e. where one can recover from the outside world. Admittance of strangers into this refuge is an admittance of the outside world from which the home owners seek refuge. This may result in the home feeling a less personal place (Ahrentzen, 1989). Such conflict may be partly resolved through further geographical separation, for example, in a small hotel it is usual to find owners' living quarters clearly distinguished from the public areas to which guests are admitted. Not everybody can accommodate receiving strangers within the home. Whilst financial motivations are attractive, there is a price to pay for the hosts in terms of loss of privacy, loss of personal space, of keeping up appearances. Cooper Marcus (1995) identifies couples who are in accord over the basic function and meaning of home as living comfortably together. She argues that beliefs about gender roles are often at the heart of relationship problems manifested through conflict over use of the home environment. Thus, 'successful' hosts are those who can integrate the receipt of strangers within the private home with minimum disruption to their life (Lynch, 1998). However, within the private home where hospitality is provided on a commercial basis, the public areas are usually shared between family and guest. One can argue that this is the case within families where the home may be a refuge from the outside world but refuge may also be sought within the refuge as one seeks to escape from other members of the family (Ahrentzen, 1989), for example escaping to one's bedroom, or to the bathroom to which one can debar access, but not necessarily shut out the presence of others. It is not surprising that tensions over the use of space have been reported in studies on private house accommodation, for instance, Stringer (1981) and Ireland (1993). In one example cited by Ireland (1993), a husband is critical of finding a guest in the kitchen which is perceived as an invasion of space, and in line with the ideas of Rybczynski (1988), the presence of the guest is a consequent loss of retreat and escape from the world. A study of territoriality in flats owned by middle class families by Sebba and Churchman (1986, p.16) identified three types of areas:

1 Those that belonged to the whole family – living room and bathroom.
2 Those that belonged to a sub-group in the family – parents' bedroom, siblings' shared bedroom.
3 Those that belonged to individuals including one's own bedroom and the kitchen.

The study of living together is a neglected area of research (Cooper Marcus, 1995). Without such study, particularly with regard to the use of the private home for commercial hospitality, it is difficult to see how we can deepen our understanding of the area.

Stringer (1981, p.363–4) in a study of bed and breakfasts identifies the importance of the home on the interactions between host and guest. The setting for the transaction, the home, can create a tension over use of space, for example, usage of the bathroom is often cited as a problem area. Tension may also arise over what the nature of the economic and social transaction entails. Does it extend to prolonged use of the bathroom, or the telephone? How integrated is the guest to be in the family household? If we consider the home as a locus of family relations, it is unsurprising perhaps that some younger guests may feel uncomfortable owing to revival of memories of their own adolescent years at home. However, we should also recognize that such tension is also a source of great appeal for guests in which the rules and behaviours and expectations of the hosts are a topic for observation and subsequent conversation.

Dann and Cohen (1991, p.163) refer to the less genuine interactions as 'commercialised hospitality' to describe 'social exchange and the profit motive, often masquerading behind a phoney front of friendliness or even servility'. This is an issue which is particularly problematical within the private home used for commercial operations owing to the strong social conventions of hospitality associated with the home combined with under-lying commercial motivations. It is also a problem within larger hospitality and tourism establishments, such as hotels, theme parks and fast food service operations.

However, whilst one might excuse unsatisfactory encounters in the latter by explaining it is only a job, in the case of commercial hospitality in the private home, a tension is created between the social expectations of the host and the obligations of commercial service. Pearce (1990), in a study of farmhouses in New Zealand, seems to identify a means of minimizing such tensions by arranging payment of the host through the tourist board rather than through the guest, thus allowing the pretence of a simple house guest to be maintained.

Conclusions

Recognition of the important concept of 'home' to the provision of hospitality may add interesting and insightful perspectives to the nature of hospitality and the hospitality product. In this chapter, the significance of home has been illustrated in the context of gender, female entrepreneurship and host–guest dynamics only. The home has been identified as a significant setting, directly and indirectly affecting the provision of commercialized hospitality.

Future research is required into this area which has surprisingly been neglected. There are many areas that have not been considered here but which impact upon the provision of commercialized hospitality in the home. Issues of ethnicity and sexuality for instance have not been addressed here. In addition, greater understanding is required on the ways that people live together, of the importance of the setting on host–guest dynamics in hospitality establishments, for example, with regard to social control, authenticity, and integration with the hosts. Furthermore, deepening understanding of the links between the home as a setting and its impacts upon entrepreneurship is required, for example, in understanding approaches to business strategy with regard to the use of personal networks for business purposes.

References

Ahrentzen, S. (1989) A Place of Peace, Prospect and . . . a PC: The Home as Office. In: Cooper Marcus, C. (1995) *House as a Mirror of Self*. Berkeley, Conari Press.

Apter, T. (1985) *Why Women Don't Have Wives: Professional Success and Motherhood*. Hampshire, The Macmillan Press.

Beioley, S. (1990) *Holiday Cottages Market Profile*. London, BTA/ ETB Research Services.

BTA/ETB Research Services (1997) *Regional Tourism Facts*. London, BTA/ETB Research Services.

Carmouche, R. (1980) Social Class in Hotels. In: Wood, R.C. (1994) Hotel Culture and Social Control. *Annals of Tourism Research*, **21**, No. 1, 65–80.

Cooper Marcus, C. (1995) *House as a Mirror of Self*. Berkeley, Conari Press.

Cowan, R. (1983) *More Work for Mother: The Ironies of Household Technology from the Open Hearth to the Microwave*. New York, Basic Books Inc.

Dahles, H. (1997) Tourism, Petty Entrepreneurs and Sustainable Development. In: *Tourism, Small Entrepreneurs, and Sustainable Development: Cases from Developing Countries* (H. Dahles, ed.). Tillburg University, ATLAS.

Dann, G. and Cohen, E. (1991) Sociology and Tourism. *Annals of Tourism Research*, **18**, No. 1, 155–69.

Ehlers, T.B. and Main, K. (1998) Women and the False Promise of Microenterprise, *Gender and Society*, **12**, No. 4, 424–40.

Franklin, A.S. (1986) Owner-occupation, Privatism and Ontological Security: A Critical Reformulation. In: Madigan, R., Munro, M. (1991) Gender, House and 'Home': Social Meanings and Domestic Architecture in Britain. *The Journal of Architectural and Planning Research*, **8**, No. 2, 116–32.

Goffee, R. and Scase, R. (1985) *Women in Charge: The Experiences of Female Entrepreneurs*. London, George Allen and Unwin Ltd.

Gurstein, D. (1989) The Electronic Cottage: Implications for the Meaning of the Home. In: Cooper Marcus, C. (1995) *House as a Mirror of Self*. Berkeley, Conari Press.

Hanson, S. and Pratt, G. (1995) *Gender, Work and Space*. New York, Routledge.

Ireland, M. (1993) Gender and Class Relations in Tourism Employment. *Annals of Tourism Research*, **20**, 666–84.

Lennon, J.J. and Wood, R.C. (1989) The Sociological Analysis of Hospitality Labour and the Neglect of Accommodation Workers. *International Journal of Hospitality Management*, **8**, No. 3, 227–35.

Leroi-Gourhan, A., La Geste et la Parole. In: Hillier, B. and Hanson, J. (1984) *Social Logic of Space*. Cambridge, Cambridge University Press.

Longman (1992) *Longman Dictionary of English Language*. Harlow, Longman.

Lynch, P.A. (1996) The Cinderella of Hospitality Management Research: Studying Bed and Breakfasts. *International Journal of Contemporary Hospitality Management*, **8**, No. 5, 38–40.

Lynch, P.A. (1998) Female Entrepreneurs in the Host Family

Sector: Key Motivations and Socio-Economic Variables. *International Journal of Hospitality Management*, **17**, 319–42.

Madigan R. and Munro M. (1991) Gender, House and 'Home': Social Meanings and Domestic Architecture in Britain. *The Journal of Architectural Planning Research*, **8**, No. 2, 116–32.

Marsden, T.K. (1979) The Socio-Economic Structure of Farming in North Humberside: A Study of the Farm in Capitalist Agriculture. In: Whatmore, S. (1991) *Farming Women: Gender, Work and Family Enterprise*, Basingstoke, Macmillan.

Morris, L. (1990) *The Workings of the Household: A US-UK Comparison*. Cambridge, Polity Press.

Northern Ireland Tourist Board (1998) *Hotels, Rooms and Bedspaces*. Belfast, Northern Ireland Tourist Board.

Novarra, V. (1981) *Women's Work, Men's Work, The Ambivalence of Equality*. London, Marion Boyars.

Oakley, A. (1980) *Housewife*. Middlesex, Penguin.

Oakley, A. (1985) *The Sociology of Housework*. Oxford, Blackwell Ltd.

Pascall, G. (1997) *Social Policy. A New Feminist Analysis*. London, Routledge.

Pearce, P.L. (1990) Farm Tourism in New Zealand: A Social Situation Analysis. *Annals of Tourism Research*, **17**, No. 3, p335–352.

Quinn, U., Larmour, R. and McQuillan, N. (1992) The Small Firm in the Hospitality Industry. *International Journal of Hospitality Management*, **1**, 11–14.

Riley, M. (1984) Hotels and Group Identity. In: Wood, R.C. (1994) Hotel Culture and Social Control. *Annals of Tourism Research*, **21**, No. 1, 65–80.

Ryan, C. (1991) Recreational Tourism: A Social Science Perspective. In: Wood, R.C. (1994) Hotel Culture and Social Control. *Annals of Tourism Research*, **21**, No. 1, 65–80.

Rybczynski, W. (1988) *Home*. London, William Heinemann Ltd.

Scottish Tourist Board (1998) *The Supply of Tourist Accommodation in Scotland 1998*. Edinburgh, Scottish Tourist Board.

Sebba, R. and Churchman, A. (1986) The Uniqueness of the Home. *Architecture and Behaviour*, **3**, No. 1, 7–24.

Sixsmith, A.J. and Sixsmith, J.A. (1991) Transitions in Home Experience in Later Life. *Journal of Architectural and Planning Research*, **8**, No. 3, 181–91.

Stringer, P.F. (1981) Hosts and Guests: The Bed-and-Breakfast Phenomenon. *Annals of Tourism Research*, **8**, No. 3, 357–76.

Tannen, D. (1991) You Just Don't Understand: Women and Men in Conversation. In: Cooper Marcus, C. (1995) *House as a Mirror of Self*. Berkeley, Conari Press.

Telfer, E. (1995) *Food for Thought: Philosophy and Food*. London, Routledge.

Walby, S. (1997) *Gender Transformations*. London, Routledge.

Wales Tourist Board (1998) *Serviced Accommodation*. Cardiff, Wales Tourist Board.

Walton, J.K. (1978) *The Blackpool Landlady – A Social History*. Manchester, Manchester University Press.

Watkins, J.M. and Watkins, D.S. (1984) The Female Entrepreneur: Her Background and Determinants of Business Choice – Some British Data. *International Small Business Journal*, **2**, No. 4, 21–31.

Whatmore, S. (1991) *Farming Women: Gender, Work and Family Enterprise*. Basingstoke, Macmillan.

Wood, R.C. (1994) Hotel Culture and Social Control. *Annals of Tourism Research*, **21**, No. 1, 65–80.

CHAPTER 7

Mediated meanings of hospitality: television personality food programmes

Sandie Randall

Department of Business and Consumer Studies,
Queen Margaret University College, Edinburgh

Key themes

- Situated and mediated culture
- Interpreting media texts – semiotic analysis
- The television personality food programme genre
- The television discourse
- Meanings about food and hospitality

In the search for a better understanding of the nature of hospitality in the modern world, it is recognized that food is of central importance. As Telfer argues, it is through the giving and receiving of food that a bond of trust and interdependency, as well as friendship and generosity, is created between host and guest (1996).

With the proliferation of media texts about food in the second half of the twentieth century, it is perhaps surprising to learn that, to date, little attention has been paid to messages about food and dining that are presented by the media. Research in this field might better inform our understanding of the function of hospitality in the contemporary world. As Strange (1998, p.301) argues in reference to one important example of these texts, the television food programme,

> this neglect suggests the assumption that cookery programmes (and other lifestyle/leisure genres such as gardening and home decoration) are transparent: that they are merely about food and the instruction of cookery methods and as such, do not merit closer examination.

In contrast to this historical neglect, the task of this chapter is to highlight the value of a closer analysis of such programmes to identify the significant contemporary messages about concepts of hospitality, as well as the ways in which these meanings are produced and circulated to ensure mass consumption.

Situated and mediated culture

In traditional societies, cultural meanings were constructed by groups of individuals to meet the needs of their individual communities. In a situated culture such as these, O'Sullivan suggests that cultural meanings are directly related to the personal conditions of experience in a specific place and time (O'Sullivan, Dutton and Rayner, 1994). However, once the technology of media production is available, communication across the boundaries of situated cultures becomes possible to varying degrees. By the late middle ages, for example, the introduction of printing technology allowed the growth of a distinctive genre of written texts that set standards about, amongst other things, what was hospitality (Castiglione, 1528/1967; Erasmus 1530; Della Casa 1558/1958):

> In my opinion it is undesirable to press food on those who are at table with you . . . most people think it is friendly and hospitable to do this, but although it is their

> way of showing concern for their guests, it also very
> often causes the guests to lose their appetite, because
> they are embarrassed to think they are being watched.
>
> (Della Casa, 1558/1958, p.98)

Although these texts were small in number, and their influence was clearly limited to the elite literate upper classes of this period, these sixteenth century examples highlight the importance of media texts as a significant source of cultural meanings and practices of hospitality.

By the late nineteenth century with its raft of technological developments, the production of written texts about food and hospitality was common in the United Kingdom: recipe books, trade publications, women's magazines (Mennell, 1996). By 1954, journals such as *Good Housekeeping* offered the reader ideas for more interesting dining as well as the possibilities of using food and hospitality as weapons for competitive display: 'Make the sauce for crepes Suzette at the table; it's a personal and elegant touch that your guests will appreciate' which Mennell translates as 'show off: impress your guests with your superior expertise; make them feel mildly inferior' (Mennell, 1996, p.257).

During the last 50 years, however, the scale and variety of media production have been profoundly transformed with the proliferation of electronic communications. As a result, individuals and groups, irrespective of literacy, have had increasing access to a large volume of different mass mediated global cultures. Moreover, the speed and quantity of mass communication, and its reception into the home itself, introduces a dynamic quality to the erstwhile stable basis for the construction of cultural meanings. As a result, as Tolson (1996, p.2) suggests:

> Not all the consumers will necessarily accept the
> experiences which are on offer, but the point about
> media saturation is that everyone, in modern societies, is
> obliged to respond in one way or another to what the
> mass media are doing.

Furthermore, Tolson argues that 'through this phenomenon ... the "situated" and the "mediated" worlds gradually but inexorably, interpenetrate' (1996, p.3).

The significance of these developments in mass communications can be better understood by a consideration of the changes in the nature of production which accompanied them. In the United Kingdom, after World War II especially, as the market for utility goods approached saturation point, capital investment was switched to the production of goods for cultural consumption (Featherstone, 1991, p.19).

> In this context, knowledge becomes important: knowledge of new goods, their social and cultural value, and how to use them appropriately. This is particularly the case with the aspiring group who adopt a learning mode towards consumption and the cultivation of a lifestyle.

Thus, entrepreneurs have harnessed the expertise of the media industry to promote innovatory consumer products not according to their use value, but with sets of secondary values in terms of their status as class markers and emotional or lifestyle meanings. These secondary values control the real exchange value of the product in the market and it is to these values that media production is targeted.

There is no doubt that the media industry has expanded by responding to the demands of, as well as exploiting, this established inflationary and competitive syndrome within industrial society. Fischler argues that faced with so much choice, the consumer becomes increasingly anxious about contemporary cultural life and turns increasingly to the media for guidance (1993, p.390). What is evident is that the role of the media has extended beyond solely that of goods promotion, to involve the production of information and knowledge that offers the consumer opportunities to acquire symbolic capital (Featherstone, 1991, p.19; Bourdieu, 1984, p.359; Finkelstein, 1989).

Significantly for our discussion then, the media industry itself is now a major producer of cultural goods, particularly of cultural information and entertainment: newspapers; books; journals; films; videos; and television programmes. The media industry, therefore, must now also continue to stimulate demand for consumption of its own products to promote its own interests (Bourdieu, 1984, p.359). This crucial symbiotic relationship integrates directly the self interests of producers of cultural goods, such as the commercial hospitality and the food industries, and the media.

If contemporary cultural meanings about hospitality are to be identified and understood, it seems clear that the ways in which the media constructs messages about hospitality and its constituent parts must be better accessed, identified and understood. The most ubiquitous of the mass mediated texts produced in contemporary British society are those of broadcast television (O'Sullivan *et al.*, 1994, p.4; HMSO, 1992). Although television produces texts about many aspects of hospitality, one component is prevalent, that of food and dining. To date there has been little attempt to examine the genre of food programmes to identify what texts are offered by television and how these texts work to produce mass mediated meanings about hospitality.

Interpreting media texts – semiotic analysis

How then can a television text be analysed for its meanings? The task is problematic in the sense that the nature of the meaning of meaning is in itself a source of continuing philosophic debate (Tolson, 1996, p.4). However, semiotic theory offers a framework for accessing meanings presented in media texts, and for identifying the ways in which the text produces and circulates these meanings to encourage audience consumption (Barthes 1957/1993, 1967, 1977). Barthes argues that media texts produce meaning with signs that develop associations in the mind of the reader/viewer (de Saussure, 1916/1974; Barthes, 1957/1993, 1977; Tolson, 1996). For successful transmission, these signs are designed to work together to invoke cultural norms that are drawn from a pool of taken-for-granted meanings within a meaning system that is mutually understood within the community (Barthes, 1957/1993, 1977; Tolson, 1996).

These meanings are constructed within texts in two complementary ways: by the distinctiveness of the words or images chosen and the particular cultural connotations that are evoked by their disposition (Barthes, 1977, p.25–7; Storey, 1993, p.80; Tolson, 1996, p.29); and by the ways in which these individual signs are combined together to produce a chain of meaning, described as a dominant or preferred reading (Fiske, 1990, p.111; Tolson, 1996, p.10). Moreover, the media design these 'chains of meaning' in ways that reduce the diversity of reality into a limited number of overarching cultural myths: 'the happy family'; 'nature'; 'the good old days'; 'romance' (Barthes, 1977, p.89–91; McDonald, 1995, p.1; Tolson, 1996, p.7). These 'myths', Barthes argues, are naturalized, 'common sense' views, that 'transforms history into nature' and disguise their origins as products of the powerful social classes in history, to become ideologies (1957/1993, p.129).

Semiotic analysis can investigate below the seeming transparency of media texts to reveal the subtler meanings in circulation (Barthes, 1977, p.89–91; Strange, 1998, p.301). Thus, media texts are able to produce and reproduce existing cultural myths, but in addition, and crucially, they can also transform cultural meanings by dropping some concepts from their chains and adding others, in an evolutionary process (Fiske, 1990, p.90). Mediated meanings also depend in part upon the context in which they are produced: 'myth is not defined by the object of its message, but by the way in which it utters this message' (Barthes, 1957/1993, p.109). Through an examination of the discourse of the message, it is possible to identify how the text invites 'participation in organised (and institutionalised) cultural practices' (Tolson, 1996, p.xv). Thus, the application of semiotic theory to television food programmes also allows the researcher to identify the particular ways the programmes seek to structure and organize meanings to ensure maximum circulation and audience consumption.

The television personality food programme genre

Since its origins in post war broadcast television, the presentation of television food programmes in the United Kingdom has been transformed from the occasional one off series, such as that of Fanny Craddock, to a range that is increasingly large and heterogeneous. Nowadays, an average week of broadcast television, such as 21–27 February 1998, offers the viewer a minimum of 12 hours of designated food programmes, as well as many other programmes which also include food items (*Radio Times*, 1998). The recent availability of cable and satellite television, with their dedicated lifestyle networks, has opened up even greater opportunities for viewing food programmes.

At the beginning of the twenty-first century, television food programmes have now become an example of a mass mediated genre. Such a distinction is recognized and used by the media itself in the marketing of television food programmes: the *Radio Times*, for example, lists all the food items/programmes for the week, together with copy on food topics, within its designated 'Food' pages. It is these frameworks, argues Neale, that organize texts into genre relationships (1980; Bennett and Woollacott, 1987). As Tolson argues, 'readers' views and expectations feed back into the production process which . . . will serve to reinforce a 'game' which is well understood by all concerned' (1996, p.86).

The television food programme genre consists of a number of 30 minute series of specific types or sub genre: the competition/game show food programme; the magazine/documentary food programme; and the travel foreign food programme (Randall, 1996, p.5–7). The Fanny Craddock series provides the original prototype of what has become the most ubiquitous sub genre, 'the television personality food programme', and it is for this reason that discussion will focus upon examples of these programmes.

The discussion in this chapter evolves in major part from the results of an in-depth semiotic analysis of one example of the personality food programme: Rick Stein's *Taste of the Sea* (Randall, 1996; 1999). This case study approach was chosen as being the most appropriate for an initial, and by definition exploratory investigation. These findings are considered within further comparative semiotic analyses of other television personality food programmes presented by BBC 2 in recent years: *Rick Stein's Fruits of the Sea* and *Rick Stein's Seafood Odyssey* (or *Stein*); *Delia's Winter Collection, Delia's Christmas Cookery* and *Delia's How to Cook* (or *Delia*); *Rhodes Around Britain* (or *Rhodes*); *Nick Nairn's Wild Harvest* and *Nick Nairn's Island Harvest* (or *Nairn*); and, *Two Fat Ladies* and *Two Fat Ladies Ride Again* (or *TFL*).

One of the features of television personality food programmes is the antimony of dominant meanings found in association with the production and consumption of food and dining: most importantly, the paradoxical juxtaposition of tradition and community with foreignness and innovation, and simplicity with sophistication (Randall 1996, 1999; Strange, 1998, p.307).

This paradox of tradition and innovation is found mainly in the contrast between the cooking and non-cooking segments, which divide the programme time approximately equally in the majority of the series (Randall, 1996, 1999, p.43; Strange, 1998). In the non-cooking segments, these programmes present images of small but traditional regional communities within the United Kingdom for their contextual settings, in ways that emphasize their distinctiveness: natural landscape; the traditional way of life and forms of work; the local accents; traditional celebrations and feasts; and distinctive local produce (*Nairn; Rhodes; TFL; Delia;* and *Stein*). Other programmes feature traditional British organizations and institutions: the WRI, the lifeboat men, the Boy Scouts (*TFL; Rhodes*). In *Delia's* case, tradition is presented through the location of her 'authentic' traditional housewife's kitchen. In addition, in some cases, there are specific references to traditional or classic British dishes (*Delia; Rhodes*).

Images of those who work to produce the food is a commonly used theme. Sometimes this is to point up a sense of the danger and dedication involved (*Stein*), and at others, to foreground the freshness and quality of the ingredients (*Stein; Nairn; Rhodes; TFL*). In this way, as Strange suggests, the emphasis upon the origin of a raw ingredient, and the labour involved in its production, invokes an 'authenticity' that contributes to the broader rhetoric of the series (1998, p.309).

In these ways, therefore, concepts of food and hospitality are produced with symbolic fictions of 'imagined communities' (Anderson, 1983; Said, 1985; Giddens, 1990; Moores, 1995). The concept of hospitality represented by the nostalgic quest for an idealized mythical past of community, tradition and belonging produces cultural meanings that clearly resonate in the contemporary world. Thus, television personality food programmes are presenting meanings that are regularly found within the television soap opera genre, where fictional constructions of community are defined in many cases by sites for the consumption of food or drink (Bell and Valentine, 1997).

In contrast, another dominant message is the promotion of innovation, experimentation and a sense of adventure as central satisfying elements of hospitality: new ingredients, new dishes, new cuisines. These representations of innovatory practices are predominantly constructed in terms of the foreign and the exotic. The nuances involve articulation of British and foreign locations and cultures within the same programme (*Stein*); and the foreignness of origins, ingredients, cooking techniques or styles of consumption within the programme: 'the whole emphasis of this dish is going to be oriental' (*Stein*, Randall, 1996). This antimony occurs in all the personality programmes: *Scottish* razor shells in an *Italian* risotto (*Nairn*); traditional *British* toad in the hole alongside *Canadian* pancakes (*Delia*); fish cooked for Boy Scouts in a *Polynesian* style pit traditionally designed for roasting humans (sic) (*TFL*). It is interesting to note that concepts of 'foreignness' are constructed with unambiguous connotations of the exotic which ignore the lived realities of poverty, degradation and exploitation (Said, 1985; Kabbani, 1986).

In these programmes, the viewers' fragmented social relations of modern life can be re-embedded into a collective identity through the assimilation of potent meanings about food and hospitality and this myth of idealized traditional community life (Said, 1985; Moores, 1995; Giddens, 1990; Anderson, 1983; Randall, 1996, 1999, pp.57–74). Through this strategy, these programmes promote innovatory concepts of food and hospitality, particularly those of a foreign nature, by concealing them within these established chains of meaning about tradition and Britishness, to seduce the viewer into unwitting consumption of the meanings on offer. Furthermore, it can be argued that this synthesis of these bipolarities of hospitality has legitimized the simulation of the parodic restaurant in the commercial sector, as an 'authentic' site for the re-articulation of hospitality, community and belonging (Finkelstein, 1989; Moores, 1995; Giddens, 1990; Anderson; 1983).

Simplicity and sophistication

This juxtaposition of tradition and innovation articulates with a second paradox, that of simplicity and sophistication. On the one hand, these programmes seek to produce images that connote naturalness and simplicity. This occurs in many ways: through the words of the local characters – 'I hope they haven't pinched our bikes' (Randall, 1996, 1999, p.56; *Stein; Nairn; Rhodes; TFL*); by the landscapes – wild seas, deserted beaches, autumn tints, and sunsets *(Stein; Nairn; TFL; Delia; Rhodes)*; with the sources of the raw materials – collecting mushrooms in the woods, digging up razor shells on a deserted beach *(TFL, Nairn)*; by the ways that the raw ingredients are depicted – raw hake posed on a boulder on the shore, fish tumbling from the net, harvesting oysters, tableaux of assembled raw ingredients *(Stein; Rhodes; Delia)*; and, through the anchoring verbal text – 'a beautiful sweet ozony sort of smell' *(Stein;* Randall, 1999, p.78). This association of food with 'naturalness' and 'goodness' embeds hospitality products and practices within a contemporary discourse of ecological correctness at a time when fear and anxiety about the purity of food and trustworthiness of production practices is high.

In contrast, many meanings in the programmes are constructed in terms of sophistication and elaboration. One way in which this is achieved is through the discourse of the presenters. Economic capital is displayed through their emphasis upon quality and expense: 'Porbeagle, the best', and 'I know its expensive but it's a flavour you'll never forget' *(Stein;* Randall, 1996) or 'you may think a rump steak is expensive' *(TFL)* or 'when you go to buy porcini, you'll think they're very expensive' *(Delia)*. This sophistication is also communicated through the presenters' disposition of what Bourdieu calls cultural capital: the type of language used; accent; references to esoteric knowledge and expertise; and especially, the demonstration of access to traditional erudite and culturally valued pursuits (Randall, 1996, 1999, pp.98–101; Dickson Wright, 1999, p.31). Significantly, it is not only the display of cultural capital that communicates sophistication, but also the naturalness, the 'habitus', with which this is done by the presenters (Bourdieu, 1984): a spontaneous quotation from Robert Herrick; and instinctive use of Latin in the girls school *(Stein; TFL)*.

The sophistication of the presenters is also demonstrated in their surroundings. The stylish aesthetics of *Stein's* restaurant reflects and reinforces his cultured tastes. The upper class associations of the venues for the *Two Fat Ladies* similarly demonstrate theirs: Prince Charles' farm; the girls' public school; the Portuguese embassy. In contrast to the others, *Delia's* didactic and pedestrian references to sophisticated ingredients or practices are more conspicuously the work of the 'autodidact', the learned mode (Featherstone, 1991, p.19), and the taste demonstrated by her kitsch conservatory kitchen, packed with every icon of idealized mythical 'housewifery' (huge vases of flowers, plants, dried flowers, antique crocks and pots, rows of preserves, trolleys of liqueurs, oils and condiments) resonates more with middle England than the upper classes. Nonetheless, the constructions of sophistication in all these programmes highlight its pivotal role in meanings about food and hospitality.

Within these programmes, differences of class in relation to food tastes are made more precise by the verbal text. By image, word or tone of voice, denigration of the food habits and taste of the lower classes are regularly signalled: 'in comparison to the sandwiches you buy for £2–3 which are filthy, this is a much better bet' (*TFL*), or 'they're just like uranium blowing on the beach, sunburnt to a crisp', and 'most of the chippies don't even clean their pans out for 3 weeks, like its ridiculous' by the Australian lifeguard in *Stein* (Randall, 1999, p.90–92).

The ways in which ingredients are transformed into dishes is another arena for the demonstration of sophistication. This message is anchored emphatically in the oral text: 'there's a clear difference to me between restaurant food and the sort of food you cook at home and vive the difference I would say' (*Stein*; Randall, 1996); 'I'm going to take a simple dish and make it special' (*Rhodes* in Strange, 1998, p.306). This transforming practice connotes sophistication through the aestheticization of food and hospitality, so that they become works of art to be consumed as cultural artefacts and practices. In these ways, as Douglas and Isherwood argue, 'the consumption of high cultural goods (art, novels, opera, philosophy) must be related to the ways in which other more mundane cultural goods (such as food and hospitality) are handled and consumed, and high culture must be inscribed in the same social space as everyday cultural consumption' (1980, 176; Featherstone, 1991, pp.65–82).

The juxtaposition of the source of raw ingredients with the final artform, a predominant feature of these programmes, points up the significance of the presenter's auteurial role: opening shots of exotic ingredients and finished cake, side by side (*Delia*). Once created, dishes are presented as sculptures turning before the camera, which lingers lovingly upon them, in ways more redolent of a still life by Chardin or Cezanne: *Delia's* Christmas puddings composed of jewel-like fruits; *Stein's* statuesque 'plateau de fruits de mer'; or *Rhodes'* and *Nairn's* architectural constructions. Thus, the personality chef is constructed as an auteur, the individual who can transform nature into an original artistic creation.

The potential power of the meanings embedded in these programmes resides in some considerable measure with the authority and authenticity of the personalities who present them. One of the crucial hallmarks of these programmes is the star or celebrity status of the presenter. The personality is established through the programme itself, but also is developed in additional ways: television food personalities appearing as celebrities in other types of shows and entertainment; newspaper articles about the celebrity (Fort, 1997, p.6; Urquhart, 1998, p.20; Fracassini, 1998a, p.5, 1998b, p.5; Gibson, 1998, p.13); newspaper articles by the celebrity about non-food matters (Futrell, 1997); their photograph as a picture question in University Challenge (BBC, 1997a); radio progammes about their choice of music and poetry (BBC, 1997b); broadcasting publications and recipe books accompanying the series; supermarket product sponsorship; and now the viewer can cruise to New York on the *QE2* with Rick Stein (*Radio Times*, 1999). As a result, the personality presenter becomes a trusted friend whose life is lived out by the viewers, who for the most part, unthinkingly accept the presenter's opinions and views on offer.

In this way, television does not rely solely upon its own productions for the promotion of meanings about food, dining and hospitality. Within the media interests, there is an incestuous arrangement of inter-textuality, or recycling of circulating messages through secondary texts. The viewers' 'reading formation' is constructed by these inter-textual references to offer 'sets of expectations through which the possibilities of reading (viewing) are organised' (Neale, 1980; Bennett and Woollacott, 1987). The scale of consumer interest in food, dining and hospitality is borne out by the massive sales of these texts and by the success of the presenter's own restaurants, and their imitators (Gibson, 1998, p.13; Randall, 1996, 1999, pp.120–121).

The role of the accompanying recipe book has an important function in that it provides the detailed recipes for the dishes shown. This is necessary because unlike earlier examples, most contemporary television food programmes do not provide explicit recipe details. This change in practice alerts us again to the possible purposes of food programmes: a greater concern now with the meanings associated with the symbolic, emotional and social values embedded in images of food and hospitality practices, rather than in the replication of the dishes.

In addition, we should note, with Featherstone, that television food personalities are no longer just cultural intermediaries, but act as 'cultural entrepreneurs in their own right' who are 'catering for and promoting a general interest in style itself, the nostalgia for past style, the interest in latest style, which in an age which itself lacks a distinctive style . . . have a fascination, and are subjected to constant interpretation and reinterpretation' (Featherstone, 1991, p.91). To sustain this role, as Bourdieu suggested, television food personalities have become the 'new' intellectuals 'who are inventing an art of living which provides them with the gratification and prestige of the intellectual at the least cost'. They apply the intellectual lifestyle and manners to 'not-yet-legitimate culture', and everyday life, with a cultivated disposition of style, distinction, and refinement (1984, p.370).

Intimacy and trust

Although largely taken for granted, the discourse of the broadcast format is another important way by which the personality of these programmes is developed for the viewer. Close ups and life-size face work, direct modes of address – you and I, and spontaneous forms of talk, are used to produce a sense of intimacy, informality and co-presence between the presenter and the individual viewer, producing what Langer calls a 'sustained *impression* of intimacy' (Horton and Wohl, 1956, p.215; Langer 1981, p.362; Ellis, 1992; Scannell, 1989, p.152). Importantly, this 'communicative ethos' constructs a complicity with the audience that fosters trust and reduces risk, to invite the viewer to unwittingly accept the messages on offer (Langer, 1981; Giddens, 1990; Moores, 1995; Randall, 1996, 1999, pp.51–6). This discourse fosters a sense of co-presence in the sharing of food and associated cultural values, to simulate, to some important degree, the interpersonal interaction of the face to face encounter of 'authentic' hospitality. The popularity of these programmes (BARB, 1995a, p.141; 1995b, p.135; 1998a, p.146; 1998b, p.148) may be due to the presentation of traditional hospitable social interaction that has been lost to a large extent within the dis-embedded social relations of the modern world (Giddens, 1990; Moores, 1995).

Thus the television food personality is constructed upon a basis of intimacy and familiarity on the one hand, and celebrities, expertise and artistry on the other to make them the architect of our desires and satisfactions within the hospitality context, to offer a contemporary model of 'mine host'.

There is one further feature of the personality food programme that should concern this discussion of mediated constructions of hospitality, and that is the conspicuous promotion of food and hospitality as self indulgent and pleasurable consumption activities.

Excitement is connoted through a discourse of iconic images: surfing (*Stein*); sailing yachts, speed boats (*Nairn, Rhodes*); fast sports cars, hot air balloons (*Rhodes*); and exotic oriental settings (*Stein*). Romance and magic are signalled with moonlight reflections; dramatic sunsets; wild seascapes; autumn colours;

elegant and glamorous restaurants (*Nairn, Rhodes, TFL, Delia, Stein*); or stylish domestic dinner parties (*Delia*).

Pleasure is also evoked by the sensuous qualities of food which offer the viewer palpable sensations of touch, smell, sight, sound and taste (Randall, 1996, 1999, pp.79–81). Food is presented and handled in ways which are very tactile: close up shots of the presenters almost caressing raw materials; eating with their hands; or close up shots of unctuous sauces tumbling over cooked dishes (*TFL, Stein, Delia, Rhodes, Nairn*). The accompanying verbal text anchors these meanings more firmly: 'it's so rich and warm ... it's so inviting'; and 'the smell is just wonderful'; 'your anticipation is rising, rising, rising' (*Stein*); 'it is really beautiful ... it is going to be succulent and juicy' (*Rhodes*). Even in *Delia* with her typically slow and rather normative style of delivery there are instances when she is clearly promoting ingredients and taste in terms of their self indulgent pleasure: 'the flavour is out of this world, I mean that literally'. Strange confirms Coward's view that the effects of these gestures and oral text serve to eroticize food and dining (Coward, 1984; Strange, 1998, p.310; Randall, 1996, 1999, pp.79–83).

Conclusions

In the modern world, a wide spectrum of media produce messages about food and hospitality. Of these, television food programmes will impact upon the greatest number of consumers at any one time. At first sight, one might think that these programmes simply offer some obvious messages about food and hospitality: cooking instruction for the recycling of traditional recipes and the presentation of new dishes. However, a semiotic examination of one particular segment of the media, the television personality food programme, reveals that such programmes offer much more complex and potentially more powerful influences about hospitality that involve social attitudes, social relations, and consumer motivations.

Television needs to produce polysemic messages that can resonate with mass audiences. In the case of television food programmes, particular strategies are adopted to ensure that this can take place: the construction of genre; the use of secondary texts and reading formations; the broadcast format and ethos of intimacy; the construction of the celebrity personality; and the production of overarching, taken for granted cultural norms, such as community, tradition, Britishness.

Within this discourse, television personality food programmes promote food and hospitality as sites where exotic commodities from all over the world are exchanged in a carnivalesque atmosphere, to become sources of fascination, longing and nostalgia (Featherstone, 1991, pp.22–3). As a result, amongst other things, consumers are offered tantalizing views of the social and emotional benefits derived from hospitable activities. In this way television food programmes have fostered the increasing democratization of dining out, and provided knowledge of the protocols needed to participate knowledgeably. In addition, it could be argued that television personality food programmes have contributed to the blurring of the division between domestic and commercial hospitality, as Mennell suggests (1996, p.330). However, analysis of these programmes suggests that the meanings produced about hospitality are still constructed and understood within an overarching ideology of social relations which relies upon subtle nuances of class taste.

In the different ways identified, meanings about food and hospitality have been transformed by television personality food programmes into artistic practices characterized by individual competitiveness, innovation and the conspicuous display of taste and social status, which generate excitement and direct bodily pleasures. It can be concluded that the dreams and fantasies of emotional fulfillment derived from the signs and symbolic uses of food and hospitality in television food programmes, produce a form of hedonic and narcissistic pleasure that has little to do with Telfer's concept of generosity, reciprocity and pleasing others (1996, p.83).

References

Anderson, B. (1983) *Imagined Communities: Reflections on the Origins and Spread of Nationalism*. London, Verso.

BARB (1995a) What the nation watched. *Radio Times*, October 21–27, p.141.

BARB (1995b) What the nation watched. *Radio Times*, November 11–17, p.135.

BARB (1998a) What the nation watched. *Radio Times*, November 7–11, p.146.

BARB (1998b) What the nation watched. *Radio Times*, November 28–December 4, p.148.

Barthes R. (1957/1993) *Mythologies*. London, Vintage.

Barthes R. (1967) *Elements of Semiology*. London, Jonathan Cape.

Barthes R. (1977) *Image – Music – Text*. London, Fontana.

BBC (1997a) *University Challenge*. BBC 2, Tuesday, December 2, 8.00 pm.

BBC (1997b) *A Night with Rick Stein*. Radio 4, Wednesday, December 3, 8.05 pm.

Bell, D. and Valentine, G. (1997) *Consuming Geographies*. London, Routledge.

Bennett, T. and Woollacott, J. (1987) *Bond and Beyond: The Political Career of a Popular Hero*. London, Macmillan.

Bourdieu, P. (1984) *Distinction: A Social Critique of the Judgement of Taste*. London, Routledge and Kegan Paul.

Castiglione, B. (1528/1967) *The Courtier*. Harmondsworth, Penguin.

Coward, R. (1984) *Female Desire*. London, Paladin.

Della Casa, G. (1558/1958) *Galateo*. Harmondsworth, Penguin.

Dickson Wright, C. (1999) Telling porkies. Spectrum Magazine in *Scotland on Sunday*, March 21, p.31.

Douglas, M. and Isherwood, B. (1980) *The World of Goods*. Harmondsworth, Penguin.

Ellis, J. (1992) *Visible Fictions: Cinema, Television, Video* (revised edn). London, Routledge & Kegan Paul.

Erasmus, D. (1530) (Cologne edn) 'De civilitate morum puerilum', in Elias, N., (1994) *The Civilising Process: The History of Manners and State Formation and Civilization*. Oxford, Basil Blackwell.

Featherstone, M. (1991) *Consumer Culture and Postmodernism*. London, Sage.

Finkelstein, J. (1989) *Dining Out: A Sociology of Modern Manners*. Cambridge, Polity Press.

Fischler, C. (1993) L'(h)omnivore: le gout, la cuisine et la corps, n.p.: Editions Odile Jacob, in Warde, A. (1997) *Consumption, Food and Taste*. London, Sage, p.30.

Fiske, J. (1990) *Introduction to Communication Studies* (2nd edn). London, Routledge.

Fort, M. (1997) 'Two fat Ladies Larder than Life' in G2, *The Guardian*, September 8, p.6.

Fracassini, C. (1998a) Delia cracks the secret of success in shops' sales. *The Scotsman*, November 19, p.5.

Fracassini, C. (1998b) Fat lady turns up heat on rector bid. *The Scotsman*, November 19, p.5.

Futrell, J. (1997) My hols: the world is Rick Stein's oyster when he's on holiday. In: Travel, *The Sunday Times*, January 12, p.18.

Gibson, J. (1998) Delia's basic recipe for book success. *The Guardian*, October 17, p.13.

Giddens, A. (1990) *The Consequences of Modernity*. Cambridge, Polity Press.

HMSO (1992) Social Trends 22, HMSO in O'Sullivan, T., Dutton, B. and Rayner, P. (1994) *Studying the Media: An Introduction*. London, Edward Arnold, p.8.

Horton, D. and Wohl, R. (1956) Mass communication and para-social interaction: observations on intimacy at a distance. *Psychiatry* **19,** No. 3, 215–19.

Kabbani, R. (1986) *Europe's Myths of the Orient*, Hampshire: Macmillan Press Ltd.

Langer, J. (1981) Television's 'personality system'. *Media, Culture and Society 3*, No. 4, 351–65.

McDonald, M. (1995) *Representing Women: Myths of Femininity in the Popular Media*. London, Edward Arnold.

Mennell, S. (1996) *All Manner of Foods* (2nd edn). Urbana, USA: University of Illinois Press.

Moores, S. (1995) TV discourse and 'time space distanciation': on mediated interaction in modern society, *Time and Society 4*, No. 3, 329–44.

Neale, S. (1980) *Genre*. London, BFI. In: Bennett, T. and Woollacott, J. (1997) *Bond and Beyond: The Political Career of a Popular Hero*. London, Macmillan, p.81.

O'Sullivan, T., Dutton, B. and Rayner, P. (1994) *Studying the Media: An Introduction*. London, Edward Arnold.

Radio Times (1998) Programme guide. *Radio Times,* February 21–7.

Radio Times (1999) Join the Radio Times on the QE2 to New York. *Radio Times,* February 13–19, 136.

Randall, S. (1996) Television Representations of Food: a Case Study of Rick Stein's Taste of the Sea, unpublished MSc dissertation, Department of Business and Consumer Studies, Queen Margaret University College, Edinburgh.

Randall, S. (1999) Television Representations of Food: a Case Study of Rick Stein's Taste of the Sea. *International Tourism and Hospitality Research Journal*, **1,** No. 1, 41–54.

Said, E. (1985) *Orientalism*. London, Penguin.

Saussure, F., de (1916/1974) *Course in General Linguistics*. London, Fontana.

Scannell, P. (1989) Public service broadcasting and modern public life. *Media Culture and Society*, **11,** No. 2, 135–66.

Storey, J. (1993) *An Introductory Guide to Cultural Theory and Popular Culture*. Hemel Hempstead, Harvester Wheatsheaf.

Strange, N. (1998) Perform, Educate, Entertain: Ingredients of the Cookery Programme Genre. In: *The Television Studies Book* (eds C. Geraghty and D. Lusted). London, Edward Arnold.

Telfer, E. (1996) *Food for Thought: Philosophy and Food*. London, Routledge.

Tolson, A. (1996) *Mediations*. London, Edward Arnold.

Urquhart, C. (1998) Knives are Always Out Among TV Chefs. *The Scotsman*, October 27, p.20.

Hospitality and hospitality management

Bob Brotherton

Department of Hotel, Catering and Tourism Management, Manchester Metropolitan University

Roy C. Wood

Scottish Hotel School, University of Strathclyde

Key themes

- Definitions of hospitality
- Management
- The hospitality industry
- The management of hospitality

Questions concerning the definition of terms such as 'hospitality' and 'hospitality management' are at the core of this book. On the one hand, a diversity of approaches to such definitions can reflect a healthy pluralism. Contra this point of view, diversity can reflect conflict and confusion, a lack of clarity. In an intellectual era dominated by relativist theories such as postmodernism, the latter position can appear as a virtue. This is not the view taken here. The discussion in this chapter seeks to circumscribe debate on the nature and relationships between 'hospitality' and 'hospitality management', and in so doing to distil a realist account of these concepts as a basis for future research. At the core of this discussion is the nature of hospitality itself, which we view as imperative to any meaningful discourse about what has come to be termed the 'hospitality industry' and 'hospitality management'.

Defining hospitality

There are two broad (and crude) approaches to defining 'hospitality': the first semantic, the second evidential. The semantic approach centres on the variety of definitions offered by informed commentators, from dictionary compilers to those engaged in research and teaching in the university subject 'hospitality management'. The evidential approach, in contrast, derives its impetus from excavation of secondary literature, theoretical and conceptual in nature, seeking to locate and define hospitality within the 'real world' of evidence. The evidential approach has not been much developed (but see the review by Wood, 1994) whereas semantic discussions are relatively plentiful, as Brotherton (1989) shows. Indeed, a notable feature of attempts to define hospitality by 'hospitality management' academics is that they have largely taken place in an evidential and empirical vacuum, without reference to generic 'real world' applications of the concept.

Semantic definitions

Dictionary definitions of terms are, by their very nature, generic in character and thus tend towards the vague. However, there is merit in reflecting upon at least some of these since it permits an appreciation of the parameters of nuance, or spin, placed on definitions of hospitality. Thus, we have hospitality as the 'friendly and generous reception and entertainment of guests or strangers' (*Oxford Quick Reference Dictionary*, 1996, p.424) and as 'kindness in welcoming strangers or guests' (*Collins Concise English Dictionary Plus*, 1989, p.604). Further elaboration of the meanings of hospitality may be obtained from related definitions. One of particular interest is the term 'hospitable' defined by *The Oxford English Dictionary* (1970, p.405) in very similar terms to 'hospitality' as 'offering or affording welcome and entertainment to strangers . . . of persons . . . of things, feelings, qualities etc. . . . Disposed to receive or welcome kindly; open and generous in mind or disposition . . . Hence hospitableness, a hospitable quality or character'. These definitions of 'hospitality' and 'hospitableness' share a high degree of commonality, especially in the emphasis they place on the attitudinal and behavioural dimensions of hospitality, notably in relation to those **providing** hospitality.

These dictionary terms resonate with both other semantic and evidential definitions of hospitality. However, it is important to reiterate that their generic character falls short of an inclusive understanding of the concept of hospitality. As we shall argue later, hospitality is neither a one-way process, nor something exclusively behavioural in nature. It involves not only the demonstration of appropriate, hospitable, behaviour, but the reciprocation of that behaviour, such that hospitality comprises a two-way exchange process. Hence, in associated terminology we have definitions for 'hospitaller' and 'host' (those who provide hospitality) and 'hospitator' and 'guest' (those who are the recipients of hospitality). Hospitality also involves the provision of physical artefacts in the form of accommodation, food and/or drink.

Turning to those definitions emanating from informed commentators in the field of 'hospitality management' we find both a greater degree of specificity, and evidence of symmetry with dictionary definitions of hospitality. One approach that has, historically, dominated the thinking of most hospitality management academics and practitioners, exhibits the tendency to take a narrow, commercial, economic and industrial perspective to defining hospitality. Hospitality is thus conceived of in terms of the activities associated with the hospitality industry. For example, Tideman's (1983, p.1) definition of hospitality as, 'the method of production by which the needs of the proposed guest are satisfied to the utmost and that means a supply of goods and services in a quantity and quality desired by the guest and at a price that is acceptable to him so that he feels the product is worth the price' is clearly rooted in this perspective. This, frankly, could be a description of almost any economic activity. There is nothing in Tideman's definition compared to other forms of economic activity to indicate anything different or distinctive about hospitality, perhaps save the reference to a 'guest'. In a similar vein Pfeifer (1983, p.191) proposes a definition of hospitality as consisting of: 'offering food, beverage and lodging, or, in other words, of offering the basic needs for the person away from home'.

Jones (1996, p.1) more recently typifies this type of product-oriented, commercial, supply-side economic perspective. He comments that 'The term "hospitality" has emerged as the way hoteliers and caterers would like their industry to be perceived. In essence hospitality is made up of two distinct services – the provision of overnight accommodation for people staying away from home, and the provision of sustenance for people eating away from home'. The main problem with this type of definition, apart from the transformative sleight of hand in substituting hospitality for hotel and catering, is that it tends to be designed to simultaneously define both the concept of hospitality and the nature/parameters of the commercial hospitality industry. It fails significantly in the former and, as a consequence, also in the latter. It is an *a posteriori* definition, focusing on effects rather than causes. Put another way, 'hospitality' is normally defined by inferring its nature from the industry activities which purportedly have grown up to service the need for (a specific kind of) hospitality, which is defined and regulated by hospitality industry practices. These kinds of definitions are highly circular and have limited utility, placing as they do the cart before the horse. To argue thus is to suggest a more effective and plausible strategy, namely defining the concept of hospitality in terms of its generic qualities (i.e. those which relate to hospitality *per se*) as opposed to using the provision of commercial hospitality as a conceptual anchor.

In this respect Cassee (1983, p.xiv) proffers a more holistic definition of hospitality as 'a harmonious mixture of tangible and intangible components – food, beverages, beds, ambience and environment, and behaviour of staff'. He contends that the hospitality 'concept comprises much more than the classical ideas of preparing good food and providing a comfortable bed'. This definition is subsequently modified slightly by Cassee and Reuland (1983, p.144) to 'a harmonious mixture of food, beverage, and/or shelter, a physical environment, and the behaviour and attitude of people'. However, although these perspectives do move the debate away from the intellectual cul-de-sac of trying to simultaneously define hospitality and the hospitality industry there is no discernible movement here from the supply-side, provider, perspectives of Tideman (1983), Pfeifer (1983), or Jones (1996) identified earlier. It is implicit in Cassee and Reuland's view that this 'harmonious mixture' is something created and provided for recipients. On the other hand, one very positive aspect of this perspective is the lack of any explicit reference to the commercial provision and/or consumption of hospitality. This serves to open up the possibility of exploring the nature of hospitality *per se*, regardless of its incidence in domestic or commercial environments. The work of Burgess (1982), Hepple, Kipps and Thomson (1990), and Reuland, Choudry and Fagel (1985), all operating from within the field of 'hospitality management', demonstrates this point. The value of these studies lies in the extent to which they both highlight the public and private contexts of hospitality, and the centrality of exchange processes within the hospitality situation (Brotherton, 1999).

Following from this, we return to the earlier noted observation that hospitality is not simply about behavioural exchange but, in addition, behavioural motivation, a view implicit in dictionary definitions of 'hospitality' and related terms such 'hospitable'. Outside of the academic area of hospitality management, the philosopher Elizabeth Telfer (1996, p.83) takes this distinction and points out that 'Hospitableness . . . is clearly something to do with hospitality' and that (1996, p.82) 'hospitableness is not based on any one motive'. Telfer (1996, p.86) also makes a clear distinction between hostship and hospitableness, suggesting that 'Being a good host is not even a necessary condition of being hospitable'. She argues (1996, p.87) that the defining feature of hospitableness is the existence of an appropriate motive, which may include desires for company, and the pleasures of entertaining, and the desire to please others, and to meet another's need. Other motives might include a person's allegiance to their perceived duties in matters of hospitality, and even ulterior motives which have nothing to do with a guest's pleasure or welfare. Telfer suggests that these different motivational roots may be employed to classify different types of hospitality.

This contribution by Telfer renders concepts of the motivation to provide hospitality as problematic. This contrasts with the taken-for-grantedness which characterizes definitions of the phenomenon current among researchers in the hospitality management field. Moreover, Telfer offers the intriguing possibility that hospitable behaviour is not a function of interpersonal competence or 'hostship', thus emphasizing the fluidity of the exchange process in the provision and perception of hospitality.

To conclude this discussion, we can see that there are sound reasons to question the rather partial and sterile view that hospitality can be adequately defined and delimited by reference to its product base and (often loosely) articulated, elements of service. The contributions that emphasize the generic essence of an exchange process, varying underlying motivations for, and alternative forms of, hospitality provision, serve to move the debate beyond existing parameters, an issue we explore further in the next section.

Evidential definitions

As intimated earlier, relatively little academic investigation has been undertaken of the concept, as opposed to the practice, of hospitality. One advantage of this is that the intellectual terrain that does exist is relatively easy to map. Another is that a high degree of clarity can be attained in focusing investigation on the relationships between generic concepts of hospitality and related terms (e.g. concepts of hospitableness) and those reflecting some 'application' (as in the case, for example, of the 'hospitality industry'). As a corollary of this, a serious limitation of current reflections on the concept of hospitality is the absence of extended theorizing about, and empirical investigation of, the subject. This not only circumscribes the potential for general-ization, but additionally undermines the credibility of any analyses which fail to root themselves in some way in that conceptual framework which does exist. Failure to attend to what we *do* know about hospitality as a social phenomenon leads, as we have already seen, to relatively arbitrary definitions of hospitality which have little value beyond the immediate context in which they have been developed.

The vast majority of academic reflection on hospitality has been generated by scholars from the disciplines of philosophy, history, and sociology (see for example Finkelstein, 1989; Heal, 1990; Murray, 1990; Visser, 1991; Mennell *et al.*, 1992; Beardsworth and Keil, 1997; and Warde and Martens, 1998) or is largely historical and descriptive in nature (Langley-Moore and Langley-Moore, 1936; Watts, 1963; White, 1968; Borer, 1972) being primarily concerned with tracing the evolution of the type and incidence of hospitality practices over time. This literature tends to be rather fragmented, differing in focus and purpose, but a number of themes and concerns of relevance to this chapter do emerge.

First, there are consistent references to the themes of order and conformity in the hospitality exchange. This is characterized by discussions of the role(s) of rules, customs, manners, rituals, and habits in regulating hospitality exchanges. For example, Mennell *et al.* (1992, p.20) encapsulate this in the phrase 'culinary cultures', which they define as 'the ensemble of attitudes and tastes people bring to cooking and eating'. Similarly, Visser (1991) refers to mutual obligations and Murray (1990) to commensality. Second, this orderliness tends to reflect the establishment and main-tenance of social relations as a central aspect of the hospitality exchange, whether this is reciprocal in nature or not. Hospitality can arise in both symmetrical and asymmetrical relationships and embrace varying combinations of the personal and social.

Third, all hospitality situations, whether public or private, are imbued with symbolic associations and significance. As a consequence it is possible to differentiate between them on the basis of either the motives underlying the provision of a particular form of hospitality (Telfer, 1996) and/or the nature of the hospitality experience (Finkelstein, 1989). Fourth, hospitality, especially in the public domain, is characterized by increasing commodification and subject to the dictates of fashion; wherein to be fashionable is synonymous with conformity on the one hand and, paradoxically, with change and innovation on the other. This tension, between conformity and change has led Visser (1991) to refer to the role of the dialectic between neophobia and neophilia in determining the dominant nature of hospitality under different socio-economic conditions. Fifth, another recurring theme in the literature is the enduring nature of the essence of hospitality across space and time in the face of different and changing socio-economic and politico-cultural influences. The key word here is 'essence'. Though the particular motives for, form of, and symbolic significance attributed to, different incidences of hospitality clearly vary across space and time, the essence of hospitality remains remarkably stable.

A possible objection to this last line of argument is that the motives for, incidence, and formats of, hospitality provision have varied over time, and continue to do so in both similar and different contemporary environments, cultures and countries. However, the fact that specific motives for the existence of hospitality and its particular manifestations do exhibit spatio-temporal variations is not a compelling reason to reject the view that the essence of the concept remains constant across time and space. As Telfer (1996, p.84) argues, this variation 'does not mean that there is no trait to discuss. Any trait will manifest itself in ways that differ according to prevailing conditions and conventions'. Beardsworth and Keil (1997, p.121) also provide support for this in stating 'that there is not necessarily a simple dichotomy between eating-in and eating-out', or in our terms domestic and commercial hospitality. Indeed, they go on to suggest (1997, p.121) that 'there is also a continuum linking domestic food [hospitality] events at the one end and public food [hospitality] events at the other'. This contention also leads them to postulate that it is not inconceivable to conceptualize a motivational dimension, 'which has eating [hospitality] events shaped by personal, social obligations and relationships at the one end and, at the other, eating [hospitality] events articulated by a commercial nexus between a consumer and a service provider'. Taking a related, but somewhat divergent line, Murray (1990, p.17) adds the view that 'although its form differs greatly between cultures, hospitality can be defined as a relationship of two social roles – host and guest. Further, it is a relationship that is both voluntary and non-commercial'. The latter point of course we would dispute, though in fairness to Murray, he seeks to distinguish between what he refers to as 'true' and 'commercial' hospitality. This distinction finds echoes in discussions of the nature of authenticity and inauthenticity in tourism and hospitality experiences (Wood, 1994).

The studies described in the preceding paragraphs contrast starkly with empirical studies of the hospitality industry conducted by researchers in the hospitality management field. One theme tends to dominate this small and fragmented body of work, namely a pre-occupation with the processual nature of and dynamics of the hospitality exchange. These studies all focus on the hospitality industry's view that commercial hospitality provision is concerned with the organization, dynamics, and management of the hospitality encounter/experience and how to improve it in various ways (but see Brotherton, 1989). This is not surprising as the agenda of such research is driven by a dominant ideological commitment in the field to 'vocational relevance', emphasizing (an industry) problem-solving approach to inquiry. The limitations of this approach have been critically appraised by many commentators over the years (see Wood, 1988; and Taylor and Edgar's nonpareil 1996 discussion which ranges over a number of the research studies alluded to here) but it still persists.

Towards a synthesis

Drawing on the above discussion of the semantic and evidential approaches to defining hospitality, it is possible to identify a number of important and recurrent characteristics ascribed to hospitality. Put simply, hospitality:

- is concerned with producing and supplying certain physical products; namely accommodation and/or food and/or drink;

- involves an exchange relationship, which may be primarily economic, social, or psychological in nature;

- consists of a combination of tangible and intangible elements, the precise proportion of each varying according to the specifics of different hospitality exchange situations;

- is associated with particular forms of human behaviour and interaction;

- is not inevitably synonymous with hospitable behaviour, which is a necessary but not sufficient condition for the existence of hospitality;

- is an activity entered into on a voluntary basis by the parties involved;

- may be provided and consumed for a variety of different motives;

- can vary in its specific form, function, and motivational basis across time and space, but in essence remains qualitatively the same;

- is an activity designed to produce commensality and mutual enhancement for the parties who engage in it;

- involves people in the process of the hospitality exchange; and

- is an exchange which takes place within an intermediate time frame, and one which reflects the close temporal connection between its production and consumption aspects.

Distilling these characteristics into a coherent definition is no easy task, but Brotherton (1999, p.168) offers the following:

> A contemporaneous human exchange, which is voluntarily entered into, and designed to enhance the mutual well being of the parties concerned through the provision of accommodation, and/or food, and/or drink.

This captures the generic essence of hospitality, placing the issue of human exchange at the very heart of the hospitality concept (see Figure 8.1). At the same time, it indicates the nature of the dimensions and parameters that serve to differentiate hospitality from other forms of human exchange.

Thus, the term accommodation is used in a wider sense than that normally ascribed to it within the context of hospitality. Here it is used to refer to any accommodation, whether permanent or temporary, used to house the hospitality exchange. Clearly this usage of the term embraces both domestic and commercial premises and posits that hospitality occurs within the context of a place. In this sense it is also capable of including the type of 'outdoor' venues sometimes used as accommodation for the provision of hospitality. For example, domestic events like barbecues, picnics, and garden parties, and commercial activities such as catering at sporting events, occur at a place and use either indoor or outdoor accommodation to house the hospitality

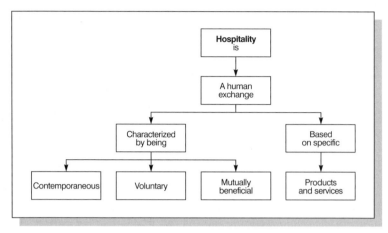

Figure 8.1 The dimensions of hospitality.

exchange. In addition, the placement of the term accommodation before those of food or drink, which is not normal practice in the literature, reinforces this contention and has further value in helping to differentiate the incidence of hospitality from other forms of human exchange involving food and/or drink.

Clearly, any precise definition of hospitality such as that proffered here is unlikely to be either uncontentious or clear cut. Nevertheless, this and related definitions are vital for establishing a consistent view of what constitutes hospitality, the hospitality industry, and hospitality management. The cavalier and unsystematic ways in which these terms have been hitherto employed demands clarity, even an artificial clarity, if progress is to be made towards meaningful elaboration and discourse on the nature of hospitality. As an intermediate step on the road to transmuting the above definition into one appropriate to hospitality management (considered in the next section) the following is offered as a new definition of the hospitality industry:

> The hospitality industry is comprised of commercial organizations that specialize in providing accommodation and/or, food, and/or drink, through a voluntary human exchange, which is contemporaneous in nature, and undertaken to enhance the mutual well being of the parties concerned.

The detail of those activities and organizations that should, based on this definition, be included within the parameters of the hospitality industry requires further thought and are generally outside the scope of this chapter, although some are touched upon briefly in the Conclusions.

Defining hospitality management

We have already noted that those operating in the academic field known as 'hospitality management' tend to employ commercially and economically specific definitions of hospitality. Such definitions do not normally admit generic understandings of hospitality as a social phenomenon. Definitions of 'hospitality management' more specifically emphasize the product/service focus of the hotel and restaurant industry. A good example of this is provided by the recent Review of Hospitality Management study, commissioned by the Higher Education Funding Council for England (HEFCE, 1998, p.2) and conducted by a panel of educationalists and industrialists. This defined hospitality management as 'having a core which addresses the management of food, beverages and/or accommodation in a service context. However, as King (1995, p.220) points out, 'Effective management of hospitality in any type of organisation must begin with a clearly understood definition of what hospitality is'. If it is accepted that hospitality may arise in both private/domestic and public/commercial contexts, it is also logical to suggest that the management of hospitality provision occurs in both contexts. Fundamental aspects of management are to be found in the management of hospitality exchanges within both domestic and commercial contexts, regardless of whether such exchanges take place primarily for social or economic motives. Whatever the context and scale of a hospitality exchange, it needs to be managed to a greater or lesser extent.

So just what is hospitality management? Precisely, nothing. There is hospitality and there is management. Both are social, economic, and political activities. Both are the products of human action. Neither can be granted any epistemologically privileged status. Both, however, can be more or less defined, or, more precisely, circumscribed. 'Hospitality management', does not exist other than as a linguistic label employed to describe programmes of study, styles of research, and so on, prevalent in higher education. However, it may be fairly objected, is not hospitality management the management of hospitality? To this we can reply 'Yes, most certainly' if we mean the application of one set of intellectual constructs and practices (management) to another (hospitality). The advantage of this explicit formulation of the term 'hospitality management' is that it frees us to determine what constructs, and what practices and applications might be studied as a form of scholarly activity in their own right (i.e. theoretically) as well as permitting of pragmatic prescription (the activity of managing hospitality). It also frees us from any predetermined context for our study. We might justifiably study how hospitality is managed in the home, or in hospitals, prisons or in commercial enterprises.

This appealingly rationalist definition lends itself to multi/inter-disciplinary study; it is above all a liberating approach. There is a problem, however, in that it clashes with another, second, type of 'definition' of hospitality management. This is the type alluded to earlier in this chapter and which currently enjoys (albeit tenuous) hegemonic grip on the community of scholars who identify themselves as being engaged in hospitality management teaching and research. In essence, this concept of hospitality management embraces two key assumptions, namely:

- hospitality management is about the management of (essentially but not exclusively) commercial organizations in the business of providing the three key related services of food, drink and accommodation; and
- hospitality management principally entails the application of management concepts and techniques to the provision of these goods and services.

The weaknesses of this approach are easy to identify. First, the use of the term 'hospitality management' in this sense is a misnomer. There may be a perception that 'hospitality' is being 'managed' (many who operate within this framework sincerely hold this to be self-evident) but we must insist that such a view is mistaken. Our second definition of hospitality management has no theory of hospitality. Rather, in an ironic methodological sense, certain 'measurement concepts' come to stand for hospitality, concepts from which we are meant to infer hospitality (or its absence) from the organizations under scrutiny. Such concepts include (most notably of late) 'service delivery models', and strategies for 'delighting the customer'. These and related concepts are the product of a strand of management thinking which properly, at a theoretical level, ought to constitute objects of study. This is because, as intimated earlier, management as a set of intellectual concepts and practices cannot be assumed to have an epistemologically privileged status. Yet those who subscribe to this second view generally do concede just such a status to 'management' knowledge. It is the old 'tool kit' problem writ large (see Slattery, 1983; Wood, 1988) – management and the social sciences being conceived of as an unproblematic set of constructs that can be readily 'applied' to a particular context.

A second problem with our second view concerns the internal contradictions that are an ever-present feature of efforts to defend the legitimacy of 'hospitality management' within academic life. There are three issues here.

The first is the utility of the term 'hospitality'. In the UK it has generally come to substitute for other terms such as 'hotel', 'restaurant' and most, especially, 'catering'. The creeping adoption of the term 'hospitality' without much thought as to its meaning may be seen as part of academics' professionalization strategies. In many societies there is still extensive institutional and wider snobbery that negatively colours attitudes towards services in general, and hotels and catering in particular. Precisely because the term 'hospitality' remains undefined and without a rationale, however, these problems have not disappeared.

This leads to the second issue which is, of course, that 'outsiders' have every right to remain sceptical of cosmetic name changes, precisely because hospitality academics continue to assert the instrumental primacy of the first assumption noted earlier.

The final issue again follows from this and is, simply, this: if hospitality management is the application of management concepts and techniques to hotel and catering organizations, why do we need special schools to do the job? The principal response of hospitality academics to this question has most often been couched in terms of the supposed 'uniqueness' of the hospitality industry – note, not hospitality management. This argument runs as follows. The uniqueness of the industry requires a selective application of management concepts and techniques, reflecting this uniqueness, in order to maximize business success. Many cling to this view (again sincerely) but they are wrong, wrong rationally, logically and empirically. There are a number of reasons for this and we do not propose to rehearse all the arguments here (see Taylor and Edgar, 1996 for the best effort so far to tackle these questions). The central problem with this position lies in the asymmetry it lends to our second view of hospitality management. Thus, the concepts and techniques of 'management' are viewed as (relatively) intellectually unproblematic and the nature of the hospitality industry as problematic. This has led to the search, if not for theories (but see Nailon, 1982) then for 'models' of hospitality management which borrow concepts from 'general' management discourse and seek to adapt these to the supposed peculiarities of the hospitality sector. This approach has profound limitations in terms of the assumptions that underpin it, a fact reflected in the remarkable sterility of hospitality research conducted according to such tenets.

The limitations of the second approach are illuminated by a third 'tradition' in the practice of hospitality management, teaching and research. This consists of the application of concepts and theories from management disciplines to aspects of the hospitality industry and management. In other words, the hospitality industry serves as a locus for disciplinary exploration. Most developed in this regard are the fields of industrial relations and human resource management. Here, researchers have explored 'hospitality' in their disciplinary contexts in much the same way as they might have explored car manufacture or yoghurt production or farming. The principal advantage of 'disciplinary approaches' to hospitality lies, above all else, in identifying characteristics of the hospitality industry while emphasizing the linkages that exist between that industry and others. The main limitation of these approaches is that in all but the most sophisticated applications of such research, the certainties of the discipline being 'applied' are assumed, and linked with equally powerful assumptions about the unproblematic nature of the hospitality industry (save that note is usually made of the 'different' characteristics of the hospitality industry in terms of models predicted on a manufacturing-service dichotomy). It should be emphasized at this point that it is not the intention to advocate here a 'back door' argument for the 'special' nature of the hospitality industry or hospitality management. The hospitality industry and hospitality management is special, even unique, in the sense that any industry has particular characteristics that differentiate it from any other. This does not prevent the analytic treatment of the industry as any other (this statement would be fatuous if not for the fact that it remains the received wisdom among certain sections of the academic community involved in hospitality management research and education).

At this point it may be worthwhile offering some diagrammatic representation of where we are in order to aid clarity. If we take the opening view then we are arguing that hospitality and management are two distinct conceptual domains as in Figure 8.2. Here, there are no assumptions as to the possible directions of research but we can build these by extending the model to produce a holistic set of possibilities as in Figure 8.3. Of course, the model can be extended and further differentiated (for example, within Figure 8.2, in the 'public provision of hospitality' there are multiple foci for study). In Figure 8.4 we have our 'second view' of hospitality management, and in Figure 8.5, the third view.

For the purposes of the arguments laid out in this chapter, Figures 8.2–8.4 are the most important, particularly with regard to any distinction between the management of hospitality and

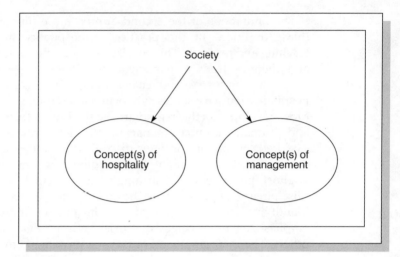

Figure 8.2

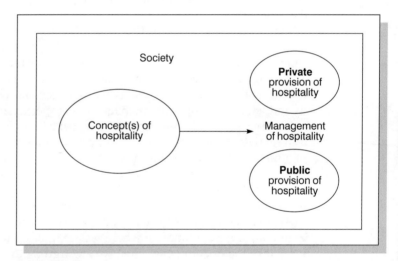

Figure 8.3

'hospitality management'. As hospitality occurs in both private/ domestic and public/commercial environments, issues concerning the management of hospitality arise, equally, in both types of environment. This is not the same, however, as 'hospitality management' in the generally accepted latter use of the term. The difference between the management of hospitality and 'hospitality management' lies in the earlier noted professionalization strategies of those engaged in the hospitality industry (taken here to also include the large academic 'industry' in hospitality

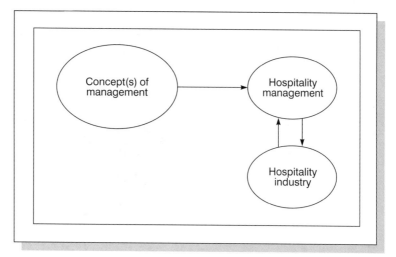

Figure 8.4

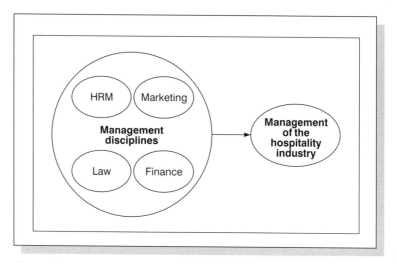

Figure 8.5

management). We can attempt some synthesis of these issues. Figure 8.6 'links' 'hospitality' and 'management' with the concept of 'professionalization'.

Hospitality, management, and professionalization strategies exist as distinct and independent concepts. The various intersections represent the following:

- **PH (professionalized hospitality).** This refers to the widely noted tendency for the domestic provision of hospitality, and

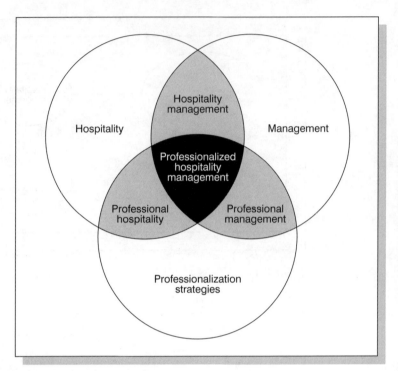

Figure 8.6

hospitality products, to be subject to voluntary regulation according to the standards laid down by third party 'advisers', notably celebrity chefs, food and drink writers/critics, and authors of manuals of etiquette (see, for example, Wood, 1995; 1996).

HM (hospitality management). This is the area we earlier referred to as the management of hospitality; it is a descriptor, nothing more, of the application of management techniques (of whatever kind) to hospitality provision and can take place in domestic and non-domestic contexts (the idea of management skills applied to domestic practice of hospitality is well-established in gender research, socio-economic aspects of time allocation and management in households and, more recently, strategic management – see Charles and Kerr, 1988; Wensley, 1996, the latter a particularly fascinating exploration of the management techniques expressed in *Mrs Beeton's Household Management*).

- **PHM (professionalized hospitality management).** This is what was termed earlier 'hospitality management' and represents those skills and techniques applied by managers employed in the hospitality industry.

- **PM (professionalized management).** This represents generic management in an industrial context.

As an exercise in model building, the heuristic value of this presentation lies in the degree to which it allows a conceptual accommodation between generic notions of 'hospitality' and 'management' while locating 'hospitality management', in its various forms, as a mutable sub-set of these categories. Furthermore, the model also has the advantage of treating the concepts and practices of hospitality, management, and professionalization strategies as *processes* and not fixed social constructs. This accommodates notions of social exchange discussed earlier and does not compromise the possibility that the essence of hospitality remains relatively stable in a spatio-temporal sense. Perhaps the greatest challenge facing those who seek to explore the relationships between hospitality and hospitality management is the need to avoid ahistoricity, to deny the processual, historical development of these concepts. Figure 8.6 offers a simplistic charting of such development in the context of issues considered in this chapter. Hospitality and hospitable-ness are concepts as old as the earliest forms of collective social

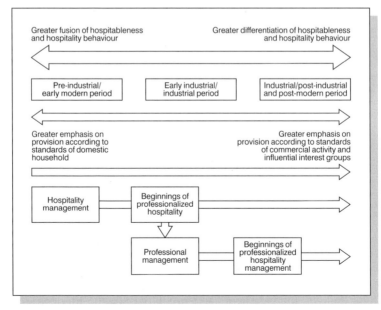

Figure 8.7 The development of hospitality in industrial societies.

Hospitality, Leisure & Tourism Series

activity but 'management' and 'hospitality management', conventionally understood, are relatively modern concepts, the product of industrialization, as are the processes they represent. Accordingly, we can define hospitality management in the industry context (professionalized hospitality management above) as: 'the professional management of the hospitality exchange process in a commercial environment'.

The industrialization of hospitality has received little direct attention but much of value can be gleaned from diverse scholarship on the industrialization of services (Levitt, 1972); industrial sociology (Braverman, 1974; Wood, 1997); and the sociology of consumption. In respect of the last of these, currently fashionable debates about McDonaldization illustrate the extremes of these debates (see Alfino et al., 1998; Wood, 1998). Future tasks include the refinement of our understanding of the interplay between societal concepts and practices of hospitality and hospitality management, and, to this end, theorizing and modelling will be insufficient to the task: there is, and will continue to be, a need for detailed empirical research in support of abstract reasoning. For such research to be meaningful, there will have to be some agreement as to the nature of the relationships between hospitality and hospitality management. More important, at least for those who make claims to scholarly seriousness in the field, a proper understanding of the concept of hospitality will be central to prescriptive pronouncements on strategy and technique in the management of the hospitality industry. In this chapter, we have sought to outline elements for consideration in both kinds of activity.

Conclusions

The aim of this chapter has been to critically review the nature of hospitality and hospitality management in order to provoke academics and practitioners alike into considering these concepts more deeply. In view of this, it is to be expected that reactions may range from a view at one end of the continuum that this is a lot of unnecessary nonsense which only serves to confuse the issues further, to that which sees this exercise as a stimulating and liberating contribution at the other. Whatever the specific nature of the reaction, the views expressed in the chapter seek to raise issues and questions to be addressed more fully in the future. The central challenge relates to the nature and scope of what should be properly regarded as hospitality and hospitality management, and we have sought to open up debate as to possible orientations, issues, and agendas for future research.

One major theme of the arguments presented here is whether hospitality research should be limited to the domain of commercial hospitality provision, within which it may be seen to be constrained by a 'tyranny of relevance' (Taylor and Edgar, 1996). A wider, more explicitly comparative perspective would help to examine systematically the nature of hospitality and non-hospitality exchanges, and the relationships between them. At the same time it would allow both intrinsically interesting as well as practical questions to be posed. On the subject of exchange for example, if hospitality is inextricably linked with the incidence of a human exchange should any form of automated food, drink, or even accommodation provision be excluded from definitions of the hospitality industry? Likewise, if hospitality is an exchange voluntarily entered into, should activities such as hospital and prison catering be similarly excluded (not withstanding that prisoners are often alluded to as 'guests of Her Majesty'!)? If, as was argued earlier, hospitality occurs within the context of a place and is contemporaneous in nature should activities such as take-away food and, more recently, home delivery and/or home meal replacement, be located within the domain of retailing rather than hospitality? Indeed, is the increasing tendency of some commercial hospitality providers in the UK to refer to themselves as 'hospitality retailers' in any way meaningful *vis-à-vis* our understanding of the term 'hospitality'? In posing these rather diverse rhetorical questions, the aim is simply to indicate the potential richness of hospitality as a concept no longer taken for granted and narrowly constrained, but dynamic, if problematic, and central to serious research enquiry in hospitality management.

A second theme of this chapter has been that in hospitality management research, attention should be shifted away from emphasis on the product elements of hospitality towards one more focused on the nature and implications of the hospitality exchange. A wider hospitality perspective could facilitate an exploration of trans-historical and cross-national and/or cultural studies of hospitality. Not only would this be of enormous intrinsic interest but it may also generate important insights for the development of new forms of commercial hospitality provision. Similarly, there is a need to explore more thoroughly the relationships between private/domestic and public/commercial hospitality. There is much to be gained from exploring the extent of reciprocity between private and public domains. For example, establishing whether commercial hospitality innovations, fashions and trends have a strong influence on the type of hospitality favoured in the private domain would parallel research in other areas of consumer studies. The reverse is also true, examining to

Hospitality, Leisure & Tourism Series

what extent, and in what ways, trends in food retailing and eating habits in general influence the type of hospitality pursued by commercial providers (Wood, 1995).

Whether agreeing or disagreeing with the views contained in this paper, there is a need for discussion and debate to be continued. These are uncomfortable times for the complacent and unquestioning researcher or practitioner. If hospitality management research and practice is to progress, those associated with it must reflect more deeply over both its essential nature and practical manifestation. Without such discourse it is unlikely that either the intellectual or vocational aspects of 'hospitality management' will progress to higher levels in the present millennium.

References

Alfino, M., Caputo, J.S. and Wynyard, R. (eds) (1998) *McDonaldization Revisited: Critical Essays on Consumer Culture.* Westport, Ct, Praeger.

Beardsworth, A. and Keil, T. (1997) *Sociology on the Menu: An Invitation to the Study of Food and Society.* London, Routledge.

Borer, M.C. (1972) *The British Hotel through the Ages.* London, Lutterworth Press.

Braverman, H. (1974) *Labor and Monopoly Capital.* New York, Monthly Review Press.

Brotherton, R. (1989) Defining hospitality, tourism and leisure: perspectives, problems and implications, Proceedings of IAHMS Autumn Symposium, The Queen's College, Glasgow.

Brotherton, B. (1999) Towards a definitive view of the nature of hospitality and hospitality management. *International Journal of Contemporary Hospitality Management*, **11**, No. 4, 165–73.

Burgess, J. (1982) Perspectives on gift exchange and hospitable behaviour. *International Journal of Hospitality Management*, **1**, No. 1, 49–57.

Cassee, E. H. (1983) Introduction. In: *The Management of Hospitality* (E.H. Cassee and R. Reuland, eds), pp.xii–xxii. Oxford, Pergamon.

Cassee, E.H. and Reuland, R. (1983) Hospitality in Hospitals. In: *The Management of Hospitality* (E.H. Cassee and R. Reuland, eds), pp.143–63. Oxford, Pergamon.

Charles, N. and Kerr, M. (1988) *Women, Food and Families.* Manchester, Manchester University Press.

Finkelstein, J. (1989) *Dining Out: A Sociology of Modern Manners.* Cambridge, Polity Press/Oxford, Blackwell.

Heal, F. (1990) *Hospitality in Early Modern England.* Oxford, Clarendon Press.

Hepple, J., Kipps, M. and Thomson, J. (1990) The concept of hospitality and an evaluation of its applicability to the experience of hospital patients. *International Journal of Hospitality Management*, **9**, No. 4, 305–17.

Higher Education Funding Council for England (HEFCE) (1998) *Review of Hospitality Management*. Bristol, HEFCE.

Jones, P. (1996) The Hospitality Industry. In: *Introduction to Hospitality Operations* (P. Jones, ed.), pp.1–20. London, Cassell.

King, C.A. (1995) What Is Hospitality? *International Journal of Hospitality Management*, **14**, No. 3–4, 219–34.

Langley-Moore, J. and Langley-Moore, D. (1936) *The Pleasure of Your Company*. London, William Chappell.

Levitt, T. (1972) Production line approach to service. In: *The Management of Service Operations* (W.E. Sasser, R.P. Olsen and D.D. Wyckoff, eds). Boston, Allyn and Bacon.

Mennell, S., Murcott, A. and Van Otterloo, A.H. (1992) *The Sociology of Food: Eating, Diet and Culture*. London, Sage.

Murray, H. (1990) *Do Not Neglect Hospitality – The Catholic Worker and the Homeless*. Philadelphia, Temple University Press.

Nailon, P. (1982) Theory In Hospitality Management. *International Journal of Hospitality Management*, **1**, No. 3, 135–43.

Pfeifer, Y. (1983) Small business management. In: *The Management of Hospitality* (E.H. Cassee and R. Reuland, eds), pp.51–6. Oxford, Pergamon.

Reuland, R., Choudry, J. and Fagel, A. (1985) Research in the Field of Hospitality Management. *International Journal of Hospitality Management*, **4**, No. 4, 141–6.

Slattery, P. (1983) Social scientific methodology and hospitality management. *International Journal of Hospitality Management*, **2**, No. 1, 9–14.

Taylor, S. and Edgar, D. (1996) Hospitality research: the Emperor's New Clothes? *International Journal of Hospitality Management*, **15**, No. 3, 211–27.

Telfer, E. (1996) *Food For Thought: Philosophy and Food*. London, Routledge.

Tideman, M.C. (1983) External influences on the hospitality industry. In: *The Management of Hospitality* (E.H. Cassee and R. Reuland, eds), pp.1–24. Oxford, Pergamon.

Visser, M. (1991) *The Rituals of Dinner*. London, Penguin Books.

Warde, A. and Martens, L. (1998) Eating Out and the Commercialisation of Mental Life. *British Food Journal*, **100**, No. 3, 147–53.

Watts, S. (1963) *The Ritz*. London, The Bodley Head Ltd.

Wensley, R. (1996) Isabella Beaton: management as 'everything in its place'. *London Business School Business Strategy Review*, **7**, No. 1, 37–46.

White, A. (1968) *Palaces of The People: A Social History of Commercial Hospitality.* New York, Taplinger.

Wood, R.C. (1988) Against Social Science? *International Journal of Hospitality Management*, **7**, No. 3, 239–50.

Wood, R.C. (1994) Some theoretical perspectives on hospitality. In: *Tourism: The State of The Art* (A.V. Seaton *et al.*, eds), pp.737–42. John Wiley & Sons Ltd, Chichester.

Wood, R.C. (1995) *The Sociology of the Meal*. Edinburgh, Edinburgh University Press.

Wood, R.C. (1996) Talking to themselves: food commentators, food snobbery and market reality. *British Food Journal*, **98**, No. 10, 7–13.

Wood, R.C. (1997) *Working in Hotels and Catering*. London, International Thomson Business Press, 2nd edition.

Wood, R.C. (1998) New wine in old bottles: critical limitations of the McDonaldization thesis. In: *McDonaldization Revisited: Critical Essays in Consumer Culture* (M. Alfino, *et al.* eds), pp.85–104. Westport, Ct, Praeger.

Managing hospitality operations

Andrew Lockwood

School of Management Studies for the Service Sector, University of Surrey

Peter Jones

School of Management Studies for the Service Sector, University of Surrey

Key themes

- The commercialization of hospitality
- The industrialization of service
- Dealing with variation
- A customer perspective

There is a story of an old man who lived high on the Lassithi plateau above Agios Nikolaos on the island of Crete and made a living out of making and selling pottery. At first, very few tourists visited him to buy his pottery, but in the tradition of Greek hospitality or 'philoxenia', those who did were provided with a drink and a snack from the old man's kitchen. As his fame spread, more tourists visited him to buy his wares and he continued to provide them with refreshment. The difficulty arose when he became an established stop for the tourist coaches and he found that he was giving out more in food and drink than he was able to make on the sale of his pottery and his business was making substantial losses. When the old man died his family took over the business, extended the pottery production, and built a restaurant capable of handling the coach parties. The business is now very successful but sometimes visitors are heard to say that it is not quite as it was in the old days.

The implication here is that while the provision of hospitality was a personal and almost peripheral act, it was in some way more genuine and better. As soon as the provision of hospitality becomes the central focus of the enterprise, it becomes commercialized and in some way diminished. By this argument, commercial hospitality can never achieve the same level of experience as hospitality in the home, and the customer may always be slightly disappointed with what they receive at the hands of the commercial operator.

However, if we turn this story on its head, a different argument emerges. Imagine that the old man had made a living out of providing hospitality and had given away pottery that he had made for a hobby. When he dies, his family successfully commercialize the pottery business and still the customers feel that something has been lost. It will always be the case, irrespective of whether the gift is pottery or hospitality, that something that is given freely will have a different status to something that is bought and sold. It is outside the scope of this chapter to compare the concepts of giving and selling; the focus here is on the selling of commercial hospitality. Commercial hospitality has emerged from domestic hospitality as a business in its own right to serve a market for food, drink and lodging outside the home as a sociotechnical business system, whose main goal is to 'create value for its customers or clients, within certain resource and social constraints' (Adler and Docherty, 1998, p.320). For both public and private enterprises, one of these resource constraints will involve continuing financial viability; in an attempt to facilitate fruitful communication between different functional specialists, businesses revert to the use of a common financial language with final accountability often resting with 'profit' as a result (Ballé, 1998).

Historical development

The emergence of commercial hospitality from the domestic and social setting provides an interesting historical perspective. Farb and Armelagos (1980) strike the first note for commercial hospitality by suggesting that there was the opportunity in both ancient Rome and ancient China to buy food on a commercial basis in urban settings.

The emergence of commercial hospitality in Britain has been well documented by Medlik and Airey (1978). However, identifying a point at which commercial hospitality takes over from social responsibility or philanthropy is still difficult. The Romans brought with them a range of hospitality operations for accommodation (*mansiones*), drinking (*bibulium*) and eating. Post-Roman Britain saw the breakdown of travel and these institutions. The few people who did travel, such as the king, were accommodated at the nearest castle at the expense (and occasional ruin) of the local nobility. Private hospitality and abbeys and monasteries were used to house the small numbers of other travellers.

The eleventh century saw a growth in travel on pilgrimages, crusades and for trade purposes. Much of this growth was accommodated by religious houses and monasteries who set up formal procedures, staff and built hostels and hospices. Some travellers still claimed their right of 'salt and fire' from the local nobility, while others stayed with private householders who started to take in strangers as well as friends and acquaintances. Over time these private houses evolved into inns. The dominant taker-in of strangers in a local area became the inn-holder. While the religious houses were happy to take in the nobility as an act of 'respect' and the poor as an act of charity, the middle classes or tradesmen 'had to go to those whose business it was to care for them – to the innkeepers' (Medlik and Airey, 1978, p.23). The business of hospitality was firmly established by the fourteenth century and the growth of these 'common inns'.

While the inns catered for the reception and entertainment of travellers by day and night, it was the taverns that provided refreshment in the form of food and drink for the local population and the ale houses who catered to a similar but more down-market clientele presumably more interested in beer than wine.

By the close of the Middle Ages, inns continued to increase in importance, as pilgrimages and the dominance of the religious houses waned. As travel increased and the new merchant class emerged, there was a system of commercial hospitality in place to cater for their needs, even if the quality was still unsatisfactory. Another boost to commercial hospitality came with the dissolution of monasteries in 1539 and the razing to the ground of a major element of competition. Inns were more in accord with the changing social and economic system and they prospered, with records showing some inns being able to accommodate more than 100 guests.

With hospitality now established as a commercial operation, further developments saw the increasing use of taverns for 'eating out' by the aristocracy and men of letters in the sixteenth century, the explosive growth of coffee houses from a start in Oxford in 1650, the growth of first inland and then seaside resorts and the first hotels, and the growth of *haute cuisine* in France following the forced redundancy of chefs previously employed by the aristocracy after the French Revolution (Beardsworth and Bryman, 1999).

These edited highlights from history are intended only to show that once established as a commercial business, hospitality has grown into a highly diverse industry consisting of all those business operations, which provide for their customers any combination of the three core services of food, drink and accommodation. The fascinating stories of the growth of down-market cafés from the once democratic coffee houses, of fish and chip shops and grand hotels, and of industrial catering as late as the 1930s are outside the scope of this study, but some insights from the growth of the eating-out market in the twentieth century will be referred to later.

The characteristics of commercial hospitality operations

The discussion attempted here compares commercial hospitality and social hospitality. Looking for similarities reveals that both are providing any combination of the three core services of food, drink and accommodation. For this hospitality to be delivered, there must be some interaction between the receiver and the provider, usually, but not exclusively, on the premises of the provider. The hospitality provision involves a complex blend of tangible and intangible elements – for both the 'products' offered – food, drink and accommodation – and the service and atmosphere that surrounds them. Both commercial and social hospitality set out to provide essentially the same type of experience using similar techniques and potentially similar technology. It is in the context of that provision that the key differences emerge, as listed in Table 9.1.

Social hospitality is essentially supply led. It is the host or hostess who invites their guests to stay for the weekend or to pop round for supper and who decides the food to cook and the drink to serve. It would be very unusual and contrary to UK cultural norms for a guest to invite themselves round. On the other hand, commercial hospitality is largely demand led. It is the customer's decision as to where and when they are going to stay or what they are going to eat or drink. This gives the customer a greater degree of choice of and a greater degree of control over the hospitality experience to which the commercial hospitality provider must be able to respond.

Social hospitality	Commercial hospitality
Supply led	Demand led
Occasional	Continuous
Small scale	Large scale
Self administered	Administered by others
Non-dedicated facilities	Dedicated facilities
Unique experience	Repeatable experience
Personalized activity	Economies of scale
Social experience	Service experience
Not for profit	Financial sustainability

Table 9.1 Comparing social and commercial hospitality

The majority of social hospitality is provided on an occasional basis, on a fairly small scale, and by the host or hostess themselves probably in their own home. In this way each social hospitality experience would be a unique experience, which would be customized or personalized for each guest. The commercial hospitality operation would be on a comparatively large scale. Even a small bed-and-breakfast establishment is likely to accommodate more customers overnight than a normal social provider could account for. In very small commercial operations, the whole workforce could be made up of the owner and their family but in many instances the service will be provided by an employee rather than the 'host' themselves. In most commercial operations, the premises will be at least partly dedicated to the provision of hospitality. Where the social experience is unique, the commercial operation sets out to maintain a standard of operation that can be repeated for every customer and in this way to benefit from certain economies of scale.

The prime focus of social hospitality is the social setting – the actual food, drink or accommodation provided is of subsidiary importance. Having a *crème brulée* where the sugar refuses to go crunchy or the *tarte tatin* falls apart on removal from its tin is unlikely to cause the guests to walk out unhappy, if the social side of the evening has gone well. If the same problems happened in the commercial setting then the customer, whose focus here is on the nature of the service experience for which they are paying, is likely to feel dissatisfied and may well complain. It would be very unusual for a guest to complain to a social host. This can be partly explained by the fact that in the commercial setting the hospitality is being offered at a price to render at least financial sustainability and perhaps profit, as well as value to the customer, while in the social setting the profit motive and money in general are not in evidence.

The nature of commercial hospitality as a service operation brings into consideration a further range of characteristics (Fitzgerald *et al.*, 1991) from which it is possible to select four key characteristics that inform any discussion of the management of commercial hospitality.

The complexity of operation

All hospitality operations require a combination of manufacturing expertise and service skill in a business that operates around the clock, 365 days a year, and is busiest when most other businesses are not. To deliver an appropriate level of product and service consistently to each customer requires the efforts of many different teams of staff who must be co-ordinated to deliver to standard every time. Catering for the needs of a single customer may be difficult enough but catering to the needs of many different groups of customers all with slightly different requirements multiplies the complexity of the problem many times over.

The reliance on service contact staff. However well planned and designed the hospitality operation and however well scheduled the resources, the success of any customer experience will be determined at 'the moment of truth' – the interaction between the customer and the service provider. The point of contact between the customer and service provider is also an opportunity for the operation to sell its services and to generate additional revenue. Hotel receptionists can significantly increase the profitability of a hotel by upselling – encouraging customers to trade up to more luxurious and more expensive accommodation – or by simply asking if the guest would like to make a reservation for dinner in the hotel restaurant.

The central importance of the customer. Hospitality cannot be delivered without the presence of the customer, who is also the source of revenue for the financial success of the operation. The customer can be directly involved in many aspects of the delivery of the hospitality service. The combination of all customers determines the demand pattern for the operation. One customer forms part of the environment for all other customers. The customer is the final arbiter of satisfaction with both the service and product elements and therefore the judge of the quality of hospitality provided.

The criticality of capacity utilization

Achieving a satisfactory balance between demand patterns, resource scheduling and operational capacity is one of the most difficult tasks facing hospitality managers. Managing customer demand to result in the optimum volume at maximum value is extremely complex. Too few customers overall and the cost structure of the business ensures financial ruin. With too many customers and without the required capacity or resources, the quality of the experience suffers and customers leave dissatisfied. Customer volume can be bought by discounting prices at the expense of value per customer. Not discounting can scare potential customers away to the competition. Yield management is crucial, both for accommodation and for food and beverage operations. Scheduling of resources is also critical. Too many staff on duty to cover anticipated demand and productivity and profitability suffer. Too few staff on duty and service levels fall along with staff morale. The key here would seem to be effective forecasting and yet unravelling these demand patterns to provide accurate predictions is often beyond the competence of many operations.

Operational complexity

The potential complexity faced by the management of any production or service process is high. Management strives through the introduction of policies and procedures, rules and regulations to reduce this potential complexity to manageable proportions. Hence the constraints imposed on operations as shown in Figure 9.1.

Decisions made at the upper levels of the hierarchy, for example at the strategic management level, place increasing constraints on lower levels of the management hierarchy. Decisions taken by management will place constraints on the

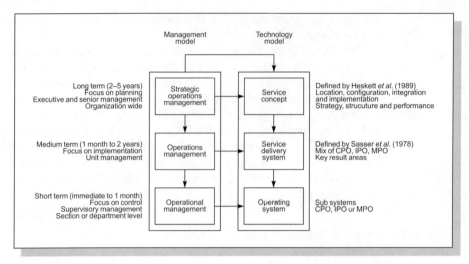

Figure 9.1 A model of operations management. *Source:* Jones and Lockwood, 1996.

functioning of the operating system and its associated technology. In practice this means that the freedom of action at the operating system level has been severely restricted by managerial decisions at the operating system level and the levels above. A decision to source a particular food product from a particular supplier for a national chain of hospitality operations may not make sense to a unit that may be able to source the same product locally at a lower price or better quality. It is only when the single unit is seen as part of the total system that the benefit to the system as a whole becomes evident.

There are four key factors that influence the operational complexity of a service or production process (Slack *et al.*, 1995). These are volume, variety, variability and customer contact. The volume factor suggests that although vary small scale production would appear less complex, it is through economies of scale that most benefits accrue. High volume in an operation allows task specialization and the systemization of the work, which in turn result in the repeatability and consistency of the operation. At the same time high volume can lead to a greater opportunity for using technology and therefore a higher capital intensity. All this leads to lower unit costs as the fixed costs of the operation are spread over a large number of products and services.

The variety factor is concerned with the flexibility in the range of products and services that an operation offers. The less variety is offered the easier it is to standardize the operation as there is little need for flexibility. Adding flexibility adds operational complexity and comes at a cost.

The variation factor is concerned with the stability of demand. The less stable the demand for a product or service, the more the operation has to adjust its capacity, the greater the flexibility in output that is needed. Demand that is relatively level allows operations to function in a routine and predictable way with a high utilization of resources and lower unit cost.

The customer contact factor argues that the higher the level of customer contact in an operation, the more complex that operation becomes. High customer contact operations need to employ staff with good customer contact skills who can deal with that fact that once customers are inside the operation they can ask for what they like and will not necessarily behave in the way the 'system' expects them to. This makes it difficult to achieve high resource utilization.

The sheer scale and scope of commercial hospitality suggest that all possible permutations of the four factors above will be evident somewhere and that some way of providing categories of operational types would be useful. One such framework mentioned earlier is that offered by Schmenner (1995). He proposes two dimensions forming a matrix contrasting the labour intensity of the service process with the degree of interaction with and customization of the service for the customer. This matrix is shown in Figure 9.2.

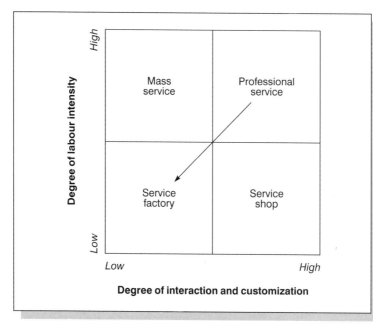

Figure 9.2 A typology of service operations. *Source:* Schmenner, 1986.

The matrix shows four operational types. Some services have low labour intensity and a low degree of customer interaction and customization. These are characterized as service factories and include fast food operations and some hotel operations. As the degree of customization increases, the service factory gives way to the service shop. In hospitality terms, this represents a wider menu range and greater employee discretion but still a relatively capital intensive operation, more typical of TGI Friday than McDonald's. Retail operations are examples of service processes with a high degree of labour intensity (or a lower level of capital intensity) but a relatively low degree of interaction and customization and therefore fall into the category of mass service. When the degree of interaction and customization increases, then mass service gives way to professional service, typified by lawyers, consultants or doctors. It is just possible that some fine dining operations or country house hotels could creep into this segment.

Schmenner (1986) also argues that there is a tendency over time for operations to move toward and indeed down the diagonal as an industrial engineering mentality is increasingly applied to service operations.

The industrialization of service

In the early 1970s when Levitt first argued that service businesses could benefit from adopting ideas from mass production (Levitt, 1972), the service sector had largely been ignored by management scholars. The service sector was growing in importance but there were cries of inefficiency, poor quality and low productivity. Specific service management models had yet to emerge. Levitt claimed that services were primitive and inefficient relative to mass-manufacturing operations, deriving largely from a focus on servitude and ministration. He argued that improvement in services would not come just from improving the skills and attitudes of service workers but more from adopting the technocratic perspective focusing on tools and systems of the 'production line approach'. The defining characteristics of this approach, exemplified in hospitality by McDonald's, include:

- **Limited discretion on the part of personnel.** Tasks are strictly defined, with clear rules and procedures to follow, resulting in standardization and consistency in meeting the specifications designed to satisfy the customer.

- **Division of labour.** The job is broken down into groups of tasks allowing skill specialization. This made possible close supervision and narrow spans of control and at the same time minimized the need for skilled staff and training time.

- **Substitution of technology for people.** Introducing technology into cooking hamburgers further eliminated the need for skilled labour, with the technology setting the pace of operation, and resulted in consistent quality and efficiency.

- **Service standardization.** This approach is only able to produce a limited range of offerings but this in turn allows for more predictability, preplanning and easier production control which in turn provides uniformity in service quality.

There is no doubt, taking fast food as an example, that these approaches have allowed hospitality companies to achieve efficient, low-cost production of customer satisfying outcomes (Bowen and Youngdahl, 1998) and the competitive advantages that follow.

In *The McDonaldization of Society,* Ritzer (1993) argues that these principles of mass production applied to services typified by McDonald's are not restricted to that one organization nor to the fast food industry. He describes McDonalidization as 'the process by which the principles of the fast food restaurant are coming to dominate more and more sectors of American society as well as the rest of the world' (Ritzer, 1993, p.3). Systems organized along the principles outlined above are seen to offer 'efficiency, calculability (or quantification), predictability and increased control through substitution of non-human for human technology' (Ritzer, 1993, p.34). There is a self reinforcing cycle at work here. As long as customers are prepared to accept mass-produced goods and services, the markets for these grow and this allows prices to be reduced through better economies of scale and scope and still allow the firms to make improved profits through the efficiency of their systems. These lower prices and the improved consistency inherent in the system result in a growing gap between the individuality offered by 'mom and pop' operations and the homogeneity of the chains. This gap further encourages customers to go where they are reassured about the standard of products and services they will receive at a cheaper price. While the focus is on 'efficiency', the industrialization of service appears to provide a dominant form that all firms, including commercial hospitality, must to some extent follow.

Dealing with variation

A strong argument in favour of production line approaches is that through clearly defined processes and procedures an operation can achieve a consistent standard of product or service; variation is reduced to a minimum and higher efficiency results in higher profits.

It has been argued however (McLaughlin, 1996), using the health care industry as an example, that this does not represent either the only or the best direction of development for service operations. He draws on the work of Boynton *et al.* (1993) who describe an alternative model of innovation, illustrated in Figure 9.3, which provides some interesting insights for hospitality. The model shows the development of operations as a simultaneous movement on the two dimensions of product and process stability. They start with an 'invention' phase where items are produced with rapidly changing designs and rapidly changing processes. It is easy to fit the development of small restaurants in this phase, where the operation is based around a craft mentality with a skilled chef offering daily menu changes to demonstrate their expertise. In time and in the process of expansion, these procedures have to be documented to ensure standards of food and service across a number of units or when the master chef is not on duty. In this way the process and the product become codified and the operation moves toward the mass production phase. However, as the hospitality operation moves further and

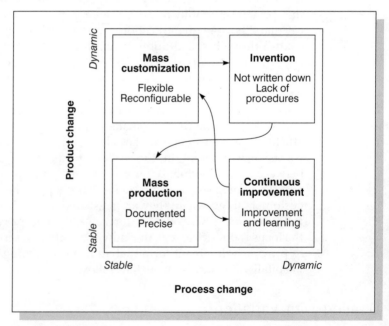

Figure 9.3 A model of product and process development. *Source:* McLaughlin, 1996.

further down this path there are expressions of dissatisfaction with the similarities of products offered – 'you can't tell the difference between hotels these days, they are all the same' – and the impersonal nature of the service being offered – 'nobody seems to care any more'.

The next phase of development recognizes that even with a stable range of products the process of their production and service can still be improved to respond to problems that have been identified and the stage of continuous improvement and learning has been entered. There can be little argument that the standards of food and service offered by the hospitality industry have improved considerably over the last ten to twenty years. Comparing an original Berni Inn with a modern day Harvester or TGI Friday would show substantial changes in technology and delivery. Through the process of continual improvement the operation evolves to take advantage of advances in technology and incorporate economical, local best practices that become inputs to organizational learning. The operation is now able to meet the demands for satisfying the individual needs of customers by offering a wider range of more customized products through the phase of mass customization.

The operation is now able to deliver a dynamic range of products but using clearly established processes, that can be optimized to meet particular client's needs. As McLaughlin (1996, p.20) explains, 'The server's role is not one of inventing service components but one of configuring available standardised components to meet individual customer needs'. The waiter would not be asked to invent new dishes but to understand how different elements may be put together to create a unique meal experience for a particular group of customers. At the corporate level, Bass UK can be seen to be moving in this direction with their restaurant operations. Using the same basic process expertise and systems, they are able to offer a range of brands – such as All Bar One, Bar Coast, Edwards, Harvester, and Browns – customized to meet the demands of a particular client group.

The manager will need to understand and accept that differences between customers and the intangibility, heterogeneity and inseparability of hospitality are givens that build variability into the system, which standardization cannot adequately cope with. Identifying ways of explicitly incorporating variability into hospitality operations is a challenge that the industry has not really started to tackle but which could make it possible for hospitality managers to make substantial improvements both in customer satisfaction and commercial success.

The predominance of the mass production paradigm in service operations has also been challenged from another direction –

from the manufacturing industry. Bowen and Youngdahl (1998) have highlighted that as early as the 1960s there was an increasing demand for product variety which traditional production line approaches could not deliver and an increasing realization of the value of engaging employees with the production process. This led to the development of 'lean production', which combines the benefits of efficiency with flexibility. The defining characteristics of lean manufacturing include combining mass production practice with flexible craft production, where flexible workers produce multiple products with standard tools and procedures; introducing just-in-time (JIT) production control to eliminate the wastes of excessive production; eliminating waste by getting rid of any activities which do not add to the value chain from product development to delivery; increasing customer focus by involving customers in designing the products they want and forming closer links with customers; empowering employees and teams to move problem solving and decision making down to the front line. In summary, lean production is claimed to pay 'more attention to customer product preferences, through increased flexibility and employee wants through higher involvement management practices. At the same time, it performs well on efficiency, quality and speed.' (Bowen and Youngdahl, 1998, p.213).

Increasing flexibility and empowerment of staff does not however mean any reduction in control. Indeed, research by Vickery *et al.* (1999) suggests that the need to be able to cope with frequent changes in product mix and volumes has in fact led to increased levels of formal control but with reduced layers of management and reduced spans of control. In contrast to the expected response of delegating authority over decision making through decentralization to cope with increased variety, there is evidence that lean manufacturing requires tight control of operations and performance concerning results in terms of cost and customer service.

Just as the ideas of mass production passed from manufacturing to service operations and into hospitality, so it was suggested that the ideas of lean manufacturing will lead to the growth of 'lean service'. Schlesinger and Heskett (1991) have highlighted Taco Bell as a leader in this development as a 'service driven company'. In the 1980s Taco Bell was a primarily food-production-focused operation with no effective decoupling of front and back of house and employees being expected to switch between the two. In the early 1990s, customer research revealed that what people really wanted was the food to be fast (F), the order to be filled accurately (A), served in a clean environment (C) and at the right temperature (T). Value chain analysis found that a considerable amount of food production could be centralized and shipped out to stores ready prepared, so allowing a new kitchen design that took up only 30 per cent of restaurant space as opposed to the previous 70 per cent. Frequent deliveries from the central kitchen matched to customer demand levels meant that stock holdings and storage space were reduced as was waste and food cost. This change changes the in-store kitchen from extensive and expensive food production to streamlined assembly, allowing the restaurant and the employees to concentrate on the real value adding activities of serving the customer. At the same time Taco Bell realized that responding to customer demands could not be met solely through technocratic solutions but relied increasingly on the employees in direct customer contact. The company introduced extensive training for both managers and employees and empowered individuals and teams to take responsibility for day-to-day problem solving.

It is suggested that the 'lean service' approach provides an opportunity for hospitality operations to move past the very successful McDonald's approach of a mass production system producing a very narrow offering of what the company thinks the customer wants, toward being able to allow the customer to 'have it their way' and still be commercially successful. As the distinctions between manufacturing and service operations continue to blur, a common paradigm and shared logic are emerging in the form of 'mass customisation'.

Mass customization is defined as 'the use of flexible processes and organizational structures to produce varied and often individually customized products and services at the low cost of a standardized, mass production system' (Hart, 1995, p.36). The services referred to here are not seen as 'anything goes at any time' but they are provided to individual choice from within a predetermined envelope of variety. The aim is to find out in advance what range of options customers would like to see provided and then guide them to that choice. There is an increasing fragmentation of markets and consequently customers are harder to see as a homogenous group and even individual wants are changing more rapidly. Taylor and Lyon (1995) see a virtuous circle emerging here as meeting customer demands leads to higher profits allowing the operation to increase its customizing potential and so being able to appeal to more fragmented markets.

Even McDonald's can be seen to be moving in this direction. Facing increased competition in the fast food market from companies such as Domino's, Pizza Hut, Taco Bell and KFC and having to respond to Burger King's 'have it your way' approach, McDonald's have rapidly expanded their product range, at least in the USA, into pizza, chicken, fajitas, submarine sandwiches, spaghetti and meatballs, carrot and celery sticks, fresh ground coffee and bottled water. In continental Europe they have expanded into a range of salads. In the UK the changes seem to be limited to a range of limited period specials often linked to film or television promotions. To achieve this McDonald's have had to find ways to reduce their product development and production times, and to generate greater flexibility and a clearer customer focus, allowing franchisees more scope in local adaptations.

A customer perspective

The discussion so far has focused largely on the service providers' perspective in discussing the pressures that commercial hospitality operations have to face. It is however also useful to consider how the customers' views of hospitality could also be expressed.

In considering some of the key themes emerging from a sociological analysis of eating out, Beardsworth and Bryman (1999) have highlighted a number of issues that are pertinent here. One important concept to emerge is that of the 'democratization of luxury' (p.233):

> . . . the transition from a situation in which eating as a leisure activity and the indulgence of a refined culinary taste are the prerogatives of an aristocratic elite, to a situation in which such indulgences are available to all those who can pay the asking price of the dishes and services in question.

They argue that the current highly developed commercial hospitality industry is a product of the linked processes of industrialization and modernization. These processes have allowed a clear move from eating out because of necessity to the firm establishment of eating out as a leisure activity in its own right. The hedonistic elements of eating out have been increasingly democratized and restaurants have blossomed in many styles and occupying a multiplicity of market niches. The food itself is now of less importance and the restaurant has become a place of entertainment and a place to be seen. In looking specifically at the development of theme restaurants, Beardsworth and Bryman (1999) highlight some key points that are applicable to all aspects of commercial hospitality provision.

Late modern society is preoccupied with issues of risk. The affluent in society can enjoy relatively low levels of risk that may result in a degree of tedium. Hospitality operators, and particularly those who use some form of themeing, can provide settings and experiences that can lift individuals out of the tedium of mundane routines. Modern production techniques allow an operation to provide a high level of stimulation but with the confines of complete safety.

It is possible to argue that the marketing activities of hospitality providers are simply a way of duping the customer and hiding the fact that these services are provided as part of a profit-oriented commercial operation. In fact it is more likely that customers know very well that the service and settings they receive are underpinned by a business ethic and that this can actually enhance the experience by the Barnum principle. This principle suggests that customers do not mind having the wool pulled over their eyes as long as they are in on the joke. The customer does not feel that the hospitality they have received is any less 'real' or 'sincere' simply because commercialization rears its head when they are asked to pay the bill or offered the opportunity to purchase merchandise. The restaurant customer is not stupid; they know what is going on.

The commercial hospitality industry can provide a tremendous range of experiences that would appear to fit the post-modern consumer but they are firmly rooted in the modern foundation of the technology that provides them. The hospitality customer may have their heads 'in the post-modern clouds, but to enjoy the experience they must know that their feet remain firmly planted on modern ground, in order to be sure of the reassuring securities of modernity: punctuality, physical safety, comfort, reliability, hygiene etc.' (Beardsworth and Bryman, 1999, p.253). Commercial hospitality has the capability to involve the customer actively and enthusiastically in the production and consumption of the hospitality experience responding to the demands of post-modern sensibilities but within an envelope of safety and the 'breathtaking potency' of late modern production techniques.

Conclusions

Hospitality operations are inherently complex both from the perspective of the technology of producing the products and services they deliver and from the inherent variability introduced by the customer and the nature of service operations in general. In order to cope with this complexity and still deliver a profit, commercial hospitality has tended to focus on efficiency as the key performance measure. This in turn has led to pressure for increased standardization and the industrialization of service.

Performance concepts	Contextual assumptions	
	Static	Dynamic
Efficiency (internal performance)	Rationalization, productivity	Development, competence
Effectiveness (external performance)	Creation of value for customers	Ability to adjust, develop, innovate
Constraining factors	Ethics, legislation, good practice, societal values	
Source: Adler and Docherty (1998)		

Table 9.2 Dimensions of performance

There is evidence however that this pressure is changing for a number of reasons. First, the focus of performance is changing. Adler and Docherty (1998) have identified changes in the dimensions of performance based on assumptions about the context of the external business environment, as illustrated in Table 9.2.

If the external business environment is stable then efficiency as an appropriate focus for internal performance would be concerned primarily with rationalization and productivity. The key focus for external performance or effectiveness would be on the creation of value for customers. It could be argued that commercial hospitality has focused on the former at the detriment of the latter. However in today's more dynamic business environment, the efficiency focus should move to be concerned more with continual improvement and the development of competence, while the effectiveness focus moves to flexibility and innovation. The pressure therefore must be on commercial hospitality to pay more attention to these aspects.

The pressure for additional flexibility and improved methods comes not only from the external environment but also from best practice in operating methods derived from lean manufacturing and taken on board by lean service in a general move toward mass customization. Mass customization offers the opportunity to be more responsive to customers and still have the advantages of efficiency and tight control through highly developed production systems that guarantee consistency and safety.

At the same time, more and more customers are now able to take advantage of the ever-wider range of hospitality services, clearly understanding that they are in a fabricated setting underpinned by the business ethic.

This chapter has attempted to establish that commercial hospitality is not simply domestic hospitality on a large scale. It is different. It is business driven and it should not make any excuses about its underlying business ethic. The challenge facing commercial hospitality is to capitalize on the highly developed technologies and systems of operation that are available, enabling employees to provide exactly the food and service that the customer wants and is prepared to pay for.

References

Adler, N. and Docherty, P. (1998) Bringing business into socio-technical theory and practice. *Human Relations*, **51**, No. 3, 319–45.

Ballé, M. (1998) *Managing with Systems Thinking*. McGraw Hill, Maidenhead.

Beardsworth, A. and Bryman, A. (1999) Late modernity and the dynamics of quasification: the case of the themed restaurant. *The Sociological Review*, 228–57.

Bowen, D. and Youngdahl, W.E. (1998) 'Lean' service: in defense of a production-line approach. *International Journal of Service Industry Management*, **9**, No. 3, 207–25.

Boynton, A.C., Victor, B. and Pine, B.J. (1993) New competitive strategies: challenges to organizations and information technology. *IBM Systems Journal*, **32**, No. 1, 40–64.

Farb, P. and Armelagos, G. (1980) *Consuming Passions: The Anthropology of Eating*. Boston, Houghton Mifflin.

Fitzgerald, L., Johnston, R., Brignall, S., Silvestro, R. and Voss, C. (1991) *Performance Measurement in Service Businesses*. Chartered Institute of Management Accountants, London.

Hart, C.W.L. (1995) Mass customisation: conceptual underpinnings, opportunities and limits. *International Journal of Service Industry Management*, **6**, No. 2, 36–45.

Jones, P. and Lockwood, A. (1996) Hospitality Operations Management. In: Hospitality Management: The State of the Art, convened by Prof. K. Michael Haywood, University of Guelph, Canada; Perry Hobson, Southern Cross University, Australia; and P. Jones, University of Brighton, United Kingdom, 10 April 1996 until 10 August 1996, http://www.mcb.co.uk/ services/ conferen/apr96/ hospitality/ conhome.htm

Levitt, T. (1972) Production line approach to service. *Harvard Business Review*, **50**, No. 5, 20–31.

McLaughlin, C.P. (1996) Why variation reduction is not everything: a new paradigm for service operations. *International Journal of Service Industry Management*, **7**, No. 3, 17–30.

Medlik, S. with Airey, D.W. (1978) *Profile of the Hotel and Catering Industry*, 2nd edition. Heinemann, London.

Ritzer, G. (1993) *The McDonaldization of Society*. Pine Forge, California.

Schlesinger, L.A. and Heskett, J.A. (1991) The service driven company. *Harvard Business Review*, **69**, No. 5, 71–81.

Schmenner, R.W. (1986) How can service businesses survive and prosper. *Sloan Management Review*, Spring, 21–32.

Schmenner, R.W. (1995) *Service Operations Management*. New Jersey, Simon and Schuster.

Slack, N., Chambers, S., Harland, C., Harrison, A. and Johnston, R. (1995) *Operations Management*. Pitman Publishing, London.

Taylor, S. and Lyon, P. (1995) Paradigm lost: the rise and fall of McDonaldization. *International Journal of Contemporary Hospitality Management*, **7**, No. 2/3, 64–8.

Vickery, S., Dröge, C. and Germain, R. (1999) The relationship between product customisation and organisation structure. *Journal of Operations Management*, **17**, 377–91.

Social scientific ways of knowing hospitality

David Botterill

School of Hospitality, Tourism and Leisure, University of Wales Institute, Cardiff

Key themes

- The 'reality' of hospitality
- Positivism and the study of hospitality
- Interpretation in the study of hospitality
- Critical theory and hospitality research

It is impossible that the domain of hospitality could have escaped the influence of the scientific revolution that has for the past 300 years provided western society with a 'new' system of knowledge. However, the low status afforded to the study of hospitality in comparison with other domains of study has until the latter half of the twentieth century tended to constrain the development of a scientific self-understanding of the field. The chapter will not, however, attempt a *tour de force* of all that scientific research in hospitality has discovered. It will, rather, seek to reach behind the claims of scientists and in particular social scientists to truths about hospitality. In this chapter, therefore, an attempt will be made to contribute to that self-understanding through an examination of debates in the philosophy of science. A major question that must be asked in all domains of scientific study is called the epistemological question or put more simply a question that asks 'How can we know hospitality?'

Words such as turn, debate, dispute and argument will often be used in this chapter to capture the inherent characteristics of any discussions of the philosophy of science. Their use deliberately conveys the sense of controversy that surrounds scientific knowledge, the competing and often conflicting schools of thought that influence debate and the unsolved and open condition of the epistemological question that continues to inspire a pursuit of a more satisfactory answer.

Pre-science, what was taken to be held as true in society, was largely understood to be vested in either (1) *a priori* knowledge – simply put the custom and practices of societies or (2) in a system of religious belief. The powerful in society surrounded themselves with the guardians of knowledge, for example the clergy, monastic brethren, 'wise' men and women. Scientists, in producing a scientific truth, challenged the authority of those in power, and, for the early eighteenth-century scientists, the struggle for authority caused them to be perceived as a radical force in society. The dispute over the authority of science continues today, particularly at what might be called the scientific frontiers, for example, in the public debates over health such as the matter of genetically modified foods. The position of scientists however has changed dramatically. No longer radical outsiders, scientists have been appropriated by the modern state and by the interests of the corporate world. The assimilation of science into the interests of governments and corporations, the modern day institutions of power, has confirmed the importance of a scientific way of knowing beyond those of the ancient regime.

The status of science in society today, however, is under question. Advances in science are often controversial and contested, particularly when they are subject to public debate. It is argued by some authors such as Ulrich Beck that the risks posed in today's society are more likely to emanate from science and technology itself rather than from the forces of nature. Science's legitimacy is challenged therefore as a result of its inability to master its own side effects: 'Until the sixties, science could count on an uncontroversial public that believed in science, but today its efforts and progress are followed with mistrust. People suspect the unsaid, add in the side effects and suspect the worst.' (Beck, 1992, p.169). The scepticism of a critical public on the claims of natural scientists is even more marked in the social sciences. The very essence of the material of social science, social life, invites public debate on claims to truth. This has resulted in the status of social science becoming ever more controversial, indeed some commentators have claimed that social science is in crisis (Delanty, 1997).

The fortunes of 'expert' social scientists, at least in Britain, have been through a difficult period over the past 20 years. Public debates about society have seldom included a social scientific dimension largely because the authority of social scientists is directly linked to the public's perception of the authority with which explanation and prediction is made. Different disciplines within the social sciences have experienced the 'crisis' to varying levels of profundity. Economics has sustained an authoritative position in public debate but even this discipline is facing difficulty. For example a hospitality researcher using the tenets of macro-economic theory may be able to predict the impact of interest rate changes on the general level of new hotel development. At the same time the individual reactions of developers and the intuitive feel of investor confidence may provide contradictory evidence. The potentially conflicting accounts of the same economic phenomenon challenges the researcher to speak with authority about this topic. The perceived weakness of authority has led the general social scientific community to engage more vigorously than their natural science counterparts with epistemology, as finding a more robust solution to the epistemic question is directly linked to strengthening the authority of the social scientific voice. It is argued, therefore, in this chapter, that the scientific way of knowing hospitality is subject as is all science to ongoing and enduring inquiry, not just about the subject of hospitality itself but also about the underlying assumptions behind our inquiry.

A major part of the chapter will be taken up with an examination of three sustained attempts to find a satisfactory solution to the epistemological question 'how can we know the social world?' in the social sciences. Attempts to answer this question have led to the development of different schools of thought. The underlying assumptions that premise the positivist, hermeneutic and critical schools of thought will be examined using examples drawn from hospitality research and the allied fields of inquiry into tourism and leisure in order to illustrate their influence on the contemporary hospitality research community's attempt to scientifically know hospitality.

This chapter begins with a consideration of the location of hospitality as a domain of scientific knowledge. It will be argued that the primary influence on the study of hospitality is and will continue to be from the social as opposed to the natural sciences. In this section we will examine the ontology of hospitality, the question of the nature of the reality of hospitality, in order to substantiate this view.

Ontology and hospitality

To speak about ontology of anything is to articulate assumptions that are made about reality. In order to propose an answer to the epistemic question of how can we know hospitality it is necessary to assume the condition of what might be meant by the reality of hospitality. For naturalistic philosophers such as Quine (1981), reality is comprised of physical entities that are assumed to be real, right down to the most hypothetical of particles. Quine's realism would be a shared assumption of scientists working in the disciplines that have been drawn to scientific ways of knowing hospitality, particularly in the domains of accommodation and food and beverages. The physical environment of hospitality accommodation has prospered under the advances of sciences in engineering, architecture, planning and design, materials sciences, ergonomics and the 'harder' information and telecommunications sciences. The physical environments associated with food and beverages have attracted a sub-set of scientific domains and disciplines – nutrition, dietetics, microbiology and biochemistry – that have informed a wide range of practices in the industry. As we shall see, realist assumptions about hospitality have lent substantial support to the adoption of positivism as an epistemic answer to research questions about hospitality.

In contrast, European idealist philosophers of the twentieth century such as William James, the influential figure in American pragmatist philosophy, argued that reality consists primarily of sensation. Consequently the ontology of pragmatism defined reality not so much by its 'real' substance but by the conception that is put upon the object, 'what effects, that might conceivably have practical bearings, we conceive the object of conception to have'. (Peirce, 1931–58, 5, p.402). The notion of the scientist authoring reality by dint of a mentalistic abstraction from a physical object is an ontological assumption that underpins much of the evolution of twentieth century social science. In contrast to the realism of the natural sciences we find in social science a constructivist solution to the epistemic question (Berger and Luckman, 1967). The social sciences' influence over studies of hospitality includes a broad chunk of disciplines – economics, sociology, anthropology, political science, psychology – and domains – health, education, business and management, development, media, leisure and tourism. The claims of truth about a social scientific view of hospitality are, therefore, predicated on a consensual constructivist abstraction that resides entirely within scientific discourse. Any resultant epistemic answer such as those provided by hermeneutics or critical theory is, therefore, in sharp contrast to the realist claims of an assumed objective reality that lies outside the discourse of science. This ontological distinction between constructivism and realism continues to play an important part in contemporary debates in the social sciences and we will return to this topic later in the chapter. But first we will turn our attention to a consideration of the epistemic question and the most influential force in providing a satisfactory answer – positivism.

Positivism in the study of hospitality

Delanty (1997) proposes five tenets of positivism: scientism or the unity of the scientific method; naturalism or phenomenalism; empiricism; value freedom; and instrumental knowledge. The influences of positivism within hospitality research will be considered under each of these five points separately although they clearly interact with more force in some studies than in others.

Scientism and the unity of the scientific method

Research in hospitality displays many of the markers of scientism. Hospitality research problems are defined as a relationship between variables; independent, dependent and intervening. The researcher classically sits outside of the phenomenon, observes and attempts to unravel the effect of interventions or treatments upon dependent variables such as consumer demand, staff motivation or service quality. It perhaps is surprising that the adoption of experimental or field-based quasi-experimental work is a relatively rare occurrence in the literature. An exception is the study by Worsfold and Griffith (1997) that is detailed in Figure 1.10. These researchers were interested in the food safety

Journal of Food Protection, **60**, No. 4, 1997, 399–406

Assessment of the Standard of Consumer Food Safety Behaviour

Denise Worsfold and Christopher J. Griffith

Abstract

An evaluation of the food safety behaviour of 108 consumers was conducted by means of an HACCP-based audit. The method employed direct observation and temperature measurement linked to a standardised risk-based scoring system based on epidemiological data. A food operation risk (FOR) score was allocated to each consumer and was based on the demerit points awarded for the violation or absence of recommended control or preventative measures. Temperature abuse during food transport and storage was exhibited by more than 40% of people. A great potential for indirect and direct cross-contamination during the preparation of food was identified. Safe cooking practices were used by the majority of consumers, however, more than half of the sample cooked well in advance of consumption and few used any method to speed the cooling of cooked food. Some consumers used potentially unsafe practices such as holding cooked food at ambient temperatures for prolonged periods and inadequate re-heating. Expressed as a percentage, the FOR scores ranged from 0 to 65% with over half of the subjects (58%) scoring below 20%.

Method

One hundred and eight subjects of whom 100 were female were recruited from the Women's Institute, church and retirement groups, and venues such as a supermarket consumer advice area and a community centre. The subjects who lived in South Wales in the UK were provided with a recipe and ingredients. The subjects were evenly distributed between the three age groups but the socio-economic profile was skewed towards the A, B and C groups. The study focused on a small range of selected food products prepared according to standardised recipes. The recipes, which included a baked egg product, a cold chicken snack, a minced beef sauce, and a fried chicken and ham dish were designed based upon food safety as well as other criteria: the ingredients should include those commonly implicated in food poisoning; the recipe should involve handling techniques which are potentially hazardous unless executed correctly; the handling techniques should include those commonly employed in the production of food in the home; the recipe should involve some element of consumer judgement about length of cooking period and about appropriate hygienic handling techniques; the recipe should be sufficiently appealing to engage the interest of participants; the ingredients should be widely available all year from major supermarkets. The ingredients should not be too expensive; and excessive demands on the cook in terms of time, experience, or equipment should not be made. Subjects selected one recipe from the bank of four recipes which had been assessed for potential food safety hazards and risks and realistic control measures. The recipe directions, typical of those found in domestic cookery books, allowed some freedom of interpretation.

Audit checklists of potential operational hazards and appropriate control measures were used to record the observations of food handling practices in the home.

Figure 10.1 A study of domestic hospitality.

behaviour of those regularly preparing meals at home and designed a quasi-experiment in order to gather data. In the field Worsfold and Griffith would come closest to the image of the scientist in the hospitality environment, characterized by the wearing of a stiffly starched white laboratory coat and clutching a clipboard upon which was mounted a series of stopwatches. In the field laboratory of the domestic kitchen observations were strictly monitored against a pre-determined list of 'food opera- tion risk demerit valuables'. Much of the full article is taken up with the 'proper' conduct of sampling regimes in a classic display of the unity of scientific method.

The questionnaire, perhaps more than any other research technique, has become the social scientist's positivist flag. The origins of the questionnaire, Delanty suggests, are to be found in the development of a professional social science in American universities, particularly in the empirical micro-case studies of functional sociology, in the early part of the twentieth century. The extent of hospitality research based on the questionnaire method is considerable. All of the major indices of domestic and international tourism demand are based on this technique and the vast majority of research in both the academic and con- sultancy spheres adopts a questionnaire instrument to make observations. Data derived from the questionnaire offers itself for quantification and statistical testing. Hospitality research has therefore assumed the 'turn' in positivist epistemology inspired by advances in mathematics. The development of logical positiv- ism was premised on the 'the ideal of a unified science based on the certain knowledge of mathematical logic' (Delanty, 1997, p.29) and the quantification present within much hospitality social science can be read as the expression of 'new' develop- ments in physics in the 1920s. This 'turn' immediately demon- strates how research in hospitality has taken its shape and form from disputes about and within positivism.

A typical study in the allied area of tourism research involving the use of a questionnaire is detailed in Figure 10.2.

In this study it is possible to locate nearly all of the traits of a positivist social science. The unity of the scientific method prevails through the detailed account of the survey method and the approach to measuring tourism described in the opening paragraph is classical reductionist social science (see below).

Naturalism or phenomenalism

Naturalism or phenomenalism implies a unity in the subject matter of science as well as the unity of method. The subject matter, reality, is external to science itself. Reality, or nature, is

The UK Tourist: Statistics 1997 (1998)

Objectives

The first objective of the UKTS is to provide measurements of tourism by residents of the United Kingdom, in terms of both volume (trips taken, nights spent away from home) and value (expenditure on those trips and nights). The second is to collect details of the trips taken and of the people taking them.

These objectives extend to:

- tourism by people of any age. The core survey includes a count of any children who accompany adults on trips, and has attached to it a separate count of children making tourist trips unaccompanied by adults.
- tourism for any purpose. Although the report naturally lays great emphasis on the important holiday sector, this is not just a holiday survey. Also covered is tourism for the purpose of visiting friends or relatives, for work or business purposes, conferences and exhibitions or indeed almost any other purpose. Trips not covered by the survey are those for reasons such as temporary removal, hospital admission or school visits.
- tourism in the sense of trips away from home which last for one night or more, up to a maximum of 60 nights. Day excursion trips are not covered by the survey at all; trips of more than 60 nights' duration cannot be adequately and representatively covered by the method of survey adopted, and are therefore excluded from coverage.
- tourism of any destination in any country of the world, using any accommodation type.

Scope of this report

This document is intended to provide **all** of the information necessary to form an overview of the **total** UK tourism market. The reader will therefore find here details of all the familiar subjects such as purpose, destination, accommodation, transport and month of trip. However, also included are other subjects such as leisure activities undertaken on the trip, methods of booking or arranging travel, and details of the types of location stayed at while away from home. Inevitably a publication of this size is selective; the "core" results of each year's UKTS run to thousands of computer tabulations, which are held by the sponsoring boards. Beyond those core tabulations, further computer analysis can provide – subject to technical limitations – any permutation of any number of parameters contained in the survey, in order to produce data on specific market sectors not already analysed. Survey results not published in this report are available from any of the sponsoring boards. Further information can be obtained from any of the survey sponsors, at the addresses shown at the back of the report.

Survey method

Each month, continuously, interviews are conducted face-to-face, in the homes of a fresh representative sample of UK adults aged 15 or more. The sample used is a two stage stratified probability sample – more commonly called a random sample. This entails drawing "first stage sampling units" (sampling points) – 540 separate parliamentary constituencies in Great Britain, and 24 wards in Northern Ireland – proportionate to population throughout the UK.

Within each of those points "second stage sampling units" (that is, individual adults) are selected by using the current Electoral Registers. From a random start point in each of the 564 sampling points, every fifteenth name on the Register is selected and passed to local interviewers, whose task it is to contact those named persons for interview. Up to four recalls are made at different times and on different days of the week, in order to obtain an interview with these selected electors; no substitutes are used in the sample.

In order to convert this sample of electors to a sample representative of adults, it is also necessary to supplement the basic sample with non-electors wherever they are encountered at addresses of selected electors.

By this method a total of 82,887 interviews were conducted with adults aged 15 or over in the course of fieldwork for the UKTS 1997, which led to the reporting of 36,115 trips.

As mentioned above, the UKTS 1997 questionnaire was administered using "CAPI" (Computer Assisted Personal Interviewing). This meant that, rather than recording respondents' answers by clerical/written method, interviewers read out the questions from, and put responses directly into, a portable computer during the course of the interview, in respondents' homes. Completed interviews were transferred electronically at the end of each day to the central computer ready for analysis. For the first time, in the UKTS 1997, this CAPI method was used throughout the whole of the UK sample. (Interviewing in Northern Ireland, sub-contracted to Ulster Marketing Surveys Limited, switched to CAPI for the first time in 1997).

In each interview a questionnaire is used which was developed for the UKTS through a combination of experience of earlier surveys conducted by the boards, pilot work, and extensive experimental work, to overcome problems of over-reporting and under-reporting of the incidence and value of tourism trips. The same core questionnaire wording has been used in the UKTS throughout the survey's history to date (1989–1997), changing only by the gradual addition of further questions, and in points of minor detail. It should be noted, however, that the change to the administration of this questionnaire by "CAPI" has probably prevented the loss from the data of some trips, which might previously have been thought by respondents to be too insignificant to record.

The questionnaire asks, each calendar month, about trips taken away from home which began in the month prior to interviews, and the month before that. This two-month memory period is adopted in the survey as the most cost-effective compromise in the use of the interviewing. It aims to maximise the sample of trips captured into the data and to minimise the risk of poor or under-reporting due to failing memory.

For each month in turn, throughout each year of the UKTS, samples of adults interviewed are computer weighted to a constant profile, in order to remove the possibility of apparent change due to periodic fluctuations in the characteristics of samples interviewed. The weights adopted for this purpose set the profile of adults in the UK, in terms of sex, age, region and socio-economic grade, to a mid-year fixed estimate. Further details can be obtained from the sponsors of the survey. (p.2)

Figure 10.2 The use of questionnaires: UKTS.

reducible to observable units or naturalistic phenomena and can be observed objectively. In Figure 10.2 the creation of a set of measurable variables enables the illusive phenomenon of tourism to be become 'real'. The variables (tourist trips, nights away from home, expenditure, purpose of the tourist trip, accommodation type, leisure activity) are the subject of quantification, agglomeration and manipulation in countless possible combinations. As the extract states, 'the core results of each year's UKTS run to thousands of computer tabulations'. The researcher is able to abstract isolated variables from the data set and to explore through the application of statistics the relationships between variables. This manipulation of the data by the researcher is underpinned by an important assumption of positivism.

Within naturalism it is assumed that the truths discovered by science have a corresponding truth-value in reality. The findings of UKTS are assumed to depict the reality of tourism, government policy is informed by these data and businesses depend on studies such as these to supplement market research. It is the perceived strength of the assumptions that underlay positivism that assert the truth value of such studies. This is a major point of dispute in epistemological argument between positivism and hermeneutics in the social sciences where proponents of the latter view have argued that the social world is too complex for such simplistic association between research findings and reality. Hospitality research, however, seldom recognizes this dispute.

Two further studies from the allied field of tourism research demonstrate that positivism still holds considerable sway in this matter. For example Emanuel (Emanuel, 1997; Emanuel *et al.*, 1996) is engaged on a substantial project of exploring relationships between the perceptions of visitors and residents (the essence of her data) and the reality of places as expressed by the shape and form of economic development. During a phase of her fieldwork Emanuel stayed as a guest at a hotel in mid-Wales. She negotiated with the manager of the hotel to undertake a series of in-depth, semi-structured interviews with guests. The interviews explored a range of topics including the guests' perceptions of the landscape in the region, their views on appropriate forms of economic development and their perceptions of the term 'health tourism'.

Gale (1996), in some ways only minimally a positivistic study, is directly seeking to 'interpret the influence of late twentieth century socio-cultural change upon the physical reality and image of Rhyl ...'. In his study Gale (1996; 1998) used resort promotion brochures, local authority committee minutes, local historical society archive material and land-use plans in order to offer a semiotic 'reading' of Rhyl as a holiday resort since 1945. The sources of data and the methods used by these two researchers would by themselves suggest a hermeneutic rather than positivist epistemology. But what binds them to positivism is the explicit claim they both make between the findings of their research and the reality they seek to explain. Without the epistemological influence of the assumption of the correspondence theory of truth in this raw form then tourism and hospitality social science research aspiration would have little credence.

The relationship between what social science creates as knowledge in its discourse and the social reality it seeks to understand or influence is a central question that we shall see distinguishes constructivism and critical realism positions in contemporary disputes. Such disputed relationships are predicated on a further trait of naturalism – objectivism. The assumption in operation here is that nature, or social reality in the case of our hospitality social science, can be neutrally observable. Facts can be collected in observable units through a process of reductionism. An objectifying attitude to social process is formed. It is possible to see this clearly in Worsfold and Griffiths' work detailed in Figure 10.1. The food operation risk (FOR) scores referred to in the abstract represent an attempt to objectify the hygienic handling of food; 'In order to evaluate consumer food safety behaviour in this study it was necessary to formulate a standard against which performance could be measured' (Worsfold and Griffith, 1997, p.401). The process of objectivism provided the scientists with a way of building what were seen as verifiable facts.

The replication of studies using a unified method on the assumption of a unity of the subject matter – a reducible, objective reality – became standard practice of positivist scientists until the challenge mounted within positivism by Sir Karl Popper. The empiricist tradition within positivism experienced a major intervention when Popper called for the deductive testing of hypotheses to replace an inductive process of replication and verification as the principal means of the assertion of scientific truths. The influences of Popperian critical rationalism are most strongly evidenced in North American hospitality research. The Popperian thesis that resulted in the proposal of hypotheses to falsify through empirical testing is evidence, therefore, of the dynamism of epistemological debate in the internal critique mounted within positivism. Essentially, Popper argued that science proceeds to truth not by a process of inductive verification but by the falsification of theoretical propositions. Research in hospitality and allied areas often displays an ambivalent attitude to the hypo-deductive approach as the studies are often predicated on a deductive theory-data axiom but without the conventional articulation of formal hypotheses. For example, echoes of Popperian thought are to be found in Emanuel's attempt to problematize the relationship between landscape perceptions and forms of economic development but without the explicit articulation of the hypo-deductive technique. Similarly, Worsfold and Griffith (1997) reported no formal hypothesis testing.

Value freedom

This characteristic of positivist epistemology is found in virtually all hospitality research. This despite the fact that hospitality researchers all, to a greater and lesser extent, have a rich stock of subjective experience that has influenced their choice of hospitality study. At the 1999 Council for Hospitality Management Education Research Conference many researchers gave presentations of their work (Lockwood, 1999). During one such presentation Lee-Ross talked about an interesting and well executed study of job characteristics amongst chefs operating large and small scale hospital catering systems (Lee-Ross, 1999).

As an aside during a period of questioning following his presentation he mentioned that he had previously worked as a chef. Yet his whole approach to conducting research described in some depth in the conference volume was to sit outside of the phenomena, to objectify it and attempt to measure it. It was as if the knowledge gained by living held little truth-value whilst the knowledge gained by researching must implicitly hold a greater authority. Likewise, Gale was drawn to his study of the seaside resort from first-hand personal experiences of growing up in urban south Wales, and the delights of a trip to the seaside. Neither of these researchers have explicitly written of these formative experiences, preferring instead to position themselves as 'outside' of and value neutral on the phenomena they study under the influence of, no doubt, 'proper' positivist science. No explicit criticism of either of these authors is meant by these comments. The crucial point is, that by the posture taken towards the reality they seek to know, they assume elements of realism and exhibit traits of positivism.

Instrumental knowledge

Positivist science has, since the ending of an ideology of scientific politics and its appropriation by the state in the early stages of the enlightenment period, sought to provide technically useful knowledge. Typically studies seek to make contribution to policy development, problem solving, near market innovation and best practice models. It is in this sense that much hospitality research also has positivist identity in that it is conducted with a view to producing technically useful knowledge.

At the outset of this section, positivism was described as the most influential force in providing a satisfactory epistemic answer for hospitality research. It is not just that the underlying ontological assumptions of realism continue to imbue hospitality social science or that the traits of a positivist epistemology are so clearly evidenced in contemporary research outputs that substantiates this claim. It is also that positivism provided the basis for a reactionary, counter, anti-positivist tradition called hermeneutics.

Hospitality, Leisure & Tourism Series

Hermeneutics and interpretation in the study of hospitality

The influences of the hermeneutic tradition are clearly to be seen in much contemporary hospitality social science research. The emphasis upon meaning and subjectivity in hermeneutics set it against the instrumental logic of positivism and has sustained an anti-positivist stance that is the bedrock of contemporary constructivist epistemology and in its linguistic form has provided the antecedents of deconstructionism.

Interpretation

Truth in the hermeneutic tradition is to be discovered through the scientist's interpretation of the data. Social structures are too complex to access using the simple act of observation, the researcher must be sensitive to the multi-layered social structure and combines intuition with interpretation. The influence of hermeneutics can be seen in those studies of hospitality where a conversational method is adopted in the early rounds of data collection. Such an approach opens the mind of the respondents and invites the researcher to sense the layers of meaning inherent within a discussion, say, of previous hospitality experiences. For example, in adopting a form of triading and laddering drawn from Kelly's repertory grid technique, Selby's (Selby, 1996; Selby and Morgan, 1996) conversations with urban tourists provided subjective accounts of experience which enable him in classical neo-Kantian style to be engaged in 'a fusion of horizons' (Gadamer as cited in Delanty 1997, p.54) between himself and the urban tourists he talked to.

The recent tendency to use qualitative in-depth interviews in hospitality research also attests to the interpretive influences in studies. The presence of qualitative data in studies of hospitality is not just a method of preferred technique, as Walle (1997) presents it, but it is indicative of the *anti-scientism* of the hermeneutic tradition. Scientism is seen as the unity of method in the natural sciences proposed by positivism and it is not just the hermeneutic conception of social structure that is anti-positivist but also the claim of the separation of method between the human and natural sciences. Selby chooses as a part of his study to develop his own technique for gathering data and in this respect rejects a number of previous attempts by researchers to capture tourism images.

This critique and origination of method is characteristic of interpretative approaches and quite unlike the science of positivism which is typified by a defence of conventional methods. The emphasis of *linguistic constructivism* is exemplified by attempts to develop a language of tourism decision making. Social action is to be understood in what Giddens (1976) has called the 'double hermeneutic' (p.162). This is achieved by researchers such as Selby at first engaging in conversations with tourists, the first hermeneutic of everyday life, and then in his own interpretation of those conversations through which he builds 'consensus constructs', the second hermeneutic. Johnson and Coupe (1999) provide another good example of the interpretative influences of hermeneutics on research into the hospitality industry. In this study the authors were interested in the nature and extent of sexual harassment in the hospitality industry and adopted a case study approach in which the subjective accounts of harassment were collected through participant observation, interviews and focus groups. The approach taken by the researchers is fully described in Figure 10.3.

The Hospitality Review, **1**, No. 2, 1999, 36–41

Sexual harassment: 'That'll do nicely, sir'

Keith Johnson and Vanessa Coupe

Our approach to research

Due to the limited literature on the topic of sexual harassment within the hospitality industry, an exploratory investigation was undertaken initially. This consisted of a questionnaire survey of all female students returning from the industrial placement year contained within a hospitality degree course. It was felt that these females would be particularly vulnerable since they were in 'trainee' roles that often involved customer contact. Some 35% of these students claimed to have experienced some form of sexual harassment during this placement year. Of these 'victims' some 70% agreed to be interviewed in order to develop detailed accounts of the offending incidents. In this way a small series of case studies of the harassment of students was established.

Having established the value of this approach as a means of successfully recording cases of harassment by customers it was decided to extend the work to cover a 'live' case study. This was considered appropriate as a method of generating preliminary, qualitative data. Participant observation was the technique chosen for research, mainly due to the sensitivity of the topic, and also for practical reasons of accessibility. The study was conducted over a period of three months. Observational data were collected and recorded in written format. Following this, informal focus group interviews were carried out among a total of 25 employees, to elicit further information on selected topics. The organisation concerned was readily accessible to the field researcher. As a part time employee within the organisation, the field researcher was accepted within its informal culture. This meant that information was elicited easily from individuals willing to confide their experiences. (pp.37–8)

Figure 10.3 A study of sexual harassment in the hospitality industry.

Throughout the hermeneutic approach there is an underlying *humanism* that presumes that human nature is meaningful and unified. The sense in which Selby is critical of the materialist determinism in accounts of the city in some studies of urban tourism is typical of the influences of humanism in his studies. Instead he proposes that tourists are in a process of negotiating their experiences through the city as an active agent. Critics of hermeneutics say that the prominence of the *subjective* in experience and the importance of cultural context in reading social structures have a tendency to produce a relativist and uncritical form of social science. It is this sense of a lack of critique that while not discounting the competition posed by hermeneutics against positivism led to the emergence of a third major force in the social sciences, neo-Marxist critical social science and theory.

Critical theory and hospitality research

The discussion of the influences of critical theory in studies of hospitality will by necessity take another line from the previous two sections. This is because the characteristics of a Marxist inspired social science are virtually absent from the study of hospitality. Questions of critique of the system of domination that gives rise to the human condition under study, the extent of the researchers' political commitment to emancipatory social change, dialectics – the interplay of theory and practice, and the account taken of historicism – the determination of economic forces in history are simply not often found in studies of hospitality.

To explore why something is not in evidence in a collective body of work is to enter a speculative frame of mind. It is, however, important to raise this question, not least because this chapter aims to map hospitality research against social science research. To omit the influence of critical theory on the search for a more satisfactory solution to the epistemological question in social science would be a serious flaw. Equally a major contribution of critical theory was to reassert the emancipatory role of social science in a rejection of the conservatism of hermeneutics and the technically useful knowledge of positivism. This 'turn' is of course central to debates about the public role of social science and by implication the public role of hospitality social science. In an attempt to account for the absence of critical theory, two potential explanations will be presented. First, is it the case that hospitality research is working itself in a closed system where critical theory is itself under represented?

Explanation 1: *Received hospitality research – a closed system?*

Interdisciplinary hospitality research, particularly that of young researchers, is influenced by a wide circle of the hospitality establishment in the roles of supervisors, advisors and examiners. The absence of certain disciplines such as sociology and political economy in British hospitality studies circles could be significant, as at least in terms of critical theory these were fertile grounds for such thinking. British geographers continue, however, to influence the allied area of the study of tourism and geography as much as any other social science was subject to the influence of critical theory. Could it simply be the case that 1990s disciplinary British social science has rejected critical theory following the collapse of the revolutionary ideal in the face of the victory of social democratic movements in the former eastern Europe and that interdisciplinary hospitality research has simply followed suit? If this is the case then at least one other allied area of hospitality research – British leisure studies – would stand against such a finding. Here, through the writings of Rojek (1997) on the authors of the Frankfurt School such as Benjamin, and feminist contributors such as Yule (1997), the perspective of power, subordination and resistance still hold influence. The proximity of leisure studies to hospitality studies is generally well understood but at least in the respect of the sustaining of an emancipatory social science there would appear to be a considerable difference.

Explanation 2: A hospitality industry prerogative in hospitality social science

The legitimacy of critical theory and the emancipatory notion within a critical hospitality social science may be under attack from the industry prerogative that pervades hospitality research. Two possible reasons for the apparent unwillingness of hospitality researchers to recognize issues of power are suggested here: naiveté, and exclusivity. It is possible that there is a naive view operating in the received study of hospitality that is ignorant of the dimensions of economic and cultural power that structure it (Morgan and Pritchard, 1998). In such a thesis it is suggested that the epistemological rationalism of positivism underpins a view of hospitality as a benign force. In the study detailed in Figure 10.3, Johnson and Coupe (1999) begin to address issues of power. 'Within this case study, female workers consider themselves to be virtually powerless since they combine a subordinate relationship to their employer with the requirement of "satisfying customer demands"' (p.41). However, against the assumptions of a critical social science their work stops considerably short of the mark in a number of respects. Firstly, there is little sense in which these researchers imagine themselves to be part of an emancipatory process for the women working in the industry. The conclusions of the study are generally confined to minor modifications of the *status quo* through redress to the law, hardly a matter of social transformation, and despite the incorporation of participant observation these researchers are not engaged in any sort of dialectics. That is, the sense in which 'science proceeds dialectically in relation to its object, constituted by it' (Delanty, 1997, p.61). Again these criticisms are not offered in destructive mode. They go to show how the different schools of thought, in tackling the epistemic questions, pre-condition assumptions about social science. This particular example also shows how hospitality research that addresses issue of power has yet to fully engage with a critical social science.

Furthermore, models of rational processes are typified by the economic analysis of hospitality. The principal challenges are set within closed system models and themes of efficient and effective deployment of resources. Typically hospitality research adopts empirically tried and tested models of organizational and business studies in an attempt to emulate optimum performance in other economic sectors. Under such an approach there is little room for a researcher to express political commitment to emancipatory social change. Alternatively is it that the industry prerogative acts to exclude any alternative conception of hospitality, as anything other than a business? The critical theorist's attack on commodification is clearly anathema to the dominant industry agenda in hospitality. Considerations of social exclusion and the marginalization of economically weaker individuals and groups, exactly the subject of the politically committed critical social scientist, are of little consequence in mainstream studies of hospitality.

Research questions to do with the conditions of those who work to provide hospitality or are so economically disadvantaged to be excluded from hospitality challenge the dominant thesis of hospitality as industry. The institutionalization of research in universities has, in Britain, increasingly become a business itself. It is not surprising therefore that the business of research in hospitality becomes the hospitality business. The spaces in intellectual life that might sustain a critical hospitality social science are therefore closed down. The professionalized hospitality research community reneges on what Bourdieu (1990) sees as the task of social science – the preservation of the autonomy of intellectual critique.

Hospitality, Leisure & Tourism Series

It is perhaps an ironic twist of fate that a question that is beginning to enter the hospitality industry research agenda might best be answered by reference to a social science founded upon the tenets of critical theory, particularly the constructivist method of Bourdieu (1995). Hospitality's economic importance is now an undisputed reality of many economies and yet its political status continues to be low in virtually all institutionalized forms. Such disparity defies all rational logic. Amongst politicians, in the executive, in intellectual circles of academy, hospitality's status remains unreservedly low. Why is it that the pound generated by hospitality although equal to the pound generated by say agriculture or manufacturing appears to have less value?

To understand the mismatch between economic importance and political status requires the researcher to retain a strong Marxist sense of the objectivity of ideological structure. In this case an ideology that clearly contains an implicit ranking of economic activity and subordinates hospitality to other dominant interests despite the fact that it has overtaken those economic interests in importance. The social actors who construct the social meaning of hospitality become, therefore, the target for the politically-reflective practice of a critical social science whose aim is to transform. The aim of the critical hospitality researcher becomes, 'the creation of a new subjectivity in its confrontation with objectified social structures' (Delanty, 1997, p.115). Critical social science promises therefore to provoke change, in this case to raise the status of hospitality and thereby elevate the interests it represents, including, ironically, the hospitality industry.

Conclusions

In this chapter readers have been introduced to the epistemic question through a very brief review of the epistemological influences in the social scientific study of hospitality. The intention has been to expose the assumptions that lie behind the claims to truth about hospitality – the hospitality researcher's way of seeing. In the spirit of this book the purpose has been to stretch the self-understanding of the hospitality research community. What should be apparent, particularly to post-graduates and experienced researchers alike, is that such an analysis exposes discomfort born out of uncertainty. Researchers deal with the uncertainty inherent in all inquiry, in part, by surrounding the process with the certainty of dominant ideas or established practices. In hospitality research the wider social scientific research community provides many of those certainties. To be alerted to disputes behind the assumptions that provide that sense of security will present a new challenge to many who read this chapter. I will end by arguing that the challenge should be perceived not in a threatening way but as an opportunity to enrich our scientific understanding of hospitality and to re-position hospitality research in relation to the social sciences.

Throughout the chapter I have maintained that the epistemic question in the social sciences remains unanswered. The opportunity, therefore, is for hospitality researchers to see contributions to the epistemic debate as legitimate outcomes of their social scientific studies. The threat might be that a self-conscious and nascent community of hospitality researchers turns inward to greater certainty by strident defence of one or more of the schools of social inquiry discussed earlier in this chapter. Such an inward looking response would in my view be counter-productive to the future of hospitality research. It might produce more sophisticated accounts of the research process but, as authors such as Delanty (1997) have pointed out, it does little to convince policy makers and the general public of the legitimacy of the outcome unless it is constructed progressively as a contribution to knowledge. Hospitality researchers are encouraged therefore to take this challenge on in a positive, constructive manner.

Furthermore, I would argue that, in living closer to the discomfort of uncertainty and looking outward for solutions, hospitality researchers could begin to re-position themselves in relation to the wider social science community. Instead of depending upon the wider community for security and legitimacy, the invitation is to imagine that current hospitality research could contribute to the pursuit of a better epistemological solution and a consequently stronger social scientific voice in society.

For those that are minded to imagine in this way after reading this chapter then the following might help to direct their thoughts. Current debates in the social sciences between constructivists on the one hand and critical realists on the other pivot on the idea, borrowed from positivism, of the correspondence theory of truth. Critical realists continue to strive for an epistemological answer that allows them to claim that an underlying social reality is accessible through science. Knowing hospitality in this realist sense assumes that what the social scientist or hospitality researcher creates in their observations, analysis and written accounts *corresponds* with the real social world of hospitality. Constructivists are less convinced. Influenced by the relativism and subjectivity of hermeneutics and following the pragmatist notion of a science of the sensation, they stop short to any correspondence claim to truth. As Ron Harré

(1998) writes, 'At best we can hope for a well described "inner" model in which something we all know how to do becomes the device by which we can come to know that the world … is wagging this way' (p.49). Hospitality researchers would do well to locate their work in the nexus of this debate.

References

Beck, U. (1992) *The Risk Society: Towards a New Modernity.* Cambridge, Blitz Press.

Berger, P.C. and Luckman, T. (1967) *The Social Construction of Reality.* Garden City, New York, Doubleday.

Bourdieu, P. (1990) *The Logic of Practice.* Cambridge, Polity Press.

Bourdieu, P. (1995) *Sociology in Question.* London, Sage.

Delanty, Gerard (1997) *Social Science: Beyond Constructivism and Realism.* Buckingham, Open University Press.

Emanuel, L. (1997) An investigation of visitor and resident place perceptions of Mid Wales and an evaluation of the potential of such perceptions to shape economic development in the area. Unpublished doctoral dissertation, Open University.

Emanuel, L., Botterill, D., Jones, G. and White, J. (1996) Visitor Perceptions and Place Image. In: *Higher Degrees of Pleasure* (Z.H. Liu and D. Botterill, eds). Proceedings of the International Conference for Graduate Students of Leisure and Tourism, 15th July 1996, Cardiff, University of Wales Institute, Cardiff, School of Leisure and Tourism, pp.38–48.

English, Northern Ireland, Scottish, and Wales Tourism Boards (1998) *The UK Tourist: Statistics 1997.* FTB, NITB, STB, WTB.

Gale, T. (1996) Semiotics and the Reading of Cultural Texts, Possible Applications in Tourism Studies. In: *Higher Degrees of Pleasure* (Z.H. Liu and D. Botterill, eds). Proceedings of the International Conference for Graduate Students of Leisure and Tourism, 15th July 1996, Cardiff, University of Wales Institute, Cardiff, School of Leisure and Tourism, pp.69–83.

Gale, T. (1998) Reconstructing the past: An analysis of landscape, brochures and local authority involvement in the seaside resort of Rhyl, 1945–97, *Concorde*, **8**, No. 2, 29–34.

Giddens, A. (1976) *New Rules of the Sociological Method.* London, Hutchinson.

Harré, R. (1998) When the knower is also the known. In: *Knowing the Social World* (T. May and M. Williams, eds), pp.37–49. Buckingham, Open University Press.

Johnson, K. and Coupe, V. (1999) Sexual harassment: 'That'll do nicely sir'. *The Hospitality Review*, **1**, No. 2, 36–41.

Lee-Ross, D. (1999) A comparative survey of job characteristics amongst chefs operating large and small scale hospitality catering systems. In: *CHME Hospitality Research Conference 1999* (A. Lockwood, ed.), pp.285–92. Guildford, Surrey, The School of Management Studies for the Service Sector, University of Surrey.

Lockwood, A. (ed.) (1999) CHME Hospitality Research Conference. *Proceedings of the Eighth Annual Conference, Volume 1 and 2*. Guildford, Surrey, The School of Management Studies for the Service Sector, University of Surrey.

Morgan, N. and Pritchard, A. (1998) *Tourism Promotion and Power: Creating Images, Creating Identities*. Chichester, John Wiley.

Peirce, C.S. (1931–58) *Collected Papers*. Cambridge, Mass, Harvard University Press.

Quine, W.V. (1981) The pragmatists' place in empiricism. In: *Pragmatism, its Sources and Prospects* (R.J. Mulvaney and P.M. Zeltner, eds). Colombia, South Carolina, University of South Carolina Press.

Rojek, C. (1997) 'Leisure' in the writings of Walter Benjamin. *Leisure Studies*, **16**, No. 3, 155–72.

Selby, M. (1996) Absurdity, Phenomenology and Place: An Existential Place Marketing Project. In: *Higher Degrees of Pleasure* (Z.H. Liu and D. Botterill, eds). Proceedings of the International Conference for Graduate Students of Leisure and Tourism, 15th July 1996, Cardiff, University of Wales Institute, Cardiff, School of Leisure and Tourism, pp.125–39.

Selby, M. and Morgan, N.J. (1996) Reconstructing Place Image: A Case Study of its Role in Destination Market Research. *Tourism Management*, **17**, No. 4, 287–94.

Walle, Alf H. (1997) Quantitative versus qualitative tourism research. *Annals of Tourism Research*, **24**, No. 3, 524–36.

Worsfold, D. and Griffith, C.J. (1997) Assessment of the standard of consumer food safety behaviour. *Journal of Food Protection*, **60**, No. 4, 399–406.

Yule, J. (1997) Engendered ideologies and leisure policy in the UK. Part 1: Gender ideologies. *Leisure Studies*, **16**, No. 2, 61–84.

CHAPTER 11

Humour in commercial hospitality settings

Stephen Ball

*School of Leisure and Food Management,
Sheffield Hallam University*

Keith Johnson

*Department of Hospitality and Tourism
Management, Manchester Metropolitan University*

Key themes

- Humour defined
- Humour, hospitality and caring
- Deliberate humour
- Unintentional humour

'What is hospitality?' has been a question which has been scrutinized and hotly debated by senior UK university academics within the hospitality research forum during the latter years of the second millennium (Lashley, 1999). Prior definitions of hospitality excluded direct reference to humour. At best connection between humour and hospitality could only be implied from indirect associations between such aspects as hospitality and friendliness and from the part that humour plays in enhancing mutual wellbeing for the parties involved through the provision of food and/or drink and/or accommodation. The ignorance of humour is somewhat surprising given that humour might in certain circumstances be regarded as an important constituent of hospitality itself and that humour abounds in the hospitality industry and other contexts where hospitality is provided.

This chapter seeks to investigate the relationship between humour and hospitality, especially within commercial hospitality contexts, and to identify and examine how, when and why humour is deliberately used by, and within, hospitality organizations. Particular reference will be made to the use of humour at the organization/customer interface. A range of different organizations and sectors within the hospitality industry will be mentioned and real-world examples will be drawn from interviews and correspondence which the authors have had with commercial hospitality personnel. The intention is to produce a rounded picture of the nature, role and potential of deliberate humour within commercial hospitality settings.

Humour defined

Humour has been defined in a number of ways. Aristotle, for example, explains humour as 'unintended ambiguity'. The suggestion that humour is inadvertant is often true. One only has to think about spelling mistakes which accidentally transform a serious word or phrase into something amusing or remember when a word is ludicrously misused, i.e. a malapropism. But in many cases humour is clear and deliberate. Koestler (1995) defines humour as a form of communication in which a complex mental stimulation amuses or elicits the laughter reflex in people. The source of this humour could be a form of oral or written verbal communication such as a joke, a book, a witticism, a slogan or a name; a sort of non-verbal communication, for instance an individual's appearance, a person's body language, the use of semiotics, pictures, whimsical objects or a combination of both forms of communication such as a cartoon strip. It could be hypothesized, that humour in all its manifestations, arises from a recognition of incongruence.

These forms of communication can facilitate humour which in turn provokes a psychological and/or a physiological response. This response to the humour stimulus could be displayed in changes in facial expression, ranging from a gentle smile through the broad grin, in varying types and levels of sound and in movements of the body. Perhaps the most extreme response would be convulsions and tears typical of explosive and prolonged laughter. Such responses could be used as indicators for the presence of humour amongst individuals or groups. This would vary according to the context. It may be someone reading a humourous passage in a book or magazine, members of an audience watching a funny scene in a staged comedy play, someone smiling at an inadvertently written, yet amusing, sign in a shop window or a group of people laughing at a joke told amongst friends. In a hospitality organization the recipients and providers of humour could be managers, employees, customers or indeed anyone else entering, or involved with, the organization. However what might be considered humourous by one person may be regarded differently by another. In extreme circumstances 'one man's humour is another man's poison'. Furthermore, humour, like hospitality, is culturally influenced. What makes a group laugh provides an insight into shared values, beliefs, behaviours and meanings. This is perhaps most noticeable at national level where differences in national cultures to humour have been proposed. Barsoux (1993), for instance, claims that:

> In Britain humour tends not to be so much action driven as personality driven. Having a sense of humour is considered a state of mind: it is personality embedded. In France or Germany, say, it is about being witty, telling good jokes or being a raconteur; and in America it is about wisecracking and one-liners. British humour, as embodied in the better situation comedies, is character-based rather than gag-based; it is winsome rather than punchy.

If such differences to humour do exist then the implications for amusing people, preventing offence or deliberately using humour in business whether it be in international organizations, in managing foreign-born or culturally diverse workers in domestic hospitality organizations or in serving international customers/guests, are significant. Humour then is more complicated than at first meets the eye.

Humour, hospitality and caring

Hospitality shares its origins with the provision of caring. Originally, both of these activities were carried out in a domestic environment. Just as the caring services and professions have moved into a social and welfare context, the provision of hospitality has gradually become more commercialized. However, the act of caring and the provision of hospitality remain as essentially therapeutic and restorative activities. The difference between them is a question of scale rather than kind. Caring involves supporting a client during their restoration from, in extreme cases, heavily traumatized conditions. The provision of hospitality is also a supporting role but in this case the extent of the client's trauma is far less severe. Clients are 'traumatized' to the extent that they are weary, hungry, thirsty, lonely, stressed by unfamiliar surroundings or some combination of these states. Hospitality is the act of enhancing a client's wellbeing by restoring him/her to at least a position of neutrality, if not actually to a positive state of mind and body.

Given this parallel, some interesting work in relation to caring has recently been published. *People Management* details the search by Barnsley Alcohol and Drug Advisory Service (1999) for common values amongst its workforce. Four groups were created, one from management, one from administrators and two from front-line counsellors and each was charged with the task of creating a list of shared values. One result was that: 'The only commonly held value among the groups was humour.' This was the only value that appeared in all four lists. Clearly, all the workers at Barnsley had identified the central role played by humour in the restorative process. Humour was seen as an essential ingredient in aiding and lubricating recovery.

If this is the case in caring, then it must also be the case in the provision of hospitality. Humour is an essential ingredient in relieving a client's trauma and restoring him/her to a position of wellbeing. Humour is pivotal in bringing about such change. It increases the 'fun factor' in situations and generates warmth, openness and trust.

Another conversion process that is central to the provision of hospitality is the act of changing a stranger, a potential enemy, into a friend. This is in fact the fundamental, historical basis of hospitality provision. Travellers came to an area and their inevitable strangeness posed a potential threat to the local inhabitants. Equally, the strangeness of their new surroundings created anxiety for the travellers themselves. Historically, religious institutions and private houses provided most of the accommodation for these travellers, many of whom happened to

Hospitality, Leisure & Tourism Series

be pilgrims. Such travellers were often housed in association with the poor and the sick of the locality, yet another link with care provision. Many of the private households gradually evolved into inns, the bedrock of early English hospitality. Such inns were staffed by 'mine host'; a character epitomizing hospitality provision. The 'host' was the pivotal figure in helping to reduce tensions on both sides by converting strangers into friends. A critical weapon in such change was the use of humour – 'sharing' jokes helped to reduce tensions and the host was the catalyst in this process. 'Mine host' continues to be seen as a warm, friendly, welcoming, jocular figure.

Today a number of tourist activities involve confronting strangeness and this is part of their appeal and excitement. Equally, this strangeness can and does involve real danger, as the number of tourists who have lost their lives over the years testifies. For tourism to be successful a balance has to be struck between familiarity and novelty so that excitement and security can both be achieved. Again humour can play a part in attaining this balance, although its role is far less central than in the conversions outlined above.

As hospitality provision becomes more and more commercialized, companies involved in the industry strive to find a competitive advantage over their competitors. Often such advantage is created from 'niche' positioning, servicing a particular market segment in a distinctive manner. Fragmenting hospitality provision into its component parts and then emphasizing a particular aspect of provision can create such niches. As humour is increasingly seen as a component of hospitality, then it is not surprising that the number of companies who place stress on this aspect of their operation is growing. Examples include: Bass Taverns' pub concept It's a Scream (see Figure 11.1), and TGI Friday's, American restaurant and bar operated in the UK by Whitbread plc (see Figure 11.2). Both these organizations have an element of humour in their operating names and use humour along with other ingredients to entertain and provide fun. They stress fun as part of their culture and pursue deliberate actions to promote and use humour in their hospitality concepts. TGI Friday restaurants use humour for the benefit of staff and guests whether it be in the design of restaurants and bars, the appearance and behaviour of staff, product sales lists, shift meetings or techniques to encourage selling. Staff are encouraged to be themselves and delight guests. Ingram and Jones (1998) write of TGI Friday:

> If employees are given a measure of control over the
> way they do their job, they are more likely to enjoy

- Promotes itself as a fun pub environment and uses humour to produce fun. Humour and fun are used throughout the organization, e.g.:
  - in meetings and in memoranda;
  - in pubs e.g. cartoons run all day, on posters, games, competitions and some live acts.
- Target market is students and like-minded people seeking fun.
- Humour is not specifically sought from new recruits, but people who have a sense of humour tend to be attracted to work in It's a Scream.

Figure 11.1 It's a Scream (Bass Taverns), deliberate use of humour. *Source:* Manager of It's a Scream public house in West Yorkshire, April 1999.

themselves and to help customers enjoy the meal experience. Staff concentrate upon 'dynamic quality' which is represented by fresh and opportunistic moments to please the customer.

Humour in commercial hospitality contexts has been popularly portrayed in numerous situation comedies on the television, such as *Chef, Dinner Ladies* and *Fawlty Towers*, and in the media more generally. In the aforementioned television comedies the hospitality context, i.e. the restaurant kitchen, school kitchen or the hotel generally, provides the backdrop. Well known comedians take the lead roles: Lenny Henry as chef, Victoria Wood as school dinner lady and John Cleese as the infamous Basil Fawlty, the Torquay hotel proprietor. Their characters tend to be exaggerated and humour is injected into hospitality-based storylines by showing the absurd in the familiar. The sources of laughter in these situational comedies vary. *Fawlty Towers*, for example, displays a host of sources. Sometimes there are situations where the part and the whole change roles, and attention becomes focused on a detail torn out of an aspect on which its meaning depended, e.g. faulty orthography on the external hotel name plate displaces attention from meaning to spelling. Other ways in which this programme creates humour include satire, impersonation and disguise, parodies, mistaken identity, the intersection through coincidence of two independent chains of events with different associative contexts, exaggeration and practical jokes. A comprehensive semiotic analysis of hospitality industry based television comedies, such as that undertaken by Randall (1999) of a popular food television programme, would reveal more

Recruitment and selection

The recruitment policy takes full account of the inherent theatricality of service delivery and the importance of 'fun' for staff and customers (Ingram and Jones, 1998). Initial interviews comprise of 'auditions' and larger-than-life characters tend to be sought with an outgoing personality of which humour is a part.

Evidence of humour in front of house

- **Appearance and behaviour of staff:** Opportunities are given for trained staff to express character and individuality, for example, in wearing a hat or braces that suit their personality or by outgoing behaviour. Different hats are encouraged and braces may have such things as badges, small dolls, etc., attached. This creates an informal working atmosphere from which both staff and customers derive enjoyment and satisfaction (Ingram, H. and Jones, S., 1998).

- **Written humour:** Elements of selling materials are used to emphasize the focus upon entertainment, e.g. an extract from a cocktail list states that 'bartenders have a special flair for showbusiness' whilst the following Friday's Fact or Fib from the cocktail list demonstrates the use of humour: 'The 1st Martini was mixed in a New York hotel by a bartender named surprisingly enough, Martini. He used Noilly Prat Vermouth and originally customers called his invention a "prat".'

- **Bric-a-brac:** Elegant American curiosities and other obscure oddities are placed in the bar and restaurant to enhance the atmosphere. The staff consider much of this to be humourous. For instance there was a replica shark hanging from the bar ceiling which had a foot dangling out of its mouth, an artificial rabbit driving a toy fire fighter vehicle and a sign fastened to the restaurant wall pointing out that 'All parasites will be removed'. On the wall behind the bar was a plaque saying 'A tea kettle sings when it's full of water! But who in hell wants to be a tea kettle?' Perhaps the best example was to be found on the entrance wall where guests wait to be seated. This was called 'Rules of the House' and went on:

  1 Cheques are accepted with a guarantee. We do accept Lilliputians, but only in small denominations.
  2 Your credit is good.
  3 We are not responsible for items left on coat hooks. We used to be responsible, but we aren't anymore.
  4 More than full occupancy is not permitted. Anything less is not tolerated by the boss.
  5 Proper dress is required. Feather boas and sneakers are optional.
  6 No one under the age of 21 is allowed inside after 8.00pm unless accompanied by a parent or legal guardian. Notes from Mother are not accepted.

Figure 11.2 TGI Friday's deliberate use of humour.

insights into the way in which humour is exploited for the benefit of the viewer. What is apparent from the consideration here is that such programmes point to a link between humour and hospitality and show that humour can be implanted or derived from events and activities in hospitality organizations, from the characteristics and behaviour of hospitality workers, from hospitality business language or from the hospitality offer itself.

Despite this portrayal in the media the role of humour in the hospitality industry has been conspicuously neglected by academics. An extensive literature search has found no research and no academic writing on the subject in commercial hospitality contexts. This neglect is the same for business more generally, according to Barsoux (1993) who is thought to be one of the few who have researched humour in business. Why then has research into humour in business and in commercial hospitality organizations in particular been ignored? One can only speculate about this. Perhaps humour in business is not regarded as a legitimate subject for research. Running a business for some is deadly serious and not a laughing matter. Practising service industry managers are often hard to convince about the value of any research (Johns and Lee-Ross, 1998). So even greater scepticism or resistance is likely over research which focuses on something which they may regard as neutral, trivial or pointless. In researching this chapter the authors came across such scepticism. A director of one hospitality organization questioned the validity of our enquiries and raised concerns regarding the funding of our activities. These were dismissed as a joke in themselves. The response from this organization was that business was a serious matter which humour trivialized.

The view that it's no joke being in business is reinforced from a survey conducted by the Aziz Corporation (Clark, 1999). Only 1 per cent of the 200 executives questioned believed that quips are appropriate in internal office meetings, while 39 per cent consider them unacceptable even in informal conversations with colleagues. Maybe the neglect of humour research relates to the failure to recognize the importance of humour in business. Whatever the reasons, the lack of research with regard to the hospitality industry seems even more surprising given the importance of groups to the working life of the hospitality industry and given the role that humour can have in cementing social relationships and to any collective endeavour. Support for the view that humour is both beneficial to the individual and to the group comes from Sir Brian Wolfson, Wembley plc:

> I think the skilful manipulation of atmosphere – because it is manipulation to some extent – is what creates an

atmosphere for people to give of their best, for people to feel good about themselves, for people to feel comfortable and warm. Laughing together is among the most agreeable and binding of human activities.

Deliberate humour

Humour has long been used by managers, employees and customers as a form of social bonding, to ease tensions, to get things done or to enable them to get their way in specific situations in commercial hospitality settings. Humour then is often deliberate and can enhance enjoyment of those present.

Humour and hospitality customers/guests

Humour certainly offers the opportunity of adding value for hospitality customers/guests and can appeal to most potential guests. Humour can evoke pleasure, a knowledge of which is described by King (1995) as one of the four general attributes of hospitality. Barsoux (1993) points to the link between being cheerful, as a consequence of humour, and eating and drinking in a restaurant when he states, 'Being merry is a natural corollary to eating and drinking . . . Eating is a convivial affair. Like humour it is a shared experience'.

Barsoux is referring in particular to the sharing of humour between customers. But given the presence of hospitality workers, humour could equally be shared between them and customers and from personal observation often is. The provision of food, drink or accommodation, which are frequently included in definitions of hospitality, is provided by people for other people. This means that service exchange is involved and that moods, feelings and emotions of the participants to the exchange process are part and parcel of hospitality. It has often been said that the concept of hospitality involves human interactions or encounters and that these include hospitable behaviour. Humour often forms part of hospitable behaviour and is key to successful relationships and interactions. Brotherton (1998) claims that hospitality is an exchange 'voluntarily entered into and designed to enhance the mutual wellbeing of the parties concerned'. If this is accepted then humour as part of hospitality can definitely smooth encounters and enhance this mutual wellbeing, whether it be between customers/guests and employees or managers, between employees and managers, between employees or between managers involved in the provision of accommodation, food or drink away from home. Friendliness and a sense of fun are particularly important in certain establishments such as theme restaurants, family pubs, night clubs and theme parks. In such contexts humour can be important to customers.

Just as humour is used within hospitality companies to influence customers, it is similarly used externally in advertising to target and persuade customers to buy hospitality products. McDonald's used humour in its TV advertising commercials during the 1998 Soccer World Cup. Swallow Hotels use humour in the company's advertising. It has been a key consideration when planning Swallow Hotels' TV and press advertising campaigns as the company believes humour helps to make the advertising more memorable. It is also believed by the managing director of Swallow Hotels that through the use of humour Swallow Hotels is portrayed as a friendly organization rather than a stuffy, faceless hotel group (see Figure 11.3).

The potential of humour in hospitality marketing and scope for raising a laugh when marketing hospitality establishments has been recognized elsewhere (Anon, 1994; Taylor, 1988). It was a major plank in the Newcastle Copthorne's strategy of stamping its identity on Tyneside early on in its existence and special promotions for recession-weary Germans, drought-hit south-erners and stressed out executives were some of the hotel's marketing ploys. Cumbria's Appleby Manor hotel has used whisky passports and hangover packs, consisting of indigestion tablets, brow cool tissues, shaky hand shaving plasters and a recovery mask, to back up a malt whisky tasting two-day break.

'Ironing made simple'

Nearly £750,000 was spent on running the 40 second and 10 second Swallow TV commercial transmitted nationally on Channel 4 in October 1999. These commercials target the ABC audience and were shown during a variety of programmes including the news, comedies, dramas and soaps.

Previous Swallow Hotel advertisements have tended to have a humorous angle and this one is no exception. The action focuses on a female guest lamenting the fact that most hotels have not got things quite right yet. Chocolate mints on the pillow are nice to have but it would be better to have something really useful like, an iron. Before anyone starts linking women with ironing, the ad turns the old male/female stereotype on the head because, here, the lady claims she does not know one end of an iron from another – she delegates it to her partner!

Figure 11.3 Swallow Hotels – use of humour in advertising a hospitality company. *Source:* Rodger Carrigan, managing director, Swallow Hotels, June 1999.

A final example is Hyatt Hotels and Resorts' London press and publicity office who have sent out socks, curry powder and packets of tea wrapped in Hyatt notepaper to promote a new hotel or a specific event (Anon, 1994). Taylor (1988) refers to the use of humour in the captions of pictures from a sales brochure selling fun weekends as part of Stardust Mini Holidays. He argues that it would be inappropriate to sell such weekends in a gloomy manner or in formal tones and, in common with Swallow Hotels' campaign, used a form of promotion to inform clients that they would not be staying with a 'stuffy' company. A word of warning from Taylor is that it is unwise to be humourous about your own specific product and that jokes should not be made about the quality of the hotel. This is a lesson that Gerald Ratner discovered to his cost when describing his jewellery merchandise (Barsoux, 1993).

Humour and hospitality staff and managers

Humour through social interaction between two or more members of a hospitality organization, or when triggered by a non-human source within the organization, can prove psychologically beneficial to individual staff or managers in numerous ways. These are skilfully analysed and in considerable detail within the general business context by Barsoux (1993). Humour could be used as a defensive mechanism (see Figure 11.4) enabling one to cope with failure, criticism and stress. It can act as an antidote to boredom and be a release for frustration and tensions. It could then be especially relevant to hospitality workers within the hospitality industry where long hours, unusual shift arrangements, stressful conditions and monotonous work are commonplace. Humour can also be beneficial to the individual when used in a more positive way. It leads to interpersonal attraction (Chapman and Foot, 1977), can be deployed to influence, persuade, to motivate, to facilitate change and so on (Barsoux, 1993). Argyle (1987) advocates the use of humour. His research (according to Ross, 1996) found that people who use humour are more likeable, which he suggests was because:

- humour breaks down social barriers and status differences;
- increases group cohesion;
- reduces anxieties and increases joy, making encounters more rewarding;
- sharing in humour is a case of close co-ordination and hearing of both thoughts and emotions.

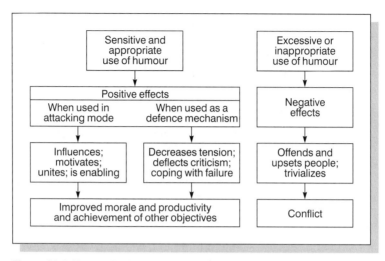

Figure 11.4 Uses and effects of organizational humour.

The importance of humour in individuals often makes them desirable for organizations to attract and retain. Figures 11.1 and 11.2 show people who have a sense of humour tend to be attracted to work in, or are deliberately sought for, environments aiming to provide fun and entertainment.

Humour has enormous potential as a lubricant to hospitality work, enabling jobs to be done and the organization to function. It offers benefits beyond those to individuals such as uniting groups, contributing to the resolution of unconstructive conflict in hospitality settings (to which attention has been drawn in previous research, e.g. Whyte, 1948 and Dann and Hornsey, 1986) and shaping and maintaining organizational cultures.

The circumstances when humour can be used between workers within commercial hospitality contexts are innumerable. It can lighten interviews and negotiations, ease meetings, facilitate training, etc. Information obtained from the managing director of Swallow Hotels showed that they have employed humour in training. Humour is used in training sessions as it helps to break down barriers and can be a very useful way of ensuring that trainees have absorbed specific messages.

Humour and the triadic relationship

Humour then can be used as a form of communication between people involved in the production, delivery and receipt of hospitality and therefore should be considered to be a fundamental element in the triadic relationship between hospitality managers, employees and customers. Evidence exists which actually demonstrates this. Terri Eastaff, director of TED Ltd, HR and training consultancy to the hospitality industry and previously director of training and development for Hilton International and vice president human resources for Radisson SAS Hotels, for example wrote in a letter to the authors in June 1999:

> Where management and employees enjoy a working atmosphere of serious FUN, stress levels are decreased as well as employee turnover figures. Employees enjoy less formal relationships with their guests which leads to the personal touch being emphasized and encourages empowered attitudes when dealing with difficult situations. One of my own memories of a shared sense of humour was during the time I was General Manager of the Amsterdam Hilton, with a full house, a visit from my Area Vice President on inspection, and a total power failure at 11pm when most of the guests were returning to the hotel! Meeting and greeting the guests at the front door with candles for them to share as they were guided up the stairs to their rooms certainly brought out the best in teamwork, camaraderie . . . and a sense of humour!

Terri Eastaff considers humour to be an essential part of her business. Others too consider it important and identify a variety of functions that humour can fulfil in hospitality organizations. For instance, Gary Palmer of Gardner Merchant in a letter to the authors indicated that there are at least three reasons why humour is important (see Figure 11.5).

Tension reliever – when staff are under pressure humour can be used to release some of the stress. The old adage of seeing the funny side is probably most appropriate.

Team spirit – the opportunity to use humour to develop a team spirit perhaps using humour as a way of attacking a common 'enemy' (the customer). Perhaps examples of this will be jokes at a customer's expense behind the scenes.

Common standards – humour can be used as a way to test the barriers of standards or approach subjects which would otherwise be difficult to approach. The classic 'you wouldn't believe what just happened to me' approach of explaining a situation pertaining to the workplace but apparently about a third party is one of the more obvious ways this could be used.

Figure 11.5 Gardner Merchant, functions of humour. *Source:* Gary Palmer, HR director, Gardner Merchant Limited, May 1999.

The skills of being humorous

An intended humorous offering in hospitality settings could be judged funny, indifferently or as offensive, partly due to taste and personal preference and partly according to the skill of the humorist. Koestler (1995) suggests that the criteria for judging humour relate to originality, emphasis and economy.

The merits of originality Koestler (1995) claims are that it provides an element of surprise which cuts across our expectations. An example in the hospitality industry would be the use of 'Eltons' and 'Olivias' which were used in Chicago Pizza Pie Factory as signs on the doors of the men's and women's lavatories. Emphasis may come from exaggeration or focus on particular concepts, idosyncrancies or figures. The Wimpy fast-food chain coined its name from J Wellington Wimpy, the dumpy hamburger-guzzling character in the Popeye cartoon strip. Wimpy use Mr Wimpy, an exaggerated beefeater figure, to advertise and promote their product both through pictures on merchandising material and in public through appearances of employees in Mr Wimpy costume. The strategy of fast-food companies associating themselves with popular cartoon characters is commonplace. The Asterix cartoon strip has been used by Asterix Burger Stores International. McDonald's, the world's largest restaurant company, have used their 'home grown' clown Ronald McDonald and friends to capture markets. Sometimes the association with humorous cartoon characters has been short-term and less linked with the brand, such as with the Simpsons at Burger King.

In contrast to emphasis, humour can be judged by its economy. This often occurs related to higher levels of humour and is expressed in the form of implicit hints or oblique references rather than in prominent explicit images. Examples include many modern pub names which pose a puzzle requiring some thought in order to discern the joke. It has been suggested that there are three critical questions which managers, or anyone else, should ask, when considering the use of preconceived deliberate humour: Is it funny? Is it pertinent? Will it offend? (Barsoux, 1993).

Unintentional humour

Humour is also frequently unintended, both in speech and writing, e.g. misspellings or mistranslations of foreign words on menus; clerical or printer's errors on hotel brochures; grammatical mistakes or ludicrous use of words in brochures, reports and personal references; anachronistic or misjudged advice in text

Hospitality, Leisure & Tourism Series

From a bill in a Little Chef: 'Mixed Gorilla £6.99.'

From a menu at the Nag's Head, Chichester: 'Food freshly prepared, so at busy times, bare with us.'

From a fish and chip shop in Gamligay: 'Wanted – a person for frying.'

From the Saffron Garden Indian restaurant: 'English dishes, all severed with chips.'

From the Blackmore Vale Magazine: 'Much of the food prepared for the customers has been handed down through several generations of the same family.'

From a hospitality student's essay: 'Too many chefs and not enough Indians.'

From countless staff in countless establishments: 'Have a nice day!'

* * * * * *

In a Leipzig elevator: 'Do not enter the lift backwards, and only when lit up.'

On the menu of a Swiss restaurant: 'Our wines leave you nothing to hope for.'

In a hotel in Athens: 'Visitors are expected to complain at the office between the hours of 9 and 11am daily.'

In a Yugoslavian hotel: 'The flattening of underwear with pleasure is the job of the chambermaid.'

In a Norwegian cocktail lounge: 'Ladies are requested not to have children in the bar.'

In an Acapulco hotel: 'The manager has personally passed all the water served here.'

In a Tokyo bar: 'Special cocktails for the ladies with nuts.'

On a Polish hotel's menu: 'Salad a firm's own make; limpid red beet soup with cheesy dumplings in the form of a finger; roasted duck let loose, beef rashers beaten up in the country people's fashion.'

Figure 11.6 Examples of unintentional humour. *Sources:* Gee (1994); the 'Peterborough' columns of various editions of *The Daily Telegraph*; the authors' own observations.

books, guide books, or conversation; the inappropriate or overuse of phrases at sales points or in service. These unintentional occurrences invariably cause those who are present or who witness them to smile or laugh. The upper section of Figure 11.6 shows some actual examples related to the UK hospitality industry while the lower section provides some amusing examples of mistranslated notices from commercial hospitality contexts around the world. These notices illustrate the potential dangers of poor translation.

Unintentional humour has the added danger of further unpredictability. In contrast to the deliberate use of humour, the events and consequently the likely victims cannot be identified in advance. Whilst the majority of instances of such humour are likely to be 'laughed off', in the sense that their unintentional nature is recognized by all concerned and hence there is no perpetrator for the victims to blame, this may not occur in all cases.

In common with many social phenomena, both context and effect define humour. Humour for one individual may not be for another. Likewise, humour in one situation may not be in another. Hence, whilst humour is a component in the provision of hospitality, it must be used carefully otherwise it might destroy hospitality rather than create it. This point must be carefully considered in any deliberate attempt to use humour as a positive contribution towards hospitality.

Humour generates victims, as every stand-up comedian will testify. Victims are victims, whether they are created by unintentional or deliberate humour. Victims create themselves in the sense that the important factor is that of effect. Victims themselves decide whether to 'laugh off' an event or to take umbrage. Therefore, there can be no guarantee that deliberate use of humour will produce its intended results. Clearly, there is a 'butt' to every joke. Care must be exercised in making sure that the butt of the joke does not take offence. The chairman of the Aziz Corporation said (Clark, 1999):

> The problem is that it's very hard to tell a joke without offending somebody. The only jokes businessmen can tell completely harmlessly are jokes against themselves.

Sharing fun with people is very different to poking fun at people, or making fun of people. For example, involving customers in the sense of fun is a means of delivering a positive message of hospitality. However, making them the butt of the joke could be counterproductive generating negative views of the hospitality provided. Likewise, humour can be used to cement relationships between work colleagues and as a lubricant to the execution of work. Equally, if it is deliberately targeted, it can drive a wedge between work groups and individuals. Figure 11.4 illustrates some of the uses and effects of humour.

As previously mentioned, humour can be used successfully to market hospitality businesses. However, not all intended humour in hospitality marketing has come off. It may be because it is not regarded as funny by the audience. An example of this is the Burger King 'Herb the Nerd' (J. Walter Thomson) advertising campaign. Herb was a badly depressed, bespectacled idiot. The idea was that Herb was the only person in America who hadn't been to a Burger King restaurant. He set out to rectify this during 1986 and there were prizes available for some of those who spotted him. The campaign was withdrawn after a few months and cost $40,000,000. The problem had been that potential Burger King customers wanted nothing to do with a nerd (West, 1992).

Another reason for the failure of humour in a commercial is when the humour swamps the selling. Humour, when used effectively, should relax the audience and put them in the right frame of mind to learn about the product and its benefits and hopefully to sell the product.

Conclusions

Humour flourishes within commercial hospitality settings, and not just in high-contact situations, because it is essentially unprivileged. It is not restricted by location, situation, time or person. Often it is unintentional and increasingly deliberate. Even so, from the little that is known about humour in the hospitality industry, it is thought to be little understood and underutilized as a management skill.

> Overall, humour is a way of changing atmosphere. That's the umbrella which covers all proactive attempts at humour. The appropriate use of humour can defuse, amuse, motivate, challenge and completely change the atmosphere. It's one of the least understood and most valid tools of management.
> Sir Brian Wolfson, Chairman, Wembley PLC in Barsoux (1993) p.182

Some enlightened organizations have realized its potential to their culture and have incorporated it in their armoury to create fun. Others realize that the power of humour to effectively convey messages and to influence is strong. This can be seen where hospitality organizations actively and deliberately use humour to advertise their offerings and in the training and development programmes for workers. Many, however, apparently see humour as counterproductive; it wastes time and is a distraction from the serious matter of running a hospitality business. Making money and making people laugh would seem to conflict. This of course could be the case; but it is argued here that it can be harnessed to positive effect within the organization. This would require an openness of mind; a clearer understanding of humour and of both its positive and negative effects; an appreciation of the circumstances when humour can and should not be used; and carefully developed delivery skills. Barsoux (1993) says that 'managers who see no need to make any concession to humour are unlikely to fail, but they may find themselves hacking their way to the green with a putter.'

This chapter argues that humour is an important element of the hospitality product and yet available experiential and observational evidence suggests that it is underexploited.

It may not form part of the core product of a hospitality organization but at the augmented level humour could be immensely significant. It may differentiate one organization from another and may also be a factor which attracts custom. Organizations which seek to entertain are, especially, discovering this.

Empirical research undertaken for this chapter was influenced by the dearth of scholarly material on humour in commercial hospitality contexts and focused upon hospitality organizations who viewed the role of humour positively to their activities. This research was driven by the desire to build upon the anecdotal and experiential evidence that linked humour with hospitality. It is clear that this work has only just begun to scratch the surface and that further investigations are required. The pursuit and exploitation of further knowledge on humour has been recognized elsewhere. 'There is humour in all things and the truest philosophy is that which teaches us to find it and make the most of it' (Anon, 1966).

References

Anon (1966) In: *Quotable Anecdotes* (L. Missen, ed.). London, George Allen and Unwin Ltd.

Anon (1994) Grabbing the Limelight. *Caterer and Hotelkeeper*, 10–16 February, 65–6.

Barnsley Alcohol and Drug Advisory Service (1999) The right stuff. *People Management*, **5**, No. 10, 20 May, 33–8.

Barsoux, J.-L. (1993) *Funny Business. Humour, Management and Business Culture*. London, Cassell.

Argyle, M. (1987) *The Psychology of Happiness*. London, Methuen.

Brotherton, R. (1998) The Nature of Hospitality and Hospitality Management: A Definitive View to Inform Research and Practice for the New Millennium? *Proceedings of International*

Journal of Contemporary Hospitality Management Internet Conference.

Chapman, A.J. and Foot, H.C. (eds) (1977) *It's a Funny Thing, Humour*. Oxford, Pergamon.

Clark, A. (1999) It's No Joke Being in Business. *The Daily Telegraph*, 31 May, p.23.

Dann, D. and Hornsey, T. (1986) Towards a theory of inter-departmental conflict in hotels. *The International Journal of Hospitality Management*, **5**, No. 1, 23–8.

Gee, C.Y. (1994) *International Hotels Development and Management*. Michigan, Educational Institute of the American Hotel and Motel Association.

Ingram, H. and Jones, S. (1998) Teamwork and the Management of Food Service Operations. *Team Performance Management*, 4, No. 2, 67–73.

Johns, N. and Lee-Ross, D. (1998) *Research Methods in Service Industry Management*. Cassell, London.

King, C.A. (1995) What is Hospitality? *International Journal of Hospitality Management*, *14*, Nos 3/4, 219–34.

Koestler, A. (1995) Humour and wit. In: *New Encyclopaedia Britannica (1995) Macropaedia*, Volume 20. London, Encyclopaedia Britannica Ltd.

Lashley, C. (1999) In search of hospitality: Towards a theoretical framework. *Proceedings of CHME Hospitality Research Conference*, April, University of Surrey.

Randall, S. (1999) Television representations of food: A case study. *International Journal of Tourism and Hospitality Research*, No. 1, 41–54.

Ross, G. (1996) Effective communication, motivation and service quality among hospitality management. In: *The International Hospitality Business* (R. Kotas, *et al.*, eds). London, Cassell.

Taylor, D. (1988) *Hotel and Catering Sales*. Oxford, Heinemann.

West, A. (1992) Fast-food marketing. In: *Fast Food Operations and their Management* (S. Ball, ed.). Cheltenham, Stanley Thornes.

Whyte, W.F. (1948) *Human Relations in the Restaurant Industry*. New York, McGraw-Hill.

CHAPTER 12

Consuming hospitality: learning from post-modernism?

Alistair Williams

*Division of Hospitality Management, The
University of Huddersfield*

Key themes

- Non-universality
- Towards a theory of post-modern hospitality
- Post-modernism
- Consuming hospitality in a post-modern era

To what extent can an understanding of post-modernism be of use in examining the theory and practice of contemporary hospitality? In this chapter I will seek to introduce the post-modern debate and demonstrate how the questions raised by the concept are critical to an understanding of theory and research within the hospitality industry, in particular those associated with marketing and consumer behaviour. In order to achieve these aims I will identify the key characteristics of post-modernism, identify post-modernism in the contemporary hospitality environment and assess the implications of this for hospitality theory and practice.

This chapter argues that as marketing reflects economic and cultural changes in society, it is to be expected that features of post-modernism will be evidenced in our choice and consumption of goods, products and services. This argument is undertaken through a consideration of the role of post-modernism in marketing and consumer behaviour within the hospitality industry. It is argued that many of the features that distinguish post-modernism are applicable to the contemporary hospitality environment. As a result the chapter argues that post-modernism offers a means of conceptualizing the changes that are taking place in the industry today. Contemporary issues such as fragmentation of markets, the growth of strategic alliances, marketing allusions to tradition and authenticity and the growth of anarchistic marketing practice can, it is argued (Foxall and Goldsmith, 1994), be viewed through the perspective of the post-modern consumer of hospitality products and services.

It is for these reasons that we must consider the potential impact post-modernism may have on practices within the hospitality industry. At a time when a number of forms of academic discipline are examining the implications of the post-modern condition, it is clear that consideration of its implications for hospitality products and services have to be investigated.

Towards a theory of post-modern hospitality

A dominant view of competitive advantage, and one that has grown in importance during the 1980s and early 1990s, has been the marketing concept, as formalized by Kotler (1980). Competitive advantage, according to this view, is created through activities such as market research, market segmentation and product positioning. It is assumed that consumers know what they want, and that if we are able to identify specific homogenous groups of consumers we are able to develop goods and services in order to match those wants. In the 1980s organizations became focused on customers, terms such as *customer-focused*, *market-focused* or *market-driven,* dominated the service literature (Carpenter *et al.*, 1997).

I do not intend here to go into detail regarding the marketing concept; I am assuming that most readers will be aware of the concept and of much of the literature pertaining to it. For those who have not studied such literature in depth and who may wish so to do I would direct them to the work of authors such as Drucker (1954), McKitterick (1957), Keith (1960) and Levitt (1960).

As is to be expected, the hospitality industry, with its focus on the consumer, has not been immune to marketing concept orientation. The marketing concept became the buzz phrase of the 1980s in the hospitality industry, with practitioners and academics directing increasing resources to the issue. The importance placed on the marketing concept in hospitality is highlighted by the work of such authors as Crawford-Welch (1988); Teare *et al.* (1994) and Mazanec (1994). Again it is to such work that I would direct readers interested in understanding more about the role of the marketing concept within a hospitality context.

Whilst the argument that we should listen to the customer and give them what they want seems correct, there are a number of problems with such a philosophy. First it is based in assumptions of consumer behaviour which may not be valid, second the question has to be addressed, if all organizations are operating in this way where is the competitive advantage? Finally, mounting evidence suggests that systematic violations of the marketing concept by consumers are the norm, rather than the exception. As Carpenter *et al.* (1997, p.81) argue:

> Buyer preferences are shown to be context dependent such that a buyer's preferences may depend on the context of choice created by a set of products available . . . buyers use a variety of decision making strategies to choose amongst alternatives, these strategies are con-text dependent. Buyers may use different rules for different occasions or choice situations.

This argument presents a challenge to many of the existing views of marketing within the hospitality industry. If consumer choice is not static but varies with context and if consumers do use a range of decision strategies, the essence of the marketing concept, i.e. to target segmented markets, becomes impossible as consumers will move through segments dependent on the context of the purchase.

Given some of the issues raised so far in this chapter, it is fair to argue that what is needed for the contemporary hospitality industry is an alternative way of looking at consumers and markets, one which is truly consumer led. It is here that perhaps the concept of post-modernism may be of value. The concept of post-modernism creates a very different model of the consumer from the information-processing rational consumer who is at the core of more traditional marketing models; the result, as Foxall and Goldsmith (1994, p.2) argue, is that:

> ... an increased awareness of the more dynamic amorphous consumer behaviour patterns requires marketeers to adopt approaches which concentrate on a willingness to listen to consumers and to accommodate marketing management to the emerging lifestyles of consumers. As such the approach of founding marketing strategies on traditional segmentation criteria is no longer appropriate.

Defining post-modernism

The debate about post-modernism 'can be precisely situated' (Seidman, 1994, p.231). Seidman argues that the first discussions regarding post-modernism took place in the late 1960s, and grew to become a major focus for sociology during the 70s and 80s, until in the 1990s post-modernism has come to be seen as a description of broad changes in our sensibilities, norms, values and beliefs.

A difficulty with investigating post-modernism and its applicability to the contemporary hospitality industry is that of defining a concept which, whilst recognized as obscure, can also be argued to offer valuable insights into contemporary consumer behaviour (Brown, 1995). The term was originally used by architects to suggest the dissolution of any distinction between high culture and popular culture. However, it has since been applied to many discipline areas and in such a diverse manner that renders common or standard usage hard to determine (Campbell, 1995). Such difficulties are summed up by Brown (1995) when he states of post-modernism 'it is essentially intangible; a mood, a moment, a perspective, a state of mind rather than a body of theory or a conceptual framework' (p.10).

Such a view is supported by many authors including Gellner (1992), Connor (1989) and Scrutton (1994). Gellner (1992, p.22), for example, says of post-modernism that it:

> ... is a contemporary movement. It is strong and it is fashionable. Over and above this, it is not altogether clear what the devil it is ... there appears to be no

postmodern manifesto which one could consult so as to assure oneself that one has identified its ideas properly.

Problems of definition are exacerbated by the fact that post-modernism has come to mean different things within different disciplines. Examples exist of post-modern design and decor; film plots; record constructions; TV commercials; magazines; critical articles and videos (Hebdige, 1986). As the range of disciplines within which post-modernism is located expands, distortion of the concepts in which it is based are inevitable, simply being a reflection of its diffusion amongst this wide range of disciplines (Brown, 1995). However, the difficulties which surround the concepts of post-modernism should not be sufficient reason to reject its use for a consideration of one of the key issues in contemporary society. Definitional problems are common in many disciplines, not least of which is hospitality. Post-modernism is a concept which is obscure and which as a result is difficult to use. However, despite these difficulties, it is possible through the work of theorists such as Lyotard (1984) and Jameson (1991) to construct the key themes of post-modernism.

The key idea that in many ways originated post-modern thought and which connects much of the literature in the field of post-modernism is that of the fragmentation of culture and an increase in importance of symbolism over substance. The basic post-modern concepts revolve around the notion of a self with multiple identities and group affiliations, which is entangled in heterogeneous struggles with multiple possibilities for empowerment (Seidman, 1994, p.136).

In order to define post-modernism in a way that makes it easier to use, Miller and Real (1998) suggest that post-modernism includes three key principles:

1 The breakdown of grand narratives that offer a framework for comprehending the world (Lyotard, 1984).
2 The centrality of new technologies in communication in providing global access to a culture of simulacra, i.e. copies for which no original exists (Baudrillard, 1983).
3 The replacement of a puritan ethic of consumption with the consumer culture of late capitalism (Featherstone, 1990).

At the centre of western society is the culture of enlightenment. This includes such aspects as the unity of humanity, the individual as the creative force of society, the superiority of the west, the notion of science as truth, and a belief in social progress (Seidman, 1994). However, it is argued by post-modernists that this perspective is under attack and that this attack is signified by such aspects as the resurgence of religious fundamentalism, the decline in the authority of key social institutions, crisis in western political ideologies and in criticism of literary and aesthetic cultural paradigms. It is suggested that a broad social and cultural shift has occurred in western society and that this is captured in part at least by the concepts of post-modernism. The terms modern and post-modern should be seen as referring to broad social and cultural patterns that can be distinguished and analysed for the purpose of highlighting perceived social and cultural trends. Authors such as Seidman (1994) suggest that these trends can be discerned in areas such as the collapse in the distinction between high art and popular art; the eclectic mixing of aesthetic codes in architecture; a nostalgia for tradition; the breakdown of traditional boundaries between social institutions and cultural spheres and the de-territoralization of national economies and cultures. As Seidman argues 'postmodern knowledge contests disciplinary boundaries, the separation of science, literature, and ideology, and the divisions between knowledge and power' (p.2).

In order to gain a working definition of post-modernism I propose to use the work of the three key authors identified by Miller and Real (1998): Lyotard (1984); Baudrillard (1983) and Featherstone (1990). Lyotard's (1984) work is seen as being pivotal in the debates over post-modernism, in particular the debates regarding knowledge. It was Lyotard who introduced one of the key themes of post-modern thought, the decline of the legitimating power of metanarratives. Metanarrative refers to the foundational or grand theories of knowledge, for example the overarching philosophies of history such as the previously discussed Enlightenment, Hegel's dialectic of Spirit coming to know itself and issues of class conflict and proletarian revolution as discussed by Marx (Fraser and Nicholson, 1988). Post-modernism suggests that such metanarratives no longer justify contemporary social practice. As Lyotard suggests 'the post-modern condition ... is one of incredulity towards meta-narratives, a refusal to accept there is one particular way of doing things and one way only' (p.88). Such a definition suggests that no single form of knowledge is privileged, no theories are ordinate or sub-ordinate to others. To Lyotard it is no longer possible to believe in a metadiscourse capable of capturing the truth of every discourse, a metadiscourse is simply one more discourse amongst others. As Lyotard argues, in order to understand post-modernism, we need to be sensitive to differences, embrace uncertainty and fragmented individuality, eschew totalizing systems of thought and avoid the suppression of heterogeneity through consensus. The value of post-modern knowledge is in making us aware of social differences, ambiguity and conflict and in developing our tolerance to this.

Lyotard focuses on one of the major themes within post-modernism, the decentering of the subject. Lyotard suggests that in post-modernism there is no centre, no coherence and little overall purpose. Post-modernism is, according to Lyotard, characterized by a lack of certainty and a decline in the belief of a unitary, coherent self. According to Lyotard the shift from metanarratives to local narratives and from general theories to pragmatic strategies suggests that we need to replace the concept of a universal, rational knowing subject, with one of multiple minds and knowledge which reflects social location and history (Seidman, 1994). In terms of our interest in post-modernism, Lyotard suggests that in addition to a shift in the way we think about knowledge we should accept a parallel decentering in the social world; whether we are referring to politics or the self, Lyotard (1984) insists that there is no centre, no unifying theme, no coherence and no order. The loss of certainty referred to above applies to the self equally as much as it does to the whole.

Baudrillard (1983) talks of post-modernism in respect of issues of simulacrity, i.e. copies for which no originals exist, and hyper-reality. Baudrillard argues that we are in an era of simulation in which the organization of society according to codes of simulation has replaced production as the organizing principle. The post-modern era, he argues, is an era of information and signs governed by modes, codes and cybernetics (Best and Kellner, 1991). To Baudrillard hyper-reality means a blurring of any distinctions between reality and non-reality to the extent that unreality becomes more real than reality, i.e. hyper-real. As Best and Kellner state (p.295):

> . . . when the real is no longer simply given, but is artificially reproduced as real (e.g. as a simulated environment) it becomes not unreal, or surreal, but realer-than-real, a real retouched and refurbished in a hallucinatory resemblance with itself.

Accordingly, hyper-reality leads to simulations coming to represent reality itself. To Baudrillard (1988) simulacrity and hyper-reality cannot be separated from advances in telecommunications, information technology, cybernetics and the mass media. Baudrillard argues that the ceaseless display of images on the mass media has removed the ability of people to discriminate between fact and fiction. According to the views of Baudrillard, post-modernism is a milieu in which there is more and more information available but it has less and less meaning. Nowhere is this tendency better seen, it is argued, than in the world of Walt Disney, as it is 'more authentic in its inauthenticity than its surrounding environment' (Brown, 1994, p.80). To Baudrillard, indeed, Disneyland has been created as imaginary in order to make us believe that the rest of America is real.

In addition to the above, Featherstone (1990) associates a post-modern society with a consumer society, an argument supported by theorists such as Kaplan (1987), Harvey (1989) and Connor (1989). As a result, a concern with consumption as a symbolic rather than instrumental activity unites much of the literature in this area. However, what individuals consume are seen not as products or services, but meanings and emancipated signs, that is signs that have no fixed meanings. In post-modern society, hyper-reality means that any object can take on any meaning.

It is not intended within this chapter to discuss at length the development and continued role of post-modernism in contemporary society. Such arguments are available elsewhere and those interested are referred to the work of authors such as Best and Kellner (1991), Baudrillard (1983), Lyotard (1984), Seidman and Wagner (1991) and Foucalt (1977). In addition Harvey (1989) and Rosenau (1992) have produced simplified texts which aid comprehension of many of the more demanding concepts. There are also a number of texts that are intended for a specifically marketing orientated audience available including those by Featherstone (1991), Elliot (1993), Firat and Venkatesh (1991) and Brown (1995).

What I am seeking to achieve within this chapter is a consideration of a number of aspects of post-modernism and the ways in which they can be seen to relate to a key feature of contemporary society, that of the consumption of hospitality products and services. In seeking an understanding of the way post-modernism relates to consumption within the hospitality industry, I intend to introduce and discuss a framework proposed by Brown (1995). Brown, whilst acknowledging the risk of oversimplifying the concept, suggests that it is possible to identify seven key characteristics of post-modernism, which aid in its definition:

1 *Fragmentation* refers to the disintegration of social organization, mass market economics, the nature and grounds of knowledge, fragmented media and the unified self.
2 *De-differentiation* involves the deconstruction of established hierarchies and the blurring of previously apparently clear cut constructs, for example philosophy/religion, science/religion, high/low culture and education/training.

3 *Hyper-reality* involves the loss of a sense of authenticity and the tangibilizing of what was previously simulation.

4 *Chronology* comprises concern for the past, or representations of the past, in a retrospective, backward-looking perspective.

5 *Pastiche* consists of the collage of available styles and mixing of existing codes in, for example, architecture, art, cinema and music.

6 *Anti-foundationalism* refers to the sense within post-modernism of deconstructionism. This factor refers to the discrediting, within post-modernism, of a search for universal truth and objective knowledge. It is also seen to represent antipathy towards orthodoxy, systematic generalizations and the establishment.

7 *Pluralism,* Brown suggests, should not be considered as a category on its own but reflects the sense in which post-modernists conclude that anything is acceptable, there are no rules and nothing is excluded. Brown also argues that pluralism should act as a reminder that in practice all of the other characteristics of post-modernism collide in a 'melange of incongruous phenomena' (p.107).

In order to investigate the role of post-modernism in the contemporary hospitality industry we will use Brown's conceptual framework and apply it to this aspect of consumption.

Consuming hospitality in a post-modern era

As I have suggested previously, it can be argued that many of the features that distinguish post-modernism are applicable to the contemporary hospitality environment, albeit that researchers may not explicitly place their studies within a post-modern framework. As I have also previously suggested the fragmentation of markets from mass product led images to smaller individualized segments is a key feature of contemporary marketing. Fragmentation can be seen to underpin much of the current debate on the disintegration of mass markets, including such aspects as micro-marketing, one-on-one marketing and the growth of software-based market databases. This fragmentation and micro-segmentation has been reinforced by the growth in distribution and media channels. Distribution has grown as locations for retailing have altered from traditional town-centre sites to out-of-town shopping malls, retail parks, ancillary locations (e.g. at airports or hospitals) and a growth in shopping from home, both from catalogues and television shopping channels (Parker, 1992). Such are the possibilities offered by new technologies in terms of hyper-sensitive targeting that it is becoming routine for marketers to talk of segments of one, and the mass customization of individual products and services, without apparently realizing the irony of such statements.

The effects of fragmentation are at odds with a suggested trend towards de-differentiated markets, i.e. the blurring of what were previously perceived as clear marketing boundaries. De-differentiation is evident in the tendency of firms to extend their product range beyond traditional boundaries, e.g. Granada's move into the hotel industry, the development of shopping centres within theme parks and the emergence of retailing hybrids such as cafes and stores within art galleries.

Perhaps the clearest example of de-differentiation in the hospitality industry, however, is the debasement of high culture through the development by many of the major national and international brands such as Tetley's and Guinness of 'museums' devoted to their history and development and the setting up of 'universities' by companies such as McDonald's.

Finally de-differentiation, it is argued, can be evidenced in a number of further areas within the contemporary hospitality industry. Such examples would include the growth in strategic alliances, joint venture relationships and vertical marketing systems. As the partnerships between Granada and Burger King or Airtours and Carnival demonstrate, traditional marketing barriers between organizations are being redrawn. Alongside this blurring of horizontal relationships between organizations, we have seen the growth of vertical marketing systems, whereby all channels of distribution are co-ordinated, operated as a unit and linked through a fully integrated network (Brown, 1995).

Chronology can be noted in the desire for authenticity and a growth in demand for traditional products, as a result there has been a growth in demand for products which are perceived as being authentic, e.g. real ale, real bread (with n'owt taken out), free range eggs and traditional holidays. The restaurant industry has seen demand for authentic foods cooked on traditional equipment, e.g. Indian tandoori ovens, Italian pizza ovens and Chinese wok cookery. The development of the Indian Balti meal provides an interesting example. Customers readily consumed the product in the belief that it was a traditional form of curry, despite it having been developed as a form of cooking by the families of migrant Indians in Birmingham in the mid–1980s. Within the public house retail sector the growth of the tavern-style pub can also be seen as an attempt to tap into the chronology aspect of post-modernism. The emphasis on authenticity in hospitality is also linked to aspects of branding, as brands are seen to offer consumers stability in markets perceived as increasingly uncertain and fragmented. Branding can be seen to be linked to the demand for authenticity as it provides security to consumers. As a result producers in turn make extensive reference to their past in order to suggest stability. This has enabled a number of producers to market a range of goods that are complimentary to their original brands and use the strength of the original brand to support the new product launch. Examples would include the wide range of luxury confectionery based ice-creams which have become such a feature of the market, the development of Guinness lager and bitter which has arisen out of the strength of the original Guinness stout brand and the growth of the Virgin hotel group. In cases where originals are not available, marketers simply create imaginary pasts, retro style. Consider the retro style McDonald's advertisements for the curry burger, or the use of retro pricing in pubs and hotels to celebrate special anniversaries.

Pastiche is available in a number of ways in the contemporary hospitality industry; indeed Brown (1995) argues that it is pastiche, more than other factors, that is the defining feature of post-modernism. Pastiche includes such aspects as irony, parody, imitation and quotation. Examples within the hospitality industry range from the growth in themed restaurants through to the latest concepts from the retail pub companies such as Bass' Bachus theme, consisting as it does of a pastiche evoking a number of eras ranging from Jacobean through Ancient Greek to Roman, Egyptian, etc. In addition to the above, pastiche is widely available in advertisements, with those for such products as Boddingtons Bitter, which mimics Chanel, and Holstein Pils that parodies those for traditional 'Irish' ales such as Caffreys amongst the best known.

Anti-foudationalism in the hospitality industry has to an extent been product rather than environment led. Anti-foundationalism is seen to include such aspects as the growth of products including alcopops and sachet spirits, along with developments such as drinking out of bottles. Anti-foundationalism can also be seen in promotions perceived as being anarchistic or subversive, such as the advertisements for Lemonhead alcopop that incorporated a man in a dress. The subversion of a traditional soft drink, such as lemonade, is a clear example of anti-foundationalism. It can also be argued that the growth in premium brands such as Sol and Budweiser is linked to the way in which they are consumed straight from the bottle, never from a glass. It has also been suggested that much of the original demand for restaurants such as Hard Rock Cafe were due to their links to rock bands, perceived, as they were by authority, to be in some ways subversive. In a similar vein the recent growth in outlets dedicated to 'hard' spirits such

Hospitality, Leisure & Tourism Series

as the Revolution vodka bars can be argued to be linked with aspects of anti-foundationalism.

It can be argued that it is in pluralism and hyper-reality that post-modernism is best illustrated in the contemporary industry. Hyper-reality refers to the loss of authenticity, a tangibilizing of simulation wherein reality and simulation become interlinked. Hyper-reality incorporates the movement away from marketing as providing product information, to one in which consumer desires, wants and needs are routinely manipulated. As a result of hyper-reality, meanings have become detached from products to be replaced by alternative signifiers. Hyper-reality is highly evident in the fantasy world created by theme parks, hotels and restaurants. The designers of such outlets often use simulacra of the past and present in order to create sanitized simulations.

Brown (1995) argues that hyper-reality subsumes most areas of branding or product image, including as it does price, perception, atmospherics, etc. As Brown suggests, however, some of the most extreme examples of hyper-reality in contemporary hospitality marketing are seen in the 'scripts, schemata and dramaturgical roles played by participants in the service encounter' (p.140). Nowhere, is this more evident than in the actor as waiter encounters one receives in heavily themed restaurants. If we consider the role of bar-server in restaurants such as Whitbread's TGI Friday chain of restaurants, it is difficult to avoid the conclusion that the participants have not based themselves on the character played by Tom Cruise in the film *Cocktail*.

As we have previously suggested, pluralism refers to the combination of many of the aspects of post-modernism identified above. Plurality refers to the inter-weaving of these aspects that is evident in much of contemporary marketing activity. Within the hospitality industry CenterParcs – an example of a combined holiday camp, health club and theme park – exemplifies pluralism in post-modern marketing, combining as it does hyper-reality and de-differentiation. Similarly the Disney Corporation's Main Street USA is central to all four of its theme parks world wide. Main Street USA is an integral theme unit, unified with a diverse merchandising system. This in turn is formed from a retro situation, that of a street Walt Disney knew as a child. Given such a scenario, it is not surprising that many commentators suggest that Disney and similar theme parks are the epitome of post-modernism (Baudrillard, 1983; Kowinsky, 1985). As Kowinsky states:

> Walt Disney based Main Street USA on the main streets
> of Marceline Missouri as it was when he was a boy

> growing up there ... but there were no sleazy bars, seedy poolhalls or dirty jail cells ... there were only pleasant, clean, colourful and nostalgic town stores which shimmered with remembered magic. (p.66)

Within the contemporary hospitality industry it is possible to identify many similar examples of pluralism, the most notable being the recently opened Irish ale houses, developed by many of the leading public house retailers. 'Traditional' Irish ale (brewed under licence in England), 'traditional' Irish food (factory produced and either chilled or frozen) and 'traditional' Irish pub entertainment (such as shove-ha'penny) are encompassed within a retro context of a perception of how a traditional Irish pub would be decorated, including manual labourers tools, e.g. paint brushes, shovels and brooms, in order to reinforce the stereotyping of the Irish as labourers.

For further examples we could look at any number of brewing companies that retain their original brewing plant, but for show only, whilst producing in huge factory plants elsewhere. Alternatively we could look at retail malls such as the recently opened Trafford Centre with its sections comprising restaurants from around the globe. Other manifestations of simulacra are widespread, from the fake sincerity of many service encounters, through the shelves full of fake books in fake libraries in pubs, to products such as alcohol-free alcohol.

It would be fair to suggest that within hospitality many commentators would argue that it is in the realms of hyper-reality and simulacrity that post-modernism is best exemplified (Brown, 1995). Authors who have considered this aspect of post-modernism include Wright (1989) who looked at hyper-reality in theme restaurants, Mourraine (1989) who identified the hyper-reality inherent in modern wine production, particularly in new producing regions, and Belk (1991) who focused on fake representations of the past in heritage sites.

Conclusions

As we have seen from the above, I have sought to argue that post-modernism offers a means of conceptualizing the changes that are taking place in the contemporary hospitality environment. In particular *fragmentation, de-differentiation, hyper-reality, chronology, anti-foundationalism* and *pastiche* are all available in a wide range of hospitality activities. Such changes as fragmentation of markets, the growth of strategic alliances, marketing allusions to tradition and authenticity and the growth of anarchistic marketing practice can easily be viewed through a post-modern perspective. Such arguments are supported by Firat and Venkatesh (1993) who suggest that, due to its emphasis on the creation and manipulation of images, marketing is at the forefront of the post-modern environment. As Firat and Venkatesh argue, the marketing concept has previously been content to portray images of normality and stereotypicality. What is required, they suggest, is a greater awareness of the huge diversity and heterogeneity of consumers.

What are the implications of this for individuals and companies involved in the hospitality industry? Elliot (1993) suggests that in a post-modern society meanings are determined not by marketers but by consumers with the result that inconsistent interpretations become the norm. This has serious implications for companies seeking to identify markets in order to determine investment, human resource and operational policies. As Brown (1995) suggests, any proposition, positioned with an emphasis on normality, is unlikely to be effective at re-focusing on post-modernity's emphasis on diversity. As Featherstone (1991) suggests, we have moved from a hierarchical system of fixed social status groups to one in which individuals are free to opt for a wide range of lifestyles. As Featherstone argues 'today there is no fashion: only fashions, no rules only choices, everyone can be anyone' (p.83).

As a result it is probably justifiable to conclude that post-modernism offers a number of opportunities for investigating the consumption of hospitality products and services. Brown (1994) offers a model which considers potential approaches and foci for such research, which I have adapted to hospitality research (Figure 12.1).

Brown suggests that research into post-modernism in marketing can follow any of the four categories highlighted in his model. I would argue that hospitality marketing research has to begin to look at many of these categories and this chapter is simply the beginning of such a process.

A number of studies have been undertaken in order to investigate consumer behaviour in purchase decisions (Tauber, 1972 and Buttle, 1986 and 1989). However, much of the research in this area, including both of the studies highlighted here, has tended to focus on the consumption of goods, and to have considered consumption an internalized state. Future research has to focus specifically on the hospitality industry and has to be grounded in a constructionist rather than a positivistic assumption, considering motives not as internalized states but in terms of descriptive or ascriptive accounts of contextualized acts. A constructionist framework would accept that individuals can be

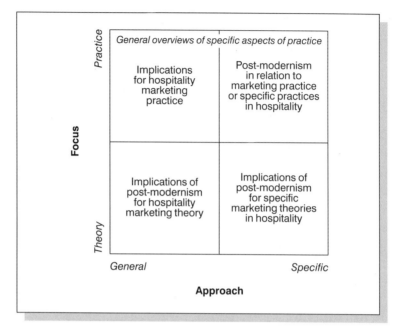

Figure 12.1 Modelling research into the consumption of hospitality.

seen as both products and producers of their individual social world. As Buttle suggests 'anyone person stands at a particular map reference with respect to a multiplicity of social systems ... each of which may construe in different ways' (Buttle, 1989, p. 352).

If companies are to be effective in the highly competitive environment that comprises the contemporary hospitality industry, it is imperative that they understand contemporary consumers and consumer decision making. As we have seen, it can be suggested that many of the approaches that are currently being undertaken are based in the arguably flawed models of the marketing concept. The industry has to recognize that in contemporary western society post-modern consumers do not adopt consistent recognizable lifestyles, but opt to experiment with an eclectic combination of goods and services in order to experience a range of, often conflicting, identities.

In answer to the opening question, what does post-modernism offer investigators in the discipline of hospitality, I would refer back to the definition of post-modernism offered by Miller and Real (1998) and argue it offers three things. First, post-modernism emphasizes uniqueness over homogeneity, offering more meaningful insights into individual consumer behaviour. Post-modernism offers us the opportunity to free ourselves in our research by breaking down and throwing aside the grand narratives that we currently use as frameworks for comprehending the industry within which we operate. Second, post-modernism offers us the opportunity to investigate the culture of simulacra, which is in many ways the very essence of the hospitality industry. Finally post-modernism offers us the opportunity to consider the extent to which the contemporary hospitality industry represents the replacement of a puritan ethic of consumption with the consumer culture associated with late capitalism.

As Brown (1995, p.178) concludes:

> postmodern marketing . . . tells us that the proponents of marketing have become product orientated . . . this implies that the fundamental issue to which we should address ourselves is not marketing myopia, but the myopia of marketing.

References

Baudrillard, J. (1983) Simulations. NY, Semiotext (e).

Baudrillard, J. (1988) *Selected Writings*. Oxford, Blackwell.

Belk, R.W. (1995) Studies in the new consumer behaviour. In: *Acknowledging Consumption* (D. Miller, ed.). London, Routledge.

Belk, R.W. (1991) *Highways and Byways*. London, Association for Consumer Research.

Best, S. and Kellner, D. (1991) *Postmodern Theory*. New York, Guilford.

Brown, S. (1995) *Postmodern Marketing*. London, Routledge.

Brownlie, D. and Saren, M. (1992) The 4Ps of marketing: prescriptive, polemic, permanent and problematic. *European Journal of Marketing*, **26**, No. 4, 34–47.

Buttle, F.A. and Coates, M. (1984) Shopping motives. *Services Industries Journal*, **4**, 71–81.

Buttle, F.A. (1986) Unserviceable concepts in service marketing. *Quarterly Review of Marketing*, **11**, No. 3, 94–102.

Buttle, F.A. (1989) Why do people shop? A constructivist perspective. Unpublished working paper, Dept. of Hotel, Restaurant and Travel Administration, University of Mass.

Buttle, F.A. (1992) Shopping motives. *Services Industries Journal*, **12**, No. 3, 349–67.

Campbell, C. (1995) The sociology of consumption. In: *Acknowledging Consumption* (D. Miller, ed.). London, Routledge.

Carpenter, G.S., Glazer, R. and Nakamoto, K. (1997) *Reading on Market-driven Strategies*. London, Addison-Wesley.

Connor, S. (1989) *Postmodernist Culture, An Introduction to the Theories of the Contemporary.* Oxford, Blackwell.

Cova, B. and Svanfeldt, C. (1992) Marketing beyond marketing in a post-modern Europe. In: *Marketing for Europe – Marketing for the Future* (K.G. Grunert and D. Fuglede, eds). Aarhus, EMAC.

Crawford-Welch, S. (1988) International marketing in the hospitality industry. In: *Strategic Hospitality Management* (R. Teare and A. Boere, eds). London, Cassell.

Drucker, P.F. (1954) *The Practice of Management.* Oxford, Butterworth-Heinemann.

Elliot, R. (1993) Marketing and the meaning of postmodern consumer culture. In: *Applied Consumer Behaviour* (M.J. Evans, L. Moutinho and F. Van Raaij, eds) (1996). London, Addison-Wesley.

Featherstone, M. (1990) *Theory, Culture and Society.* London, Sage.

Featherstone, M. (1991) *Consumer Culture and Post-modernism.* London, Sage.

Finklestein, J. (1989) *Dining Out: A Sociology of Modern Manners.* Oxford, Polity Press.

Firat, A.F. and Venkatesh, A. (1993) Postmodernity; the age of marketing. *International Journal of marketing, 10,* No. 3, 227–49.

Foucalt, M. (1980) *Power, Knowledge and Other Writings 1972–1977.* Hemel Hempstead, Harvester Wheatsheaf.

Foxall, G.R. and Goldsmith, R.E. (1994) *Consumer Psychology for Marketing.* London, Routledge.

Gellner, E. (1992) *Postmodernism, Reason and Religion.* London, Routledge.

Harvey, D. (1989) *The Condition of Postmodernity.* Oxford, Blackwell.

Hebdige, D. (1986) Postmodernism and the other side. *Journal of Communication Inquiry,* **10,** No. 2, 78–98.

Jameson, F. (1991) *Postmodernism or the Cultural Logic of Capitalism.* London, Verso.

Kaplan, E.A. (1987) *Rocking Around the Clock: Music, TV, Postmodernism and Consumer Culture.* London, Methuen.

Keith, R.J. (1960) The marketing revolution. *Journal of Marketing,* 24, Jan.

Kowinsky, W.S. (1985) *The Malling of America.* New York, Morrow.

Kotler, P. (1980) *Marketing Management: Analysis, Planning, Implementation and Control.* Englewood Cliffs, Prentice-Hall.

Levitt, T. (1960) Marketing myopia. *Harvard Business Review,* **38,** July–August, 45–56.

Lyotard, J.F. (1984) *The Postmodern Condition: A Report on Knowledge.* Manchester, Manchester University Press.

Mazanec, J.A. (1994) *Marketing in Hospitality and Tourism.* London, Cassell.

McKitterick, J.B. (1957) What is the marketing management concept? In: *The Frontiers of Marketing Thought and Science* (F.M. Bass, ed.). Chicago, American Marketing Association.

Miller, G.R. and Real, M. (1998) Postmodernity and popular culture. In: *The Postmodern Presence* (A.A. Berger, ed.). London, Sage.

Mourrain, J.A.P. (1989) The hyper-modern commodity form. In: *Marketing Theory and Practice* (Childers *et al.*, eds). Chicago, American Marketing Association.

Ogilvy, J. (1990) This post-modern business. *Market Research Today,* Feb., pp.4–22.

O'Guin, T. and Belk, R. (1989) Heaven on earth: consumption at Heritage village. USA. *Journal of Consumer Research, 15,* 227–38.

Parker, A.J. (1992) Retail environments into the 1990s. *Irish Marketing Review, 5,* No. 2, 61–72.

Piercy, N.F. *et al.* (1993) Strategic and operational market segmentation. *Journal of Strategic Marketing, 1,* 123–140.

Rosenau, P.M. (1992) *Postmodernism and the Social Sciences.* Princeton, Princeton University Press.

Scrutton, R. (1994) *Modern Philosophy: An Introduction and Survey.* London, Sinclair-Stevenson.

Seidman, S. and Wagner, D. (1991) *Postmodernism and Social Theory.* Oxford, Basil Blackwell.

Seidman, S. (1994) *The Postmodern Turn – New Perspectives on Social Theory.* Cambridge, Cambridge University Press.

Tauber, E.M. (1972) Why do people shop? *Journal of Marketing, 30,* October, 46–72.

Teare, R., Mazanec, J.A. and Crawford-Welch, S. (1994) *Marketing in Hospitality and Tourism.* Cassell, London.

Wright, T. (1989) Marketing culture. In: *Marketing Theory and Practice* (T.L. Childers *et al.*, eds). Chicago, American Marketing Association.

Consuming hospitality on holiday

Hazel Andrews

*School of Tourism and Hospitality Management,
University of North London*

Key themes

- Understanding hospitality in context
- Ethnography of consuming hospitality
- The interface between guest and host
- Commodified hospitality

Wood (1994a) has argued that there have been few attempts to understand what the concept of hospitality actually means. For the purpose of this chapter the definition supplied by Telfer will be used, with the addition of the provision of entertainment. She states '[w]e can define hospitality as the giving of food, drink and sometimes accommodation to people who are not regular members of a household' (1996, p.83). This accords with the meaning offered in the *Shorter Oxford English Dictionary*. Implied in Telfer's description is the idea of an outsider, a stranger. She goes on to say that through the meeting of the needs of the stranger, bonds of trust and interdependency are established. These bonds are based on ideas of reciprocity and exchange, which have been explored in relation to gift giving by Malinowski (1967) and Mauss (1954). The basic tenet of their arguments is that gift exchange structures and represents the material and moral life of the community, establishing relationships based on mutual obligation. In this respect another basic maxim to an understanding of hospitality is established – that of turning a stranger into a friend.

In both the studies of hospitality and tourism, the appropriateness of the motives behind hospitality have been cast into doubt as the question of the commodification of the exchange between 'host' and 'guest' has been examined. In terms of hospitality Wood (1994a) cites Muhlmann (1932) and Heal (1990) as contending that, due to the introduction of financial transactions within the hospitality nexus, it can no longer embody the principles of obligation and reciprocity. In short these are done away with by the payment of money.

In anthropological studies of tourism, the 'host–guest' relationship has been situated in a general framework that has considered tourism in terms of commodification. The general thrust of this argument has been to suggest that non-western cultures have been turned into commodities for sale as a package to be purchased by tourists. The seminal work in this respect is Greenwood's (1977) paper about the Alarde festival in the Basque region of Spain. Although Greenwood later revised his work (Selwyn, 1996a), the focus of attention has remained on the 'host' population (see for example Boissevain, 1996; Abram *et al.*, 1997[1]).

With specific focus on the nature of the host–guest relationship in tourism (which appears to have been favoured rather than hospitality *per se*), the suitability of the terms have been called into question, because, it is argued, the meeting is not one of equals. This premise is due to two assumptions: (a) the tourist-guest occupies a superior financial position, and is purchasing the goods and services which make up the tourist experience, and (b) the tourist-guest is at leisure whilst the host is at work (Crick, 1989; Ryan, 1991; Burns and Holden, 1995; Zarkia, 1996).

The theme of commoditization in the host–guest encounter has also been discussed in relation to O'Rourke's film *Cannibal Tours*. The film depicts wealthy, middle-class, white westerners in Papua New Guinea consuming locals via the souvenirs they buy, and the photos they take. Dean MacCannell comments on the film 'the relationships between tourist and recent ex-primitives[2] are framed in a somewhat forced, stereotypical commercial exploitation model characterised by bad faith and petty suspicion on both sides'. (1992, p.27). However, Selwyn suggests that when towards the end of the film the tourists are seen helping each other to decorate their bodies with paint and then to dance the night away to Mozart they can be seen to have 'a passing interest in dimensions of social organization other than commodity-based activity'. (1996a, p.15). That is, they are concerned with sharing their experience and building relationships in which no financial transaction takes place.

To return more specifically to hospitality, Wood has criticized Muhlmann's and Heal's approach 'as highly romanticised and nostalgic'. (1994, p.739). He suggests that not all commercial provisions of hospitality can be assessed solely as an exchange of money. Instead he turns to the work of Burgess who has discussed hospitality through the metaphor of gift exchange and its use in structuring the social world as suggested by Malinowski and Mauss (see above). Thus Burgess states '[s]imilarly, hospitality has been concerned with social interaction, the extension of relationships, and thereby social stability' (1982, p.49–50). In light of this, Wood (1994a) calls for more attention to be paid to the 'mechanisms' by which hospitality is delivered in the commercial world.

To summarize, ideas of hospitality are premised on an understanding of caring for a stranger in order to establish a relationship based on reciprocity and exchange. In both the studies of hospitality and tourism, the nature of this exchange has been questioned based on the notion that financial transactions remove the real motives behind hospitality.

The main problem with the approach adopted in tourism studies has been to assume that the host is the local resident of the destination. Such a paradigm does not fit the charter tourist experience in which the potential local host has been supplanted by the charter organizer – the tour operator. This leaves the question of what is the nature of the relationship between the tourist and the operator. The next section, taking its cue from Wood (1994a), will describe the mechanism by which operators extend hospitality to the tourist-guest.

Ethnography of consuming hospitality

This section, by focusing on three elements of the tourist experience, seeks to describe some aspects of the nature of hospitality, and its implications for the host–guest relationship in Palmanova and Magaluf. Central to ideas of hospitality is that of being made welcome. Thus the starting point of the ethnography is the 'welcome meeting'. From here, two tour operator outings will be considered; the first takes the tourists out of resort and the second is within resort. Before considering these details there is a brief overview of tourism in Mallorca.

Mallorca – background and tourism history

Tourism development began slowly at the beginning of the twentieth century with the 1950s and 60s seeing a boom. By the mid-1970s mass tourism was firmly established. The offer is mainly one of sun, sea and sand. Tourism is the main source of income in the Balearics. In 1996 it accounted for 58 per cent of GDP (Bardolet, 1996, p.18), and generated a figure of 700,000 million ptas or approximately £3 billion per annum (p.23). By 1995, 6 million of the 8 million annual visitors to the Balearics visited Mallorca (p.25), which is the largest of the Balearic Islands.

Palmanova and Magaluf are in the municipality of CalviB located in the south west of the island. It receives visitor numbers in the region of 1.6 million per annum (Selwyn, 1996b, p.97). Not only is CalviB the richest municipality in Spain, it is also one of the richest in Europe with money being derived mainly from tourism (Selwyn, 1996b, p.96).

Magaluf and Palmanova, which are two of the six coastal resorts in the municipality, are predominately 'British' resorts (the other resorts also have their own national flavour, notably Peguara as German and Santa PonHa as Irish) in that the majority of tourists derive from England, Scotland, Wales and Northern Ireland. They can also be characterized as mainly white, heterosexual, and 'working class'.

This is a landscape characterized by signs of Britishness. On a surface level as well as a deeper symbolic one there is an overt display of ethnicity. Overwhelmingly it is British, but within that statements of being English, Scottish, and Welsh also exist. Therefore one encounters advertisements for British food and drink: the fry-up (both English and Scottish), roast beef and Yorkshire pudding, fish and chips, Boddingtons and Tetley's (which can be purchased as an imperial pint), and invitations to spend pounds sterling. The food and drink can be enjoyed in café-bars, sometimes British owned or run, which refer directly and indirectly to their British origins – for example Eastenders, The Tartan Arms, The Willows, and Sospan Fach to name but a few. In addition the sheer volume of British visitors ensures that English appears as the dominant language added to by the broadcasting of British sporting fixtures, and British comedy, most notably Only Fools and Horses, but also Roy Chubby Brown and Jim Davidson. Menus are written in English (and other tourist languages, for example French and German), but by law they must also appear in Spanish. It is also possible to catch up with news from home by reading a British daily newspaper or watching Sky TV news.

There are a number of activities in which tourists can participate. These include day trips ranging from visiting a pearl factory, through scenic island tours, to horse riding, and going to the island's main markets. Other activities include paragliding, diving, riding inflatable bananas, and using amusement arcades. Shops sell plastic sex toys, buckets and spades, clothes, watches, jewellery, knives, leather goods and porcelain, and a range of other souvenirs.

The majority of tourists arrive on a package that has been organized by one of the leading British tour operators, for example Thomsons, Airtours, or First Choice. It is not the purpose to discuss here the economic characteristics or structure of tour operators, but there are some general points about the way in which they are organized that need to be made in order to locate as it were the package holiday experience. Vertical integration is a feature of modern business practice, which involves businesses buying related companies or offering related services, for example supermarkets providing credit and banking facilities. Over the past few years vertical integration in the tourism industry has enabled operators to increase control over the tourist expenditure. What vertical integration means for the tourist is that they may buy from a travel agent owned by a tour operator, will almost definitely travel on a tour operator owned airline, and may stay in a tour operator owned hotel (Burns and Holden, 1995). In their role as provider of the package, their influence over the tourist has begun before the actual holiday takes place in that through the provision of brochures they provide the image which informs people's expectations, and feeds into their cognitive understanding of where they are going to. As Dann notes it is '[t]he images [that] define what is beautiful, what should be experienced and with whom one should interact' (1996a, p.79). He also contends that tourism is a language that must be learnt, requiring a process of socialization. The tour operator is key in orchestrating the socialization process involved in the resort through the likes of welcome meetings and the organized bar crawls.

The extent to which the operator dominates and mediates the landscape the tourists find themselves in is suggested in the following example. The majority of hotels provide some form of entertainment for the tourists. This runs during the course of the day with in-house entertainers encouraging people to join in games. In the evening the entertainer is usually a guest comedian or singer. During the summer of 1998 in one hotel dominated by one British tour operator the advertising of the evening entertainment extended a welcome to the entertainer not by the destination, or hotel, but by the tour operator itself.

The concept of 'welcome' is inextricably linked with ideas of hospitality and is frequently used in tourism advertising discourse denoting friendliness, caring and security. In the package tourist experience under discussion here, the tour operator in the form of 'welcome meetings' makes a display of this aspect of hospitality. The welcome meeting is crucial for establishing a relationship between the tour operator representative (rep) and the tourist. The rep is a key mediator of the tourist experience continuing the role already established in the brochures of directing the tourists and hopefully ensuring that any additional monies spent in resort will be with the operator. Clearly the rep is also the mediator between the tourist and the powerful transnational tour operator.

Welcome meetings

Once the tourists have cleared customs and collected their luggage at the airport they encounter a row of reps holding signs which display the name of their company. The tourists approach the appropriate rep, have their names ticked off against a list and are given instructions as to which coach to board and where to find it. Once everyone is boarded, the transfer rep joins the coach, and greets everyone over the PA system. During the transfer to their accommodation tourists are advised to adjust their watches and to avoid drinking the local tap water. Alongside this information they are also asked to ensure that they attend the welcome meeting organized for them by their resort rep. The importance of the meeting is stressed, of being essential even for those who have visited the island before because 'your rep will be able to tell you of new and exciting things to do'. In some cases the tourists receive personally addressed hand written invitations from the resort reps detailing the time and place of the meeting and the rep's name.

The resort reps have more than one unit[3] to look after, and visit these at set times on set days of the week. The welcome meetings are scheduled for the day after the tourists arrive and can start (depending on where the unit fits in to the rep's timetable) as early as 9.15am, regardless of the time of arrival the previous day. Thus if a flight delay has caused the tourist to reach their unit in the early hours of the morning there is still an expectation (although the reps will be aware of the unrealistic nature of this) that tourists will attend the early morning meetings. If tourists do not attend the welcome meeting it is not uncommon for messages to be left at the unit reception advising of the rep's next visit and the services on offer. One company expected its reps to visit the tourists in their rooms if they did not appear at the meetings.

Attitudes towards the tourists can be based on whether they attended the meeting or not, and therefore the degree of helpfulness tourists receive. A tourist left his coat on the transfer bus and it ended up in one of the operator's offices. The tourist in question neither attended the welcome meeting, subsequent visits nor responded to the notes left for him. It may well be that the tourist has a case to answer in terms of his manners having not responded to the messages, perhaps he just did not care about the coat. The day of departure was approaching and the question of what to do with the coat remained. Short of physically delivering the coat to the tourist, the rep felt that he had done everything he could to return it. On consultation with management it was decided that the coat should be taken to the airport lost property, and the tourist left to deal with its retrieval for himself. The justification for this course of action was that the tourist had not attended the welcome meeting, and, perhaps more crucially, not bought anything from the rep. Although this is an extreme example, what the story does indicate is something about the nature of the relationship between the tourist and the tour operator, which the coat came to symbolize. The operator felt able to dispense with care of the coat, in effect the tourist, based on the fact that a commercial transaction in resort had not taken place.

What of course this story also suggests is that the motives behind welcome meetings are governed by a desire to facilitate a commercial transaction rather than a warm friendly gesture. As already stated, the welcome meetings take place the day after the tourists arrive. Those tourists who do attend are gathered in the appointed meeting place, which is usually the unit bar. The names of those attending are ticked off against a list held by the rep. The information that follows is derived from welcome meetings conducted by two reps working for two different companies. The first took place in the summer of 1997 and the second from observations made over several meetings in the summer of 1998.

Meeting 1 • • •

Everyone is welcomed, and the rep gives a short autobiography of herself. She explains that the purpose of the meeting is so that everyone can get to know each other. She goes on to say that everyone staying in the hotel is on a package organized by the same tour operator and that whilst the UK is now viewed as a multi-cultural society everyone has started their journey in the UK, and speaks English. It is therefore 'safe' to talk to people in the hotel. Emphasis is also given to the friendliness of the (Spanish) hotel staff, their ability to speak English, and their cheerful acceptance of the mispronunciation of their names.

The talk continues with some practical information, for example not to take glasses out to the swimming pool, the location of chemists, and the expected code of dress in the dining room. Then the rep goes through the list of excursions and activities available for the tourists to buy from her. These range from an afternoon playing fantasy golf to an evening of cabaret entertainment, to sightseeing tours and trips to the island's main markets, and the organization of car hire. Emphasis is placed on the danger and discomfort that trying to reach some of the venues independently will entail. For example the local bus service is described as overcrowded and full of pickpockets, thus the advice given is that the tourists should let the tour operator (always referred to as 'we' or 'us') organize the excursions for them. Reassurance is given that for the night out at the cabaret 'we all go together and we all sit together'. Throughout the proceedings, the availability of food and drink, but especially the latter is emphasized, along with the numerous opportunities to consume it, including the rep emphasizing her own enjoyment of it. During this time the complimentary welcome drink of a small glass of sangria is being prepared at the bar. It is brought around to people as the meeting draws to an end. Some people stay in the bar to look at the information they have been given, and possibly go on to buy a trip.

Meeting 2 • • •

The following is derived from meetings that take place in units in which more than one operator is working and with a smaller number of tourists.

The tourists are welcomed: 'My name is Paul, on behalf of Sun and Sea Tours let me welcome you to the island of Mallorca and more importantly to unit Sea View.'[4] The welcome drink of bucks fizz, sangria or orange juice has been organized, the rep and the tourists share a toast of 'cheers' and the meeting begins. An information pack is distributed that details the excursions – price, place and day that the tourists can go on them.[5] The meeting begins as before with some practical information, for example where to exchange money, sun safety and the unit facilities. With reference to the information pack, details and advice about the excursions are given. The rep tries to anticipate the likes and dislikes of the tourists and only talks to them about those things in which he thinks they will be interested, so for example for a group of young men he will not detail the market trips. He also informed me that he adjusts his own language and manner to appear to be on equal terms with the tourists.

When describing the excursion to the weekly leather market at Inca in the centre of the island, the rep does not advise the tourists about the local train service. Instead he explains that the local buses to the market will be overcrowded, the number of buses from the market will be few and people will be faced with having to get an expensive taxi back to the resort. The message is clear: do not undertake the journey independently. The reason given for omitting the information about the train is that knowledge of it would deter tourists from buying the trip from the rep.

An expectation regarding tourist behaviour was highlighted in the tale of the coat. For this rep there was a further expectation about the way the tourists should behave during the welcome meeting. They are not expected to talk among themselves, and although invited to ask questions are not encouraged to raise complaints, rather these should be brought to the attention of the rep in private. In general complaints by tourists are not welcomed and the majority of the reps I spoke to felt that the tourists had paid little for their holidays, and therefore had no right to complain. Of course the rep is in an ambiguous position in that they must balance the satisfaction of the tourists without compromising the position of the company they represent. Stories of revenge taken on persistent complainers include arranging to have them strip-searched on their return to the UK, or deliberately misdirecting their luggage. The relationship between the tourists and the reps can certainly be one of tension, which can work both ways. For example one tourist who felt that his complaint was not being dealt with adequately remarked 'they herd you in like sheep take your money and then give you a bad package', and reps report stories where they have been confronted with violence by dissatisfied customers including one who had her face pushed against a window with the threat that she would be thrown through it. By contrast other tourists express genuine gratitude for the help afforded to them by the reps, for example the 'honesty' in describing the contents of some of the outings, and it is not unknown for reps to have a collection of tourists' home addresses.

The reps are under pressure to meet weekly sales targets. In some cases, failure to meet the target is punishable by withdrawing the rep's only day off during the week. As already suggested, the rep is in an ambiguous position, is a representative of the host and must answer to loyalty of the host first. Clearly, the ability to collect contact addresses and become friends with some of the tourists suggests that relationships outside of commercial exigencies can and do exist.

Having set the context in which the hospitality takes place I now wish to turn to consider some of the entertainment offered by the tour operators for their guests. The first focuses on a trip that takes tourists out of the resorts and the second looks at bar crawls that happen in resort.

Travels with My Aunt ▪ ▪ ▪

In Meeting 1, described above, an excursion is promoted that does not form part of the standard set of excursions offered by the tour operator or other tour operators. The trips that are on offer do not take people into Palma or visit Bellver Castle, on the outskirts of Palma. Palma is accessible by bus, but as already described, people are warned against their use because of pickpockets.[6] It is possible to access the castle by taking a bus and then walking uphill for about 1(CA)km. A trip to the castle independently is discouraged by emphasizing the awkwardness of getting to it, the steepness of the hill, and the expense of a taxi. The way to take in the castle and go to the cathedral in Palma is to go on a half-day excursion run by a woman 'we call Auntie Pam'.[7] Soon after the announcement of her name 'Auntie Pam' walks into the meeting and there follows some jocular banter between her and the rep. The following are accounts of the trip given by two sets of tourists.

The first is a middle-aged couple from Birmingham. They explained that Auntie Pam equated the position of the seats on the mini-bus to old style money, for example shilling or half crown. The price of the seats was taken to indicate the 'quality' of the customer. This couple had been in two of the cheaper seats, but they had not been bothered by this or the ribbing that went with it because Pam, who is from their neck of the woods, had made them laugh so much.

A slightly younger, but still middle-aged woman, from Newcastle made the second report. She was travelling with her husband and two children. She did not recommend the trip calling Pam 'Auntie Pat' by mistake, and screwing up her face. She said that the view from the castle was fabulous, but that the trip had ended with a visit to a shop selling expensive leather goods. She felt that the purpose of the whole trip was really to bring people to the shop in the hope that they would buy something and was sure that Pam would earn commission on any items that the tourists might purchase.

There are two main points to consider here; one concerns the use of the term 'Auntie', and the other is about the nature of the tourist experience. First, in the meeting much emphasis is given to the shared background of the tourists, and that they are all with one tour operator. The implication is that they are all part of one family. Pam, who does not work for the operator, must be presented as acceptable and she is therefore represented as a kindly aunt figure who will effectively baby-sit for the tour operator on a trip they do not offer. This fictive kinship relationship is established to inculcate feelings of safety and dependency. Also the humour is used to develop a sense of common bonds as Ball and Johnson show in Chapter 11.

The second observation to make is between the contrasting appreciation of the tourists described above. Clearly the second informant was unimpressed by the trip and placed it, if not within, at least parallel to commercial transactions. The first couple had not discussed the trip in these terms but had emphasized the fun they had had on the trip. This indicates that, within what is essentially a commercial nexus, as the second respondent would seem to suggest, there are opportunities for other kinds of relationships or experiences to be formed. The following discussion of an organized outing within the resort will demonstrate this point further.

Bar crawls ● ● ●

During the high season summer months bar crawls[8] are organized by the majority of tour operators, and take place mainly in Magaluf. The number of people joining in bar crawls can be as large as 200. Like the welcome meetings, their purpose is two-fold. First they are used to show tourists around the resort, and second they provide another opportunity for reps to earn commission. This is derived not only from the sale of tickets (1000 ptas each) to the tourists, but also from the fee (in the range of 170–350 ptas per tourist) that the bars pay to the reps for being included on the crawl. In addition, by joining in on the bar crawls, the reps are able to give the impression that they are on an equal footing with the tourists with the hope that this will encourage the tourists to spend more money with the rep. In this respect, as in trying to direct their actions in the welcome meeting, the reps are trying to exert some form of control over the tourists which is exemplified in the games that are played throughout the evening. Further, the participating bars, by focusing their attention on to a particular group of tourists for an hour, have the opportunity to demonstrate why the tourists should visit that bar again during the course of their holiday.

A free 'shot' (i.e. small cocktail) is handed out to tourists on arrival at the bar after which they must buy their own drinks (on some bar crawls a 'free' bar has been arranged at one of the venues and more free cocktails are available at others). After about half an hour the tourists are gathered in one place and told of the rules that will govern their behaviour during the evening. For example, all personal names are to be dispensed with and they can only refer to each other as either Fred for men or Wilma for women; these may be interchanged with other names from popular culture. Another rule is that opposite sex toilets are to be used, i.e. men in the ladies and vice-versa, and permission to use the toilet must be gained from the rep. Drinks are to be held in either the right or left hand as indicated by the rep; this rule like the others can be changed as the bar crawl progresses. In some cases the tourists are asked to swear an oath in which they promise to get drunk on that night and on every night of their holiday. The reps also have to follow the rules themselves and any transgression either by tourist or rep is punishable. The penalty is usually to down a drink in one and then to buy another.

As the tourists move from bar to bar they are welcomed by the rep to the bar telling them the name of the bar they are in and often proclaiming its importance as one of the top night spots in Magaluf. The in-house DJ will take over the proceedings and seek to establish a rapport with the tourists based on, for example, their place of origin. That is, asking where people are from: country, city or region and encouraging them to cheer when they hear the place appropriate to them. The time allocated in each bar is approximately an hour with the final stop usually being made at the fifth bar.

Clearly, the dominant feature of the bar crawls is a commercial transaction of several layers in which money exchange occurs between tourists and reps, tourists and bars, and bars and reps. Ultimately the exchange also occurs, via the reps, between the tour operator and tourists and tour operator and bars. Thus the tour operators increase their income from the tourists.

However, there is also something else going on. It is during the bar crawls that many of the friendships between reps and tourists are established. Further, the tourists also speak of the bar crawls as offering an opportunity to join a group and meet people. Magaluf has a reputation for a place to visit in order to find sexual gratification on a casual basis; it has the nickname of 'Shagaluf'. The bar crawls also facilitate such an exchange and the stripping of the tourists' own identity through the removal of their name goes some way to allowing this to happen. In Stanley Kubrick's (1960) film *Spartacus*, when Spartacus first enters the gladiator school he asks one of the other trainees for his name he is told that it is not a suitable question to ask because if they were to confront each other in the ring they would not be able to kill each other. The implication is that knowledge of someone's name is a sign of intimacy and bonding. Whilst lasting relationships cannot be precluded, it would not seem unreasonable to suggest that the lack of intimacy suggested by the use of aliases eases the passage towards short-term, fleeting relationships that do not require the commitment of knowing someone's name. In addition the removal of own names and the associated removal of self identity coupled with the games that make the tourists answerable to the reps places the reps in a position that allows them to exert power and control over the tourists.

Encouraging the consumption of alcohol to the point of being made to feel unwell, or physically being sick, can be interpreted as another method by which the reps attempt to exert control over the tourists. Mary Douglas (1987) has noted that among alcohol's many social uses are that it can make the drinker more malleable. However, there is an ambiguity that occurs if people are vomiting. Many of the bars have a faint smell of vomit, and it is not unusual to see tourists being sick or puddles of vomit on the streets. Vomiting is both an act of violence and rebellion and one of care and compliance. Physically it is the act of the gut forcibly repelling substances that do not agree with it, either through there being too much of it or it is potentially damaging associated with poison or disease. The violence is the force involved in ejecting the material and the care is that of the body looking after itself. Thus it is both rebellion in that it rejects what has been taken into the stomach and compliance because in some circumstances it allows the consumption of more.

The point of bringing up vomit here is to illustrate something about the nature of the relationship established in the guise of hospitality. It is not unknown for tourists to be evicted from their hotels or expected to pay for damage that they have caused during their stay. The establishment of obligation and reciprocity through hospitality demands that the guest behaves 'by the rules'

Hospitality, Leisure & Tourism Series

which in a situation of personal hospitality does not normally include smashing up the host's furniture and being sick everywhere. However, in commercial hospitality the tourist has paid for the use of the facilities and effectively dispensed with the obligation. In addition there is an incongruity with the pressure to conform or behave in a certain way at a time that is supposed to be free from the constraints of society. This in itself might incur acts of rebellion.

The examples discussed above reflect only certain aspects of the tourist experience. The welcome meeting, or certainly its availability, is common to all tourists arriving on a charter trip. It is of course up to the tourists if they then participate in any of the trips offered or organized by the tour operators. Some will seek to go on excursions organized by independent travel agents or hire a car. Other tourists will stay largely within the confines of their unit feeling that their needs are being met in that way. The next section seeks to draw the ethnography and theory together to try and understand what the nature of the relationship between host and guest is as manifest in the above examples.

The interface between guest and host

The first part of the chapter provided a brief theoretical context for the present study. This section will return to some of the issues raised, and, along with the consideration of other sociological debates, there will be an analysis of the ethnography presented above. I shall consider how the hospitality displayed to the tourists relies on ideas of incorporation of the stranger, particularly through the use of drink, and what then are the types of relationships facilitated by this.

To return to Telfer's (1996) definition of hospitality, implied in her statement is the idea of the stranger. Both Simmel (1950) and Schutz (1944) have discussed the stranger as someone who is outside of an 'in-group'. In many respects the category of the stranger is necessary to the in-group's understanding of itself, in that it allows an other against which the in-group can be defined. The position of the stranger is also one of ambiguity as the etymology of the word linking it to both guest and enemy demonstrates (Zarkia, 1996). Further, as Schutz (1944) notes, the lack of knowledge of the stranger about the assumptions held by the in-group engenders a feeling of insecurity and disorientation.

It is this combination of ambiguity and disorientation that demands that the stranger must somehow be incorporated into the in-group. Heal (1990) argues that in early modern England the head of the household used hospitality to display their authority within that household. The gate or door to the house was obviously a boundary marker, and the ability to grant its transgression, and incorporate the stranger into the household was one of power. Thus the idea of 'enclosure' was more important than that of openness.

The translation of these ideas to the situation described above takes place firstly in that the tourist exhibits many of the characteristics of the stranger. She/he is an unknown quantity and a person out of place, unfamiliar with the practices she/he now finds her/himself in. For many there is a feeling of disorientation as many tourists express confusion about exactly where they are staying, for example questioning where exactly they are on the island or even not knowing that they have come to stay on an island. Similarly guidance is sought on functions that in the home-world might be described as 'everyday' – for example a visit to the bank. The tourists' journey to their destination represents the transition into the new environment and their incorporation into it truly begins once they are in resort.

Palmanova and Magaluf form a clearly bounded area. In land they are demarcated by a motorway that runs between Palma and Andratx, and on the coast the sea forms a natural marker. The enclosure that these borders produce is added to by the concerted efforts on behalf of tour operators to ensure that the tourists remain within the confines of the tour operator 'family'. As we have seen, efforts to deter tourists from making independent travel arrangements are made, premised on the contrast between safety and danger. The latter is applied to the world outside that of the tour operator, for example the pickpockets on the buses.

This feeling of envelopment is added to by the attempts to overplay familiarity and friendliness: the use of the title 'Auntie' to establish a fictive kinship relationship that offers with it ideas of security and reassurance; and the reps' own attempts to appear like the tourists through their language and behaviour on bar crawls. The disorientation and lack of knowledge attendant with the category of the stranger tourist requires that they undergo a process of socialization and are brought into an understanding of the rules that govern the environment they now find themselves in.

An understanding of the rules and a concomitant obligation to abide by them brings the role of the socialization process in line with Dann's (1988, 1996b) and Wood's (1994b) arguments about tourism and hotels as a form of social control. The former contends that the process begins before the holiday starts in the images projected in the tour operators' brochures and continues in resort in hotels and on the excursions made. For example, he comments 'the tourism establishment exerts control over time in the scheduling of events and timetabling the holiday experience' (1996b, p.77). Wood claims that the hotel star rating system and related codes of behaviour exerts controls over the guests by establishing 'boundaries of inclusion and exclusion' (1994b, p.67).

The main rule that appears in the tourist setting described here appears to be concerned with consumption. Consumption is no less of a difficult concept to consider than hospitality, and its meaning ranges both between and within disciplines (Bocock, 1993). However, it is possible to say that it includes actions that range from the purchase of goods and services to eating and drinking.

In the tourist setting of Palmanova and Magaluf, emphasis is placed on the constant availability and opportunity to consume food and drink. Telfer contends that it is the giving of food that is of primary importance to hospitality because 'giving, receiving and sharing food is a symbol of the bond of trust set up between host and guest' (1996, p.83). In the cases discussed above it is drink, and particularly alcoholic drink, that is of central importance to the hospitality displayed. Its part in attempts to form bonds of trust is no less important than that of food. As Gurr points out, 'offering or accepting a drink is an indication of a social relationship, the acknowledgement of social obligation' (1987, p.230).

The contention here is that at the welcome meeting and on the bar crawls the complimentary drinks offered are an attempt to establish a bond between the tourist and the operator or bar owner. The complimentary drink is free; it is a gift. Mauss (1954) argued that the object of gift giving is to produce friendly feelings between the parties involved in the exchange, as well as establishing bonds of reciprocity. Both friendliness and reciprocity are inherent in the concept of hospitality. However, it is also the case that as Malinowksi (1967) demonstrated gift giving facilitated other forms of exchange. During the Kula subsidiary 'ordinary' trading of items of great utility were carried out.

The parallels are clear, the giving of the welcome drink is side by side with other forms of trade, that is, the potential to enact a commercial transaction in the form of buying an excursion. Telfer (1996) claims that genuine hospitality arises when the motives behind it are selfless and based on the desire to please the guest. The hospitality exhibited by the reps and the bar owners is not selfless, rather it is based on the need to earn commission and gain repeat visits. In addition the tour operator wants a loyal customer base and so it is within their interests to ensure that the tourists have an enjoyable holiday.

Clearly the commercial interests of the tour operator are prominent. However, in a similar way that the Kula allowed other forms of trade to take place, in the context discussed here the 'buying into' the holiday by the tourist also allows bonds of reciprocity and friendliness to occur. Heal's observation about the displacement of free hospitality by a monetary transaction illustrates the point '[e]ven if they [the guest], rather than the hosts, provided the alcohol at a local inn, they still welcomed the opportunity to drink with the "better sort" of inhabitants as a way of achieving temporary incorporation into the community' (1990, p.208). Thus, although having had to buy the outings, many tourists clearly enjoyed the feelings of social solidarity that arose out of their participation in either the bar crawl or trip with Auntie Pam.

Conclusions

The main purpose of this chapter has been to present ethnographic material that enables the mechanisms (Wood, 1994a) of hospitality to be examined. Hospitality is essentially about the creation and extension of relationships. In the commercial hospitality of a package holiday the main concern of those mediating the experience is to encourage additional expenditure by the tourists as well as trying to maintain a client base through the provision of a 'good time'.

The way that this is undertaken is to use 'devices' of hospitality; for example, the welcome, and the gift. Thus the providers of hospitality, reliant on notions of obligation and reciprocity, attempt to disguise what is essentially a commercial transaction. The success of such attempts works to varying degrees as the relationship between the tour operator (host) and the tourist (guest) can be both one of animosity and amicability. In addition, the experience that the tourist has 'bought' in to enables feelings and relationships to develop that are not based on rational economic criteria.

The emergence of monetary payment in place of reciprocity and obligation have given rise to the questioning of whether such practices can in fact be hospitality. In anthropological studies of tourism, the concepts of host and guest have been challenged partly on this premise and also because the meeting of the 'host' and 'guest' is considered to be one of unequals in which the tourist-guest has the superior position. In the examples discussed here powerful companies in the form of tour operators have supplanted the local host. The tourist has the ability to withdraw their custom but this is most likely to be after the holiday by not using the same operator again. However, the extent to which the operator controls or attempts to control the tourist experience shifts the balance of power away from the guest in this situation.

Wood has argued that within commercial hospitality the social nature of the event is maintained. He contends hospitality management is about the management of reciprocity and exchange (1994a, p.741). The nature of commercial hospitality places it within a framework of economic concerns. To suggest that economics could be separated from a social context would be misleading. However, even if the commercial practice of hospitality incorporates elements of its archaic form, it is the motives behind it that will determine whether it can be considered genuine or not.

Notes

1 For notable exceptions see Passariello (1983) and van den Berghe (1994).
2 The term used by MacCannell (1992) to describe the local population.
3 Unit is the word used for accommodation. It encompasses both hotels and apartments.
4 False names have been used to protect informant confidentiality.
5 The larger tour operators have particular times allocated for going on the excursions, thus in Meeting 1 the rep is able to tell tourists that they will all sit together because they will go to the cabaret on the night allocated to their company. Smaller operators tend to have to fit in around this.
6 It is not the intention here to deny the presence of pickpockets, but they probably pose no greater or less a threat to the tourists than on any other transport system in the world.
7 Although the title Auntie is real, the name given is again an alias.
8 The bar crawls take place in both bars and venues that might more properly be described as nightclubs.

References

Abram, S., Waldren J. and Macleod, D. (eds) (1997) *Tourists and Tourism: Identifying with People and Places*. Oxford, Berghahn Books.

Bardolet, E. (1996) *Balearic Islands General Information*. IBATUR Conselleria de Turisme Govern Balear.

Bocock, R. (1993) *Consumption*. London, Routledge.

Boissevain, J. (ed.) (1996) *Coping with Tourists: European Reactions to Mass Tourism*. Oxford, Berghahn Books.

Burgess, J. (1982) Perspectives on gift exchange and hospitable behaviour. *International Journal of Hospitality Management*, **1**, No. 1, 49–57.

Burns, P. and Holden, A. (1995) *Tourism: A New perspective*. Hemel Hempstead, Prentice Hall.

Crick, M. (1989) Representations of International Tourism in the Social Sciences: Sun, Sex, Sights, Savings and Servility. *Annual Review of Anthropology*, **18**, 307–44.

Dann, G. (1988) Images of Cyprus Projected by Tour Operators. *Problems of Tourism, 41*, No. 3, 43–70.

Dann, G. (1996a) The People of Tourist Brochures. In: *The Tourist Image: Myths and Myth Making in Tourism* (T. Selwyn, ed.). Chichester, John Wiley and Sons.

Dann, G. (1996b) *The Language of Tourism: A Sociolinguistic Perspective*. Wallingford, CAB International.

Douglas, M. (1987) Introduction. In: *Constructive Drinking: Perspectives on Drink from Anthropology* (M. Douglas, ed.), Cambridge, Cambridge University Press.

Greenwood, D. (1989 [1977]) Culture by the Pound: An anthropological Perspective on Tourism as Cultural Commoditization. In: *Hosts and Guests: The Anthropology of Tourism* (V. Smith, ed.). Philadelphia, University of Pennsylvania Press.

Gurr, L. (1987) Maigret's Paris, conserved and distilled. In: *Constructive Drinking: Perspectives on Drink from Anthropology* (M. Douglas, ed.). Cambridge, Cambridge University Press.

Heal, F. (1990) *Hospitality in Early Modern England*. Oxford, Clarendon Press.

MacCannell, D. (1992) *Empty Meeting Grounds, the tourist papers*. London, Routledge.

Malinowski, B. (1967) Kula: The circulating exchange of valuables in the archipelagoes of eastern New Guinea. In: *Tribal and Peasant Economies Readings in Economic Anthropology* (G. Dalton, ed.). Garden City New York, The Natural History Press.

Mauss, M. (1954) *The Gift Forms and Functions of Exchange in Archaic Societies* (trsl Ian Cunnison). London, Routledge.

Muhlmann, W.E. (1932) Hospitality. In: *Encyclopedia of Social Science* (E.R. Seligman, ed.). New York, Macmillan.

O'Rourke, D. (1987) *Cannibal Tours* (film). Canberra, O'Rourke and Associates.

Passariello, P. (1983) Never on Sunday? Mexican Tourists at the Beach. *Annals of Tourism Research*, **10**, 109–122.

Hospitality, Leisure & Tourism Series

Ryan, C. (1991) *Recreational Tourism: A Social Science Perspective.* London, International Thomson Business Press.

Schutz, A. (1944) The Stranger: an essay in social psychology. *The American Journal of Sociology, 49,* No. 6, 499–507.

Selwyn, T. (1996a) Introduction. In: *The Tourist Image: Myths and Myth Making in Tourism* (T. Selwyn, ed.). Chichester, John Wiley and Sons.

Selwyn, T. (1996b) Tourism Culture and Cultural Conflict: a case study from Mallorca. In: *Sustainable Tourism in Mediterranean Islands and Small Cities* (C. Fsadni and T. Selwyn, eds). Malta, Medcampus, in European Tourism Project.

Simmel, G. (1950) The Stranger. In: *The Sociology of Georg Simmel* (H. Wolff, ed.). Glencoe, Illinois, The Free Press.

The Shorter Oxford English Dictionary on Historical Principles (1973) Oxford, Oxford University Press.

Telfer, E. (1996) *Food for Thought: Philosophy and Food.* London, Routledge.

van den Berghe, P. (1994) The Quest for the Other: Ethnic Tourism in San Cristobel, Mexico. London, University of Washington Press.

Wood, R. (1994a) Some theoretical perspectives on hospitality. In: *Tourism: State of the Art* (Seaton *et al.*, eds). Chichester, John Wiley and Sons.

Wood, R. (1994b) Hotel Culture and Social Control. *Annals of Tourism Research, 21,* 65–80.

Zarkia, C. (1996) *Philoxenia: Receiving Tourists – but not Guests – on a Greek Island. In: Coping with Tourists: European Reactions to Mass Tourism* (J. Boissevain, ed.). Oxford, Berghahn Books.

CHAPTER 14

Working in the hospitality industry

Yvonne Guerrier

School of Hotel Management, South Bank University

Amel Adib

School of Hotel Management, South Bank University

Key themes

- The context of hospitality work
- Service or servile: relationships with guests
- Who am I? Identity and hospitality work
- Managing the hospitality worker

What does it feel like to work in the hospitality industry? Over 50 years of research into working lives has bequeathed us many and mixed images. One of the most persistent of these is of the actor (or con-artist) waiter who emerges from a squalid back of house to deliver a wonderful performance to the guest. The guests are made to feel that they are in control but all of the time it is the waiter who is calling the shots. This image is perhaps best summed up in the following, much quoted, extract from Orwell's (1933) description of his life working in hotels in Paris in the 1930s:

> It is an instructive sight to see a waiter going into a hotel dining-room. As he passes the door a sudden change comes over him. The set of his shoulders alters; all the dirt and hurry and irritation have dropped off in an instant. He glides over the carpet with a solemn priest-like air . . . And you (cannot) help thinking, as you (see) him bow and smile, with the benign smile of the trained waiter, that the customer (is) put to shame by having such an aristocrat serve him.

The same ideas can also be found in Goffman's (1959) description of a Shetland hotel in the 1950s, in Mars and Nicod's (1984) work on the cons and scams of waiters and in Whyte's (1946, pp.132–3) work on American popular restaurants in the 1940s which poses the question: 'Does the waitress get the jump on the customer, or does the customer get the jump on the waitress?'

Contrast this with the image of the host who is genuinely concerned about the welfare of his or her guests. The hotelier Derek Picot (1993, pp.42–3) tells the following story that portrays the hotelier as hero:

> Being in the Middle East can be an exciting experience both for the hotelier and the hotel guest . . . When the Iraqis decided to move into Kuwait overnight in 1990, Hermann Simon, an Austrian, was in charge (of one of the international hotels) . . . The hotel eventually became a barracks, but not before Hermann . . . had delivered each of his foreign guests to their respective Embassy compounds. The hotel car was bedecked with an enormous Austrian flag across the bonnet, and he personally drove his clients to the diplomatic area until the wheels were shot out by a zealous Iraqi guarding a road junction.

Picot's book paints a picture of hotel work as exotic and amusing: dealing with bizarre problems, mixing with the rich and famous and occasionally, as in the example above, requiring real bravery.

At the other extreme, however, there is an image of hospitality workers as the dregs of society: doing dirty, tedious and hard jobs for little pay because they have no alternative. The following quotation from Gabriel's (1988) book on the working lives of those employed in the less glamorous parts of the catering industry illustrates this perspective: 'You keep on washing up and they keep bringing you more. Day in day out I hardly do anything else.' (Kitchen porter in a London hospital quoted by Gabriel, 1988.)

Gabriel describes his respondents as victims of dehumanizing work, demeaning management styles and inadequate pay: far from the glamour of hospitality work as experienced by Picot.

The development of new concepts, technologies and management approaches has brought new ways of exploiting employees. As Fordism represents the routinization of work in the manufacturing sector, so McDonaldization represents the routinization and commodification of hospitality work. Routinized hospitality work has its own special ways of demeaning employees in that it involves controlling not just what people do but how they interact with other people (customers). The following quotation from Leidner's research into McDonald's workers in the USA illustrates just one of the ways in which employees can be made to feel silly:

> During a special promotion of 'Shanghai McNuggets', . . . (McDonald's workers) were forced to wear big Chinese peasant hats made of styrofoam. Most of the workers felt that the hats made them ridiculous: Katie says that McDonald's ought to pay another ten cents an hour for making them wear the hats: 'No one should have to wear those. It's TORTURE.'
>
> (Leidner, 1993, p.183)

Rather than focusing on the ways in which hospitality employees 'get the jump on the customer', more recent research, following from Hochschild's (1983) study of airline cabin crew, has focused on the way in which new management approaches with their mantras about 'doing whatever it takes to satisfy the customer' have made hospitality employees increasingly vulnerable to abuse from customers. At the least, they have to cope with the psychological pressures of smiling and keeping their tempers in response to verbal provocation. At most, they may be routinely subject to more serious abuse as the following quotation from a study of restaurant workers in Texas illustrates: 'I do not go through a shift without someone . . . pinching my nipples or poking me in the butt or grabbing my crotch . . . It's just what we do at work' (Waitress in a restaurant in Texas quoted by Giuffre and Williams, 1994).

However, a contrasting view is that the entry of large and sophisticated companies into the hospitality sector has led to an improvement in the quality of management and the quality of the work available. Jobs are no longer, or no longer universally, demeaning and unrewarding. Work in the hospitality sector can be conducted by well-trained and empowered teams of staff, as Lashley explains in the following description of the organization of work in the Harvester restaurant chain:

> At restaurant level, the Team Manager and Team Coach were no longer 'managing' the staff but were responsible for enabling and facilitating staff to be more self-managing and empowered. Each restaurant is organized around three teams which reflect the key operational areas (bars, restaurants, kitchen). Each team has its own *team responsibilities*, that is, those aspects of business performance for which it will be accountable. In the restaurant, for example, the team will be responsible for guest service, guest complaints, sales targets, ordering cutlery and glassware, cashing up after service and team member training. In the more advanced cases, members take part in the selection and recruitment of new team members.
>
> (Lashley, 1997, pp.44–5)

There is a real mix of messages here. Are hospitality employees heroes, villains or victims? Is work in the hospitality sector a career of choice or a job of last resort? Is the work interesting and rewarding or routinized and demeaning? Is it a 'macho' male activity, dealing with tough and even dangerous problems, or a feminine one, about caring and looking after people, the province of women and gay men?

Given the range of organizations and jobs within the hospitality sector all of these images at the same time carry an element of truth and are highly misleading. This chapter explores some of the paradoxes of work in the contemporary hospitality industry. It begins by setting the context of hospitality work. It then uses examples drawn from previously published studies as well as examples from interviews with hospitality management students to look at the relationship between hospitality staff and customers, the way hospitality employees see themselves, and the way they are managed. In conclusion, it explores the extent to which the nature of work in the hospitality industry is affected by the nature of the hospitality exchange: that is, that the work is concerned with the provision of food, drink and accommodation rather than some other service.

The context of hospitality work

The hospitality industry, in all its forms, employs an increasingly large proportion of the working population. It has been estimated (BHA, 1998) that about 2 million people are employed across the commercial and non-commercial sectors of the industry in the UK. Whilst there is a broad range of different jobs available in the industry, the majority of those employed are unskilled, semi-skilled or skilled manual workers (Lucas, 1995).

The types of companies offering employment in the hospitality sector have changed immeasurably during the last two decades. The 1980s and 1990s have seen a growth in the UK of hotel brands, the chain budget hotel, fast food outlets and themed restaurants and pubs and the increasing dominance of a small number of large, sophisticated firms operating across a range of sectors in the industry (Granada, Whitbread, Ladbroke, Bass). Nevertheless the hospitality industry also includes a very large number of small, often family run, businesses. The average establishment size in the industry as a whole has been estimated at 4.5 employees (Lucas, 1995).

Employment in the hospitality sector shows interesting patterns by gender, age and ethnicity. A first impression would be that hospitality work is naturally women's work (Novarra, 1980) in that it involves those domestic activities – cooking, clearing and cleaning – which have traditionally been women's domain in the domestic sphere. However, in the grander hotels and restaurants, chefs and waiters have traditionally been men with women confined to roles such as chambermaid and breakfast or tea waitress. Overall, the hospitality industry employs a large proportion of women but they tend to be confined to the less skilled roles whilst men are employed in higher numbers in craft skilled work (as chefs) or as managers.

The hospitality industry, particularly the restaurant sector, also employs a high proportion of young people. Restaurant work provides the first work experience for many and an extra income for students. A study in the USA claimed that a third of Americans under the age of 35 say their first job was in food service, and a similar pattern might be found here. Further, although hard data on this is sparse (Lucas, 1995), the industry employs a high proportion of staff from the ethnic minorities and migrant staff, particularly in the least skilled jobs. The picture generally is of an industry which employs large numbers of people from groups who are disadvantaged in the labour market and are confined to less skilled and less well paid positions.

This summary of the hospitality labour market might equally apply to other service sector industries, notably retailing. Are there any particular aspects of work in the hospitality sector which distinguish it from work in other service industries? Of course, hospitality work is not entirely service work. It comprises both service activities and production activities; service in the restaurant and production in the kitchen, for example. In that respect it is different from pure service operations such as shops.

Hospitality work involves the production and serving of food and drink and the provision and servicing of accommodation in an activity which mirrors the domestic. For the guest, eating a meal or staying in a hotel is a leisure activity (even if it is undertaken as a part of work). Urry (1990) quoting a study by Marshall (1986) notes the 'complex intertwining of labour and leisure' (p.74) in hospitality work, and to that might be added the intertwining of the domestic and the commercial. Marshall (1986) observed that the restaurant workers he studied 'were convinced that they weren't really "working" for their pay packets at all' (p.40). Employees were friends or relatives of customers, mixed freely with them in slack times and spent much of their leisure time drinking in the restaurant bar. The appeal of running a guest house, pub or restaurant as a life-style choice is that appeal of mixing leisure and work.

But, by contrast, being employed as a hospitality worker, as compared with running one's own hospitality business, is not regarded as such a desirable occupation. This may be a response to labour market conditions: hospitality jobs are regarded as undesirable to the extent that they are badly paid and can only attract people with no option of better work. In situations where the labour market conditions are better, then, one might expect to see hospitality work as having a higher status and, to some extent, this seems to be true in resort areas and developing countries with large tourist sectors.

But are there more fundamental problems with the nature of hospitality work? It is often claimed that people dislike the notion of giving service: doing the best for the customer implies a status difference between the service provider and the customer which people may find uncomfortable in egalitarian cultures. Leidner (1993) comments, in relation to the States, that working class men associate masculinity with 'toughness, gruffness and pride ... For such men, deferential behavior and forced amiability are often associated with servility, and occasions that call for these attitudes ... may feel humiliating' (p.200). Thus interactive service jobs in the hospitality industry may be perceived as essentially female roles, with a lower status because of that. (And where men do them they may often be assumed to be homosexual.) It is notable that the hospitality roles most associated with working class men are craft roles in kitchens, where the culture is tough and there is no requirement to be polite to customers.

However, the requirement to be polite to customers or guests is no different in the hospitality industry than in the retail industry, for example. One distinction is that the hospitality sector is much more concerned with the guests' intimate bodily functions: eating, drinking and sleeping and the clearing up after those activities. In that sense, hospitality work is 'dirty work' (Saunders, 1981). It is interesting that the contrast that both Goffman (1959) and Orwell (1933) make between back-of-house and front-of-house is not just between the authentic and the staged but between the dirty and the clean. The role of the hospitality worker is to manage the 'dirty' and to keep it, as far as possible, out of view of the guest. In that sense, hospitality work has much in common with nursing, also a relatively poorly paid, low-status, feminized activity but one which carries a certain extra nobility because it involves working with the sick.

Hospitality workers are also required to confront certain aspects of life which are often taboo. Although hotels and restaurants provide 'domestic' services for people outside their homes, the fact that people are not at home sometimes allows them to engage in activities which would not be acceptable at home. Services provided in hospitality organizations are contested in the sense that there is a conflict between providing guests what they want and policing their behaviour. This policing relates to the type of food that people are allowed to consume, their consumption of alcohol and drugs and their sexual behaviour. A hotel room, for example, is not just a place to sleep, but also potentially a place for sexual activity. As Hearn and Parkin (1987) point out, 'hotel and guest house managements explicitly or implicitly have to be aware of the sexual possibilities for residents, to impose visiting or time restrictions, "turn a blind eye", make arrangements for blue movies, "call girls" or whatever' (p.77). This connection with the 'less respectable' aspects of life may be another reason why hospitality work is accorded low status.

The relationship between hospitality employees and their employers is also problematic. Many jobs in the hospitality sector still attract tips and to the extent that the tips form the main part of the reward, 'employees' could almost be seen as self-employed operatives whose only relationship with the 'employer' is to provide an environment in which they can ply their trade. The high turnover of staff in many hospitality organizations also attests to a relatively loose relationship between employer and employee. However, many hospitality jobs also involve working

Hospitality, Leisure & Tourism Series

unsociable hours when other people are at leisure and may involve living in. It is sometimes argued that hospitality employees see themselves as part of an occupational community (Salaman, 1973) where work merges into leisure and where, because there is little opportunity to develop outside friends and interests, one's identity as a hospitality worker if not one's attachment to a particular employer is central to one's life. In this context, relationships between co-workers may be more intense than in other work settings.

But hospitality employees, at least those in customer-service roles, are both providing a service and part of the product. Far from being allowed to behave as independent operators, much recent research has emphasized the ways in which the hospitality organizations are concerned to control every detail of the behaviour and attitude of their staff: selecting staff who can project the right image, choosing their uniforms, scripting their behaviour. Once again, this approach can be seen across a variety of different service settings and is not unique to the hospitality sector.

The picture is that of contradictions. Where are the boundaries between staff and guest, between work and leisure, between the commercial and the domestic? Where are the boundaries between friendship and friendliness, between being one's own person and representing the company? How do hospitality employees manage the conflict between serving the guest and policing the guest? How do they see themselves in a situation when others may look down on what they do? How does their gender, ethnic background and sexual identity affect their self-image and how they are seen? Where are the boundaries between what an employee is paid to do and the extra they will do to serve the guest?

These are big questions and this chapter cannot do more than explore some of these contradictions. This will be done partially through stories collected from students of hospitality management about their experience during their year's industrial placements. These stories are not intended to provide a comprehensive picture of all aspects of work in the industry. They focus particularly on incidents that the storyteller found surprising or uncomfortable; that is, on the paradoxical elements of the work. Hospitality students on placement have an interesting perspective on these paradoxes as their own situation, as educated people who have made a commitment to a career in the hospitality industry but who are doing operative level jobs as part of their training, is itself paradoxical. On their return to university, they are also able to reflect on their experiences distanced from the work itself.

Service or servile: relationships with guests

Nick, working as a receptionist in a budget airport hotel, described his attitudes to his guests as follows:

> Well sometimes you don't care what the guest is thinking, you're just there. As long as they think you're listening and you care that's all that matters ... Of course, you never portray what you're feeling inside otherwise you'd be dead by now ... Big smile and nodding all the time, just agreeing – um yes I understand ... They really chat a lot. I assume it's in all hotels. It's so different from when you work in Tesco's and sometimes you don't even look at the guest, you just do the work and they walk away. In a hotel they just talk, talk, talk ... I think that maybe because they are away from home or they don't know people in the place and want to make themselves more relaxed or wanted, belonging somewhere.

This is a good description of the process of providing emotional labour. It has long been recognized that this is an important element of interactive service work (Hochschild, 1983). The service worker requires technical skills certainly – the waiter has to be able to carry the dishes without dropping them, the receptionist has to be able to work the computer system – but beyond this there is a requirement to manage the encounter so that the customer feels good. This may involve, as in the example quoted above, the service worker displaying emotions that are not genuinely felt. He or she smiles and nods while secretly wondering when the next break is due or when the customer will finally get bored and go away.

This need for service workers to manage their emotions is not new. Orwell's Paris waiter of the 1930s described at the beginning of this chapter clearly demonstrates his skills in managing his emotions. Stearns and Stearns (1986) describe the way that in the States from the 1920s onwards, service sector companies became concerned about training their customer service staff to manage their emotions:

> For female sales personnel, the cheerful smile in the face of the most aggravating upper-class customer became a standard badge. Department store super-visors, concerned with imparting to their sales-force a veneer of middle-class culture, included anger control in their goals. (p.117)

Hospitality, Leisure & Tourism Series

Over the 1980s and 1990s, however, large service sector organizations have become more sophisticated in their attempts to manage the customer–service worker interaction (Hochschild, 1983; Leidner, 1993). Some commentators may feel that such managed emotions, delivered only because the service worker is being paid, compare poorly to freely given hospitality, friendliness that is genuinely felt (see for example Taylor, 1996).

It can be argued that the nature of the emotional labour required by hospitality employees has changed over time and varies from culture to culture. Within more traditional and formal hospitality settings the ideal service employee is emotionless, indeed scarcely human:

> Typically the waiter is someone who is present, but whom others treat as he (sic) is not really there – as if he were a 'non-person' – this means that a waiter must not be seen eating, drinking, smoking, sitting, talking, burping, farting – or anything else which signifies being human . . .
>
> (Mars and Nicod, 1984, p.695)

This traditional role strongly emphasizes the status distinction between the customer or guest and the service worker and this poses difficulties on both sides in more egalitarian cultures. Whyte (1946) commented in his classic study of restaurants that European waiters create fewer problems than American waiters because the former are more accustomed to class differences and low social mobility and therefore less resentful of social distinctions (see also Shamir, 1980). A traditional approach by customers to staff may be resented by those staff used to a different culture, witness the following comments made by a waiter working in a four-star London hotel:

> Probably in the olden days . . . they used to click for a waiter but I thought that was rude but I don't know . . . I thought this is like being a slave but I'm not a slave I'm a waiter . . . You can put your hand up fine. Clicking is not good. It's like in the past when they click for a dog.

However, in less formal, more modern hospitality settings, the hospitality employee as non-person has been replaced by the hospitality employee as friend. Leidner (1993) describes the importance of a friendly welcome within American culture:

> Whereas other cultures might see indiscriminate friendliness as presumptuous, invasive or an attack on legitimate social distinctions, here those who resist friendliness risk condemnation for snobbery or coldness. (p.221)

This service style solves some of the problems about status differences between service worker and customer and may act to make the work more enjoyable and raise the self-esteem of the hospitality employee. Kirsten, working at an exclusive health farm, described the normal relationship with the guests as follows:

> If you are in a business like a health farm where you know all the people, it is so personalised. I mean you call Emma Thompson, Emma, and it is all kissy, kissy, you know. That is when you are not professional any more . . . It's like you can combine yourself and you can really, you know, like a flower that's open.

However, a different experience of hospitality work emerges if the guest decides not to be friendly. Kirsten, a German national herself, describes an encounter with a German guest in the same health farm:

> This lady was very, very rude . . . She was purposefully trying to incite me and she said in English to everyone in the restaurant that I was being an incompetent person and unwilling to work and typical German and I had a German attitude problem and I was not suitable for that business and how they could dare putting such an unco-operative person like me into the restaurant, that I was the reason why so many people wouldn't come into the dining-room . . . then later on when I was alone, she was waiting for me outside the room and she said I was ugly as well and unintelligent.

This guest's abuse of Kirsten continued throughout her stay. Kirsten described her difficulty in continuing to deliver emotional labour in these circumstances:

> The person in front of me (in a hotel) could have had an accident before they arrived or could have had a terrible, terrible morning . . . the worst thing you can do is be rude yourself, isn't it . . . Comfort the person, that is the professional side. So maybe in what happened to me I should have stayed calm and not given a damn, but because it had reached such a stage I just couldn't separate it any more because this was too incredible, this was too personal.

A different problem emerges when guests step over normal boundaries and ask for a service that is not provided. Nick, working on reception in a budget airport hotel claimed the following situation was relatively common:

> People just come down and say 'I've had a long day, I'm very stressed out, do you know where I can get a blow job or ... At the front desk, they don't shout it out because, of course, they don't want other people to hear ... Well I don't really know of places like that and I just went – I'm being serious, you try not to laugh or anything – 'um I don't really know I'll just ask a colleague' or sometimes I'll just go and forget about it.

Nick nevertheless felt that it was inappropriate to be rude to the guest:

> You're scared they might complain and say he wasn't being helpful but they won't say why he wasn't helpful. You just think if they trust in you saying that to you at least you can respect it and just not be rude to them and say 'go away, I don't know that stupid information'. If you really don't know you just say 'I'm really sorry I can't help you' and not be rude about it. Everyone's different.

He kept in role even when asked for a service that was even more outrageous:

> One guest, oh my God, he comes down and goes 'Do you have any entertainment?' and we said 'hm'. 'Can you send one of your colleagues up to my room?' and I just went 'Hm – no I don't think she'll come up to your room' and he goes 'well you'll do anyway' and I said 'No, we don't provide that service' and walked away. He was really serious. He goes 'well you'll do, just come up' like we're obliged to do it . . . He just thought it was a service we should provide him.

In this context, exhortations by hotel management that staff should do whatever it takes to ensure that guests are totally satisfied take on an ironic meaning. In reality, hospitality service involves a series of complex negotiations between guests and service providers about what is and what is not acceptable behaviour. When the expectations are in line with each other, the interaction is a satisfying experience for both but the service provider is extremely vulnerable if guests choose to step over the boundaries. Again, this is also the case in many other customer service occupations but the hospitality worker is more likely to be required to negotiate boundaries to do with sexual behaviour or alcohol consumption. In many hospitality settings, the relationship between guests and staff is a relatively long term one and it may be more difficult for staff to avoid further contact with abusive guests (as Kirsten discovered). (It is worth also pointing out that guests can feel equally vulnerable if staff overstep boundaries.)

However, by way of contrast, it is possible to find examples of work in the hospitality industry which is rewarding (intrinsically and extrinsically) and high status. Pauline, working as a receptionist in a five-star London hotel, described the role of Peter, the concierge:

> It's so specialist that a concierge will earn a basic £20,000 on paper but their take home pay is probably close to £80,000. Because they send people to restaurants where a party of four are going to pay £1000 to £2000, so they're tipped by that person leaving the hotel 'That's the best meal we've ever had, thank you.' And it's easily £100 just to say thanks for the evening. And then of course, the restaurant will thank them because they've sent so many people over to them, after a time. . . . Women would love the idea of the concierge organising their theatre tickets for them, recommending where to go for dinner, where to be seen. I think they liked the idea of Peter, who looked absolutely suave and gorgeous, a pink English man, from the country, silvery hair, they loved the idea of speaking to somebody like Peter who would say to them 'of course, if you go to the Aubergine, you don't do this or this.' . . . you could see the way they were sort of melting.

One may question in this context is whether Peter may be regarded as working for the hotel or working for the guests given that tips form such a major part of his earnings. Shamir (1980) discusses what he terms the intersender conflict that the hospitality employee faces in trying to match the demands of organization and guest, especially where the guest has recourse to a tip. Lashley (1997) quotes the following example from an employee of TGI Friday:

> I like the relationship with customers. I like to feel that I have given them a good time whilst they are in the restaurant. Last week I had a party in from one of the theatres, I didn't rush them. I took time and we had a good laugh with them. After the meal one customer asked me for a cigar. We don't sell cigars, so I went next door to the tobacconist and bought one for him. He was

> really grateful. Afterwards they thanked me for a great
> time and left a £20 tip. Management wanted me to hurry
> them through so as to bring in more customers, I don't
> like to rush people. (p.122)

In this example the employee resolves the intersender conflict in the favour of the customer, apparently not just because the customer tips (and for such an employee, according to Lashley (1997), tips would contribute around 50 per cent of his income) but also because the customer is fun. When the relationship with the guest is good, it is the guest contact that makes the job enjoyable.

Who am I? Identity and hospitality work

The examples quoted above demonstrate the tension between the professional self and the personal self in hospitality work. When the relationship with the guest is good the hospitality employee may feel that it is he or she as a person that is relating to the guest, that there is something approaching genuine friendship (as in Kirsten's description of her dealings with Emma Thomson). On the other hand, the professional self is a mask that the employee can hide behind, especially when an encounter with a guest is going wrong. The uniform, the role definition and the script all allow the employee to believe that if he or she is under attack it is as a representative of the company and not as an individual. But a uniform does not disguise someone's gender or ethnicity. It was not accidental that Kirsten's German guest-from-hell chose to bully a German waitress and that much of the abuse focused on Kirsten's German identity. Indeed, it was the fact that the abuse was so clearly targeted at Kirsten as a person rather than as an employee of the health farm that made it so difficult to handle. Similarly, Nick was probably more likely to be asked to recommend a prostitute as a male receptionist than his female colleagues. Further the implication from the guest who asked him to come up to the room that he would do as well as one of his female colleagues reflected assumptions about his sexual identity. Nick reflected on the fact that his job role encouraged him to adopt a camp style so he was often assumed to be gay (although he was not).

> I say to people 'why do you think that?' (that he is gay)
> and they say 'you know, you talk about women's things
> or you're always with women all the time, not like a lad
> "oh, let's go for a beer" and things like that'. Macho men
> – I don't think they would be any good working in

reception, or on the telephone or things like that because they don't have an ear for listening or talking, I don't know.

Gender dynamics in the hospitality work have been relatively well explored but there has been less discussion of either sexual identity or ethnic identity. If, as Telfer (1996) argues, people have duty of hospitality to those who are 'in one's circle', ethnic identity, as part of an in-group or an out-group, is certainly not irrelevant.

Rachel, an Israeli working in a hotel in Washington, described the issues that she faced when dealing with Israeli guests:

> They came up to me ... I wouldn't speak Hebrew although I knew they were Israeli, I could hear them talking and I wouldn't. The main reason why I don't is because they would say 'What! Do you think I can't speak English, why are you talking to me in Hebrew?' The second thing is once they know you speak the same language they are going to bug you non-stop. You know 'you're one of us, you can do this for us, you can do that.' I would try but if my manager was there he would say 'no, deal with other people as well,' which is right.

Rachel remarked that her ethnic background also meant that some guests were less willing to be served by her:

> I did notice that a lot of people of colour, especially American – you have discrimination, racial discrimination – and you know if you were black and the person dealing with you was black, yes they were happy to deal with you but when I tried to deal with somebody they weren't very pleasant to me ... I don't want to make generalisations but for the first time in my life I was actually approached by that and that really hurt, and there was a black person next to me, one of the people who worked with me, and so when they left I said to him 'Don't tell me that wasn't a racial thing' and he said 'No, you're right.' He even noticed it so it wasn't like I was paranoid.

Pauline, a Jamaican woman, was the first black receptionist in an exclusive five-star London hotel. She told the story of one regular guest at the hotel who refused to deal with her at all, he would not speak to her and refused to acknowledge her existence. So whenever the guest was due to book in her manager would come out and handle the check-in. If the guest telephoned down to reception and spoke to her, not recognizing who she was, he was charming.

Ethnic identity also affects the way someone is seen by other staff. Pauline recalled the assumptions that were made about her when she was first appointed:

> Of course all the maids are black, or the majority of them are black, and you know a couple of them said to me 'Oh, you're going to be our new housekeeper' so I said 'No, actually I'm going to be working on reception.' And they said 'Oh god, how long has it taken.' This prompted me to ask my manager 'Is there any reason why you've never had a black receptionist before?' and she said she'd never thought about it to any degree but 'when you came to your interview and I wanted to offer you the job the general manager said "I would love to be able to employ her straight away but I just want to toss something up with the Head Housekeeper. How do you think her life would be with the other girls?" That was his only concern which I thought was quite interesting . . . Would I almost be seen as some kind of traitor? Why wasn't I in housekeeping?' I thought that was amazing.

Amy, an English woman working in a hotel in Guernsey, found that her ethnic identity, different from that of her co-workers, did cause her problems:

> I hated house-keeping because all the staff working in house-keeping were Portuguese and they didn't speak English to me. I told the housekeeper how awful it was, they basically had this impression that all English girls are tarts and they, straight off, didn't want to know . . . In a department where there are eight Portuguese maids and the head is Portuguese me complaining isn't going to get me anywhere . . . After a while I just got on with it, I just knuckled down and worked cleaning my rooms, prove that I can do the job . . . It got better from there on.

Managing the hospitality worker

It is clear from the previous discussion that managing hospitality work is problematic for a number of reasons. Hospitality employees may have only a loose allegiance to the organization in which they are working as their skills are relatively easily transferable to other organizations and, in any case, guests, through tips, may provide a large proportion of their earnings. Hospitality workers may be perceived as low status, low skill employees but it is difficult to envisage a way of 'making' hospitality employees be genuinely hospitable through the types of control normally used with operative workers. Hospitable behaviour depends on subtleties of facial expression, nuances of verbal tone, or type of eye-contact, which, as Du Gay and Salaman (1992) point out, 'are difficult to enforce through rules, particularly when the employee is out of sight of any supervisor' (p.621).

Thus it is obvious that the 'hospitableness' of hospitality employees is influenced by the way they perceive they are treated by their employers as well as the way they are treated by the guests. Indeed, senior industry figures often explicitly acknowledge the link between their company's profits and the attitudes of staff, as in the following quotation from Rocco Forte:

> In a service industry, the most important ingredient in the product is the people. The quality of our people determines the quality of the service we give to customers and thus our success in the market place.
>
> (Forte, 1982, p.2)

However, in a commercial hospitality business, front-line staff are both a means to provide hospitality and a business cost and there is always a balancing act between how much hospitality is provided and how much guests are prepared to pay. When business is bad, the sentiments top managers express about valuing their staff are not always matched by their actions. This is illustrated in the following story from Steve who was working in a provincial three-star hotel:

> The hours were very long over Christmas, we were doing an average of 70 hours a week. The thing I found most difficult was management's attitudes, the management seemed to have a very blasé attitude about staff. Our hotel came second to bottom of 21 hotels in their internal reward scheme and after Christmas, one of the hardest periods, we ended up over budget. The management seemed to acknowledge that the staff were working so hard but they repaid us by cutting our wages (the wage budget) in January by £10,000 and a lot of the staff were very demotivated and they left . . . The hotel was left with a skeleton staff that made it difficult for everyone . . . They (top management) knew what the staff were feeling but they chose to ignore it deliberately.

Steve none the less argued that the pride of first-line managers in the hospitality provided in the hotel ensured that standards did not completely collapse:

> Without them (the department heads) motivating their staff to get on with their jobs under difficult circumstances ... the hotel wouldn't have been where it was ... A lot of them were demotivated but it was their character to be perfectionists ... they wanted to offer that service because in the end they were proud of their department.

Certain hospitality companies have made a conscious effort to build on this pride many hospitality employees feel in the service they provide to customers by introducing a more consultative and participative style of management which encourages staff to use their initiative for the benefit of guests (and the company). Lashley (1997) quotes examples from Harvester restaurants (a family restaurant chain) and from Marriott hotels of strategies based on empowerment. Employees, organized in autonomous work groups, are given power to resolve problems without recourse to managers. A member of the unit management team at Harvester described the way they worked as follows:

> A few years ago if the freezer broke and I was away for a couple of days, it stayed broken. Now we say to everyone in the kitchen, if the freezer breaks down what do we do ... get it fixed. OK, how do we get it fixed? ... now we get it fixed, there is no alternative, even if costs £1000.   (quoted in Lashley, 1997, p.47)

This type of approach to employee management can only work if companies are prepared to invest in the training and development of their staff, so that they are capable of taking on this additional responsibility, and also if staff are very clear what the limits of their authority are. Not all hospitality organizations provide this type of training. Alison, working as a receptionist in a four-star hotel in Edinburgh, commented on the way she learned her job:

> I never knew how much decision-making I was allowed to do or how much authority I had, what I could do and what I couldn't do because I was never really trained. I was just put on the reception desk with another person to start with, another shift leader in the first three or four days, and from then on I was left on my own.

In this context, Alison was ambivalent about being empowered to solve problems herself, even those she felt capable of solving, feeling that she was not paid to take on the role of a supervisor:

> Sometimes you have really stressful days where you just get abuse throughout the whole morning, a busy Sunday morning checkout for example, and if I then get somebody shouting at me, I will say I do not have time to deal with this, it's not my job to deal with this. If he's complaining about the restaurant for example and I'm not interested in dealing with this, I'll call the duty manager straight away. It could have been dealt with by me there and then, by listening, apologising and offering to speak to the restaurant manager perhaps and I'd have solved the whole situation there and then. But sorry, no, not interested, don't want to speak to you. I'm going to call someone else.

Alison, as a way of protecting herself from the stresses of her job, places clear boundaries around what she is paid to do and what she is not. Her attitude may also reflect her perceptions of how she is valued (or not valued) by her employer. It is interesting to contrast this attitude with the following example of a room attendant who is prepared to step beyond these boundaries:

> A guest at a hotel asked Marlene Abbott, a guest room attendant, to arrange for items of clothing to be laundered. The timing of the request meant that it would be difficult to fulfil, so rather than telling the guest this, she took the guest's laundry home and did it herself.
>
> (Hubrecht and Teare, 1993, p.iv)

This example can be interpreted in many ways. It can be seen as a demonstration that the hotel company's empowerment practices are working (which was the interpretation the authors placed on the example). It can be seen as a demonstration that employees working in a late twentieth century large hotel group can still behave in a way which is genuinely hospitable. However, it also raises issues about the boundaries of expectations about staff. Should a low-paid hotel worker be expected to use her own time, washing powder and electricity to provide this level of hospitality in a commercial company? (See also Lashley, 1997, p.104 who quotes this example.)

Hospitality, Leisure & Tourism Series

Conclusions

We have particularly chosen, in this chapter, to highlight those aspects of hospitality work which often remain hidden and barely discussed on hospitality management programmes: dealing with unreasonable requests and behaviour from guests, balancing professional behaviour and personal feelings, dealing with gender and racial discrimination, dealing with hidden (or not so hidden) sexuality and dealing with exploitative and incompetent manage-ment. It is only fair to point out that the respondents, whose stories have been quoted here, generally enjoyed their work experience in the hospitality industry and that where difficult incidents have been described they are usually relatively isolated problems, all the more memorable because they are uncommon. However, it is our contention that these examples do contribute to a picture of what it feels like to work in the hospitality industry, or at least in sections of it. It is also our contention that ignoring these, less pleasant, aspects of hospitality work makes it harder to find ways of dealing with them.

Most of the incidents described in this chapter could have occurred in other industry settings. It remains difficult to pinpoint any aspects of work which are uniquely associated with the hospitality industry. There are some aspects of the relationship between the hospitality employee and the guest that do seem different in character from those between a shop worker and customer, for example. The relationship tends to involve more personal matters, it tends to sustain over a longer period, it is susceptible to countless ambiguities and misinterpretations. But again these differences may depend on the particular industry setting considered. Serving hamburgers in a fast-food restaurant is more like operating a checkout at Tesco's than like being a waiter at the Savoy. The commodification of hospitality has, it may be argued, made work in this industry more similar to work in other industries. It is only in those organizations where a more personalized approach towards the commercial provision of hospitality persists that it is possible to identify these particular characteristics of hospitality work.

References

British Hospitality Association (1998) *British Hospitality: Trends and Statistics 1998* London, BHA.

Du Gay, P. and Salaman, G. (1992) The cult(ure) of the customer. *Journal of Management Studies*, **29**, No. 5, 615–33.

Gabriel, Y. (1988) *Working Lives in Catering*. London, Routledge and Kegan Paul.

Giuffre, P. and Williams, C. (1994) Boundary Lines: Labeling Sexual Harassment in Restaurants. *Gender and Society, 8*, No. 3, 374–401.

Goffman, E. (1959) *The Presentation of Self in Everyday Life.* London, Penguin.

Hearn, J. and Parkin, W. (1987) *'Sex' at 'Work': the power and paradox of organisation sexuality.* Brighton, Wheatsheaf.

Hochschild, A. (1983) *The Managed Heart.* Berkeley, University of California Press.

Hubrecht, J. and Teare, R. (1993) A strategy for partnership in total quality service. *International Journal of Contemporary Hospitality Management, 5*, No. 3, i–v.

Lashley, C. (1997) *Empowering Service Excellence: Beyond the Quick Fix.* London, Cassell.

Leidner, R. (1993) *Fast Food Fast Talk: Service Work and the Routinization of Everyday Life.* Berkeley, University of California Press.

Lucas, R. (1995) *Managing Employee Relations in the Hotel and Catering Industry.* London, Cassell.

Mars, G. and Nicod, M. (1984) *The World of Waiters.* London, Allen and Unwin.

Novarra, V. (1980) *Men's Work, Women's Work.* London, Marion Beyars.

Orwell, G. (1933) *Down and Out in Paris and London.* London, Penguin.

Picot, D. (1993) *Hotel Reservations.* London, Robson Books.

Salaman (1973) *Men and Work in Britain.* Blackwells.

Saunders, K. (1981) *Social Stigma of Occupations: the Lower Grade Worker in Service Occupations.* Farnborough, Gower.

Shamir, B. (1980) Between Service and Servility: Role Conflict in Subordinate Service Roles. *Human Relations, 33*, No. 10, 741–56.

Stearns, C. and Stearns, P. (1980) *Anger.* Chicago, University of Chicago Press.

Taylor, G. (1996) Put on a happy face. In: *Tourism and Culture: Towards the 21st Century* (M. Robinson, N. Evans and P. Callaghan, eds). Conference Proceedings, University of Northumbria.

Telfer, E. (1996) *Food for Thought: Philosophy and Food.* London, Routledge.

Urry, J. (1990) *The Tourist Gaze.* London, Sage.

Whyte, W. (1946) *Human Relations in the Restaurant Industry.* New York, McGraw Hill.

Education for hospitality

David Airey

School of Management Studies for the Service Sector, University of Surrey

John Tribe

Faculty of Leisure and Tourism, Buckinghamshire Chilterns University College

Key themes

- Origins and early influences
- Current provision and curriculum
- Hospitality knowledge
- Future directions and dangers

To a large extent the development of hospitality education has been driven by what Tribe (1997), writing about tourism, has referred to as an agenda of 'vocational action'. *Action*, here is used in the sense of the counterpart of *reflection*. Hence a *vocational action* curriculum is focused on enabling students to do, or, in Tribe's words (1999, p.119), 'It is getting on with things, involvement with the world of doing, and engaging with the world as lived'. The prevalence of training restaurants, production kitchens and industrial training placements as a part of the students' learning experience all provide tangible evidence of this focus. Given its history, origins and development, this vocational emphasis is not surprising. In its origins, the education developed from on-the-job training in hotels. The vocational orientation was further supported by a strong vocational ethos nationally which emphasized the important links between an educated workforce and a strong economy and it was given added impetus by student demand anxious about future employment prospects. At the same time, as a new field of study, the basis of knowledge about hospitality originally drew strongly from studies generated directly from the industry and the world of work rather than from the many disciplines or other fields of enquiry which help to explain hospitality.

The outcome of this emphasis on vocationalism and action contains both strengths and weaknesses. In many ways it has been helpful to the development of the subject. The vocational orientation provided fairly clear boundaries which during the early stages of development gave a helpful framework within which the subject could develop and justify its existence. Similarly the emphasis on action, rather than on reflection, helped the subject area to gain credibility, particularly with its stakeholders in industry. Yet at the same time, this fairly clear focus has provided some important constraints. In particular, as understanding and research about the subject area has grown and as the boundaries have expanded, evidenced in part by the shift in name from *hotel and catering* to *hospitality*, an emphasis on the vocational and on action have come to be a restriction on development. They have tied curriculum development too closely to the needs of industry and have prevented the subject from expanding into a consideration of the wider issues which are raised by and underlie hospitality.

At the start of the century therefore hospitality education is at an important stage in its development. It has proved itself as a popular and worthwhile subject of vocational study. But it is still, to some extent, caught in a *vocational* and *action* mould. There are strong arguments now for breaking the mould if the subject area is to take its place as a proper focus of study in higher education in the twenty-first century. These arguments are given added force by recent developments in the study of the related area of tourism. While enrolments on courses in tourism, which is seen as less narrowly vocational, have boomed, the demand for hospitality has been less buoyant. However, there are equally strong arguments that point to the dangers of moving away from the traditional core, not least the dangers of fragmentation and ceasing to have relevance to the core stakeholders in industry.

Against this background of change and 'breaking away' from *vocational* and *action* education, this chapter will explore the development of hospitality education and of the hospitality curriculum as a background to considering the nature, problems and pressures associated with the current provision. This will then lead to a consideration of the future developments, directions and dangers. The focus is on hospitality in higher education, which today in the UK is provided in the universities or other higher education institutes (HEI) and the emphasis is particularly on the experience in the UK.

Origins and early influences

Until the 1950s training for the hotel and catering industry, including for management, took place on the job, with 'insistence on a long and thorough practical experience ... and working experience on the Continent was regarded favourably' (Medlik and Airey, 1978, p.161). The same source suggests that those who had any formal training, largely technical rather than managerial, had received it at Westminster Technical College which had opened in 1910 yet was still the only hotel school in the UK, at the Swiss Hotel School at Lausanne or in one of the armed services. Medlik and Airey identify three early influences on this pattern which subsequently set the stage for what has become the study of hospitality in higher education. The first was the emergence of professionalism in the industry, manifested by the formation of the Hotel and Catering Institute (HCI) in 1949 and earlier by the Institutional Management Association (IMA) in 1938. These provided courses as well as professional examinations which marked the beginning of recognized standards of education and training for management in the industry. The second was pioneering work by a number of colleges in developing diploma level courses. By 1960, diploma level awards were offered at some 20 colleges. Third, within the industry itself there was the beginning of management training.

One outcome of these developments was that formal courses quickly became the main route for potential managers to gain entry to the industry and not surprisingly the courses were strongly geared to these employment needs. This strong vocational orientation was seen in the first two degree courses which were introduced at the Universities of Surrey in 1964 and Strathclyde in 1965 as well as in the 12 courses which were introduced in 1969 in England and Wales leading to the Higher National Diploma in Hotel and Catering Administration and the eight courses in Institutional Management. It was also seen in the six degree level courses which were offered outside the universities by 1977. The strong influence of industry was also felt through the work of the Hotel and Catering Industry Training Board which was established in 1966 and subsequently by the work of the then Hotel, Catering and Institutional Management Association (HCIMA) which was formed in 1971 by the merger of the HCI and the IMA. This organization played a prominent role in setting out a corpus of knowledge for professional management in the industry (HCIMA, 1977) which subsequently helped to influence the content of degree programmes.

The outcome of these developments is that by the late 1970s there was a range of degree and diploma courses at colleges and universities providing various levels of education and training for management. Partly as a result of their origins and with the continuing influence of the professional body and industrial training board the needs of the hotel and catering industry remained the key influence on the curriculum.

Current provision and curriculum

Since its early development the numbers of students, courses and institutions have shown fairly consistent growth, although this has flagged in the last few years. From just two degree courses in the 1960s and fewer than ten at the end of the 1970s, by 1995/6, as given in Table 15.1, there were an estimated 79 courses offered by 27 HEIs and enrolling more than 8000 students. An indication of growth during the period is given by one of the official reports

Source	Students	Courses	Institutions
Litteljohn and Morrison	8356	79	27
Cooper *et al.*	8512		

Source: HEFCE, *Review of Hospitality Management* (1998)

Table 15.1 Estimates of the scale of provision of hospitality management degree courses 1995/6

(HMI, 1992, p.6) which suggests that 'As the number of degree courses ... has increased, student enrolments have expanded to fill the places available' and it gives a measure of the growth suggesting that 1989/90 degree enrolments in hotel and catering courses were almost double their 1987/8 level. In other words hospitality management education has been a buoyant area of education provision growing faster than the average growth in enrolments into higher education.

As far as the curriculum is concerned the origins and the influence of the industry are prominent. This can be seen in the example of the contents of a BSc degree course provided in Table 15.2. Like most of the courses, this is offered as a four-year thick sandwich including one year of supervised work

Subject	Total supervised hours per year
Year 1	
Food studies	45
Food preparation techniques	45
Economic environment	90
Quantitative business analysis	90
Building and facilities	90
Communication studies	90
Year 2	
Catering systems and technology	45
Organization behaviour and management	45
Financial accounting	45
Accommodation and facility management	45
Food and beverage operations	90
Sales and marketing facility	45
Planning and development	45
Year 3	
Industrial placement	
Year 4	
Corporate and research project management	150
Operational strategy	150
Option	45

Source: HMI, *Hotel, Catering and Tourism Management.*

Table 15.2 Outline of a BSc (Hons) hotel and catering management course

experience. The emphasis on practical and industry-oriented content is clear in module titles such as *Food preparation techniques*. The HMI report (1992, p.7) at the beginning of the 1990s suggested that a common aim of the courses 'is to equip students with the understanding and skills required to be effective managers in specific catering ... contexts and as adaptable members of society'. Further they comment that 'Most hotel and catering courses share an emphasis on management of practical food preparation, food service and accommodation operations' and 'all courses are set in an appropriate framework of applied business studies'. This theme is also picked up in the review conducted by the Council for National Academic Awards (CNAA) (1992, p.7) which suggested that:

> Typically ... courses include business studies components, such as marketing, law, economics, information technology, behavioural studies, quantitative techniques, accounting, employee relations and personnel management as well as management in a more generic sense. These are combined with inputs of specific hotel and catering studies which invariably include a science element.

With this background, practical work in food preparation and service is normally an important ingredient of hotel and catering higher education and most degree and diploma courses include a period of industrial placement lasting between 18 and 48 weeks. Again quoting from the CNAA Review (1992, p.11) 'There is general agreement about the need for degree courses to include the acquisition of certain operational, technical and craft skills'. This industry influence is also demonstrated clearly in the 1998 report by HEFCE (1998) which provides a definition of the subject strongly couched in vocational and action oriented terms. This is outlined in Figure 15.1. The industry emphasis is further stressed in the report with the comment that the practical element is a defining characteristic which differentiates the subject from other business and management courses.

One interesting change that has occurred in the past decade or so is the shift from the common use of *Hotel and catering* in the title of degree programmes to the use of *Hospitality*. By 1989/90 for example, according to the CNAA (1992), of the 24 degree courses running, half had 'hotel', 'catering', 'food' or 'accommodation' in their titles and a further eight used the term 'hospitality'. An early comment on this in the UK was made by Nailon (1981, p.2) who suggested that:

Hospitality management is characterised by a core which addresses the management of food, beverages and/or accommodation in a service context.

Courses offer a mix of the following, the balance varying with the student market and the industry sector which the provider targets:

- technical knowledge of the core areas of food and beverage management and/or accommodation management, with optional add-ons such as food science, microbiology, nutrition, and so on

- a practical element of hands-on experience of operational areas, this being a *combination* of college training and supervised work experience

- personal skills, such as communication, teamworking and self-confidence (which have implications also for recruitment to higher education courses)

- generic hospitality management skills, such as financial management, human resources, management information systems, marketing, operations management (including service quality management), business and corporate strategy

- applied hospitality management skills, such as yield management and specialised software systems

- industry sector specialisms, such as contract catering, licensed retailing, fast food, public sector provision, hotels and so on.

Figure 15.1 Definition of the academic subject. *Source:* HEFCE, *Review of Hospitality Management.*

the provision of foods, beverages and accommodation away from home involves a more comprehensive range of activities than is implied by the traditional description of 'hotels and catering'.

He goes on to suggest that *'hospitality* describes the unifying factor or binding thread'. From this he proceeded to develop a conceptual framework for hospitality which drew upon broad areas of knowledge from the external environment, management information systems, human resources and the technical infrastructure. These are set out in Figure 15.2. In many respects this provides an outline of the ways in which the present hospitality management courses have developed. The move from the name 'hotel and catering' therefore is significant in that it represents a move to put the studies in a conceptual framework although at the same time it is clear that the vocational orientation remains at the core of the curriculum.

The hospitality curriculum

The idea of curriculum space has been developed by Tribe (1999) with specific reference to tourism. It also provides a helpful basis on which to understand the development and current nature of the curriculum in hospitality. Tribe (1999, p.111) explains the curriculum space as 'the expanse or area that contains the range of possible contents of a curriculum'. Further he goes on to suggest that the curriculum represents a contested space over

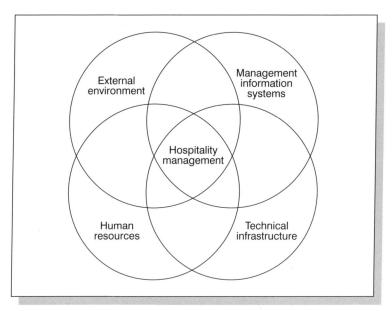

Figure 15.2 Framework for hospitality management studies. *Source:* Nailon, 1981.

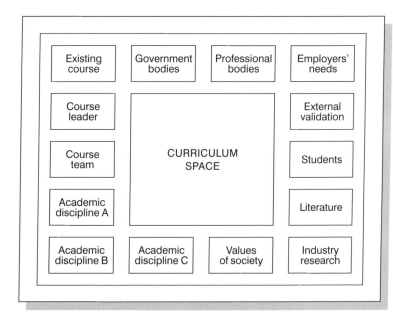

Figure 15.3 Curriculum space and influences. *Source:* adapted from Tribe, 1999.

which a number of stakeholders seek to exercise influence. This is set out in diagrammatic form in Figure 15.3.

Since the curriculum space is ultimately limited by, for example, the length of the course, or the capacity of the students to develop their knowledge, or the resources of the institution, decisions between competing influences, about the use of the space, inevitably have to be taken and in the process the curriculum is framed so that some items are included, and, just as importantly, some are excluded.

In the case of HEIs in the UK these curriculum framing decisions are normally taken by those working within the institutions, course teams, course leaders, validation bodies, etc. In other settings a national curriculum may be set. This national approach is under discussion for higher education generally in the UK but it is still a long way from introduction. However, while the decisions about the framing of the curriculum in the curriculum space is taken within institutions, those taking the decisions are far from having a free hand in the process. They are all subject to the same wide range of influences with the result that most curricula end up with a similar content. As the CNAA report commented on these courses (1992, p.2) 'there now appears to be a consensus about the core curriculum' and the added comment 'Hotel and catering degree courses have been developed to meet a vocational need' provides the flavour of that consensus.

From what has been said and from the examples of courses provided, a number of key influences have helped to determine the existing curriculum in hospitality management. The needs of industry and employers have clearly been key influences as has the professional body in outlining, at an early stage, a corpus of professional knowledge (HCIMA, 1977). The resulting curriculum, once established, then continued with relatively minor changes – reflecting changes, for example in industry practices and in industry-related research. As a result new areas of study such as information management have joined the curriculum but basically once the curriculum became established this in turn became the so-called *corpus of knowledge* which in turn has become enshrined in textbooks, in the minds of external validators and in many of the other influential sources. The end result of this process has been a hospitality curriculum offered in most institutions which bears a resemblance to that provided in Table 15.2 and which contains the ingredients set out in Figure 15.1. Tribe (1999, p.35) identified a similar process in tourism commenting that:

> A normalisation process is underway where a vocationalist curriculum is establishing, defending and replicating itself . . . A key challenge . . . is to explain this emerging

> orthodoxy and subject it to external scrutiny. The question emerges as to whether the tourism curriculum that was developed is an education that serves us well. This is not answered by the literature . . . which lacks a philosophical perspective.

There is nothing particularly exceptional about this process as far as hospitality management is concerned. All courses are subject to ongoing influences which mean that there is a similarity in the curricula content even without a national curriculum. What is perhaps distinctive about the hospitality curriculum is that it appears to be confined to a relatively small part of the total curriculum space. Again, Tribe's (1999) analysis of tourism education provides a framework for examining this.

Tribe has divided the curriculum space along two axes: the vocational–liberal axis and the reflection–action axis. The first represents the different ends of the curriculum, essentially the degree of vocational focus, and the second the different stance or modes of study and expression which the curriculum employs to achieve its ends. In Tribe's words (1999, p.112):

> A vocational curriculum is a curriculum for action. It is a curriculum to equip students to engage in the vocational world and to participate in it. A liberal curriculum is a curriculum for study and reflection.

He goes on to suggest that:

> the vocational and liberal not only have different aims in the world of business on the one hand and the field in general on the other, they also equip students to take different stances. These can be identified as an active stance towards the world of work (vocational) and a reflective stance towards the field of study (liberal).

The vocational–liberal axis runs from curricula that are concerned with the world of work to those that focus on the world of study. The action–reflection axis extends from curricula where students are involved in the world and are engaged in putting ideas into practice to those where the engagement is with the cognitive processes of the mind. The relationship between these two axes are set out diagrammatically in Figure 15.4.

As far as the curriculum for hospitality management is concerned, the issue from this is the extent to which the curriculum is confined to the *vocational action* quadrant. From the outline of the course given in Table 15.2 and from the definition

Stance Ends	Reflection	Action
Liberal	Reflective liberal	Liberal action
Vocational	Reflective vocational	Vocational action

Figure 15.4 The use of curriculum space. *Source:* Tribe, 1999.

of the academic subject provided by the HEFCE report (1998) and presented in Figure 15.1, *vocational action* appears to be the dominant component of the curriculum. The existence of training restaurants and production kitchens all point to the importance of the action elements of the curriculum, as do the inclusion of work-based learning and supervised work experience. The HEFCE report (1998) draws attention to the fact that all the institutions covered in their survey include laboratory work of which the lion's share, 64 per cent, is to do with food and beverage management. Similarly the involvement of industry representatives in the courses bears witness to the vocational orientation. Again the HEFCE report (1998, p.15) provides comments on the closeness of the links with industry:

> We find that, in general, the subject has widespread and mature links with its industry . . .

> Many departments have specialist links with individual companies – providing staff development programmes, in company training and awards.

> Most departments invite employers to contribute to the assessment of modules or particular activities, and just over half have industry representatives as external examiners.

In brief, the hospitality management curriculum is very much focused on the *vocational action* area of the curriculum. Given the subject matter and the aims of courses this is hardly remarkable. Hospitality management education has developed a long way from the on-the-job training orientation of its origins through to the sort of theoretical framework set out by Nailon (1981) and in the process the participants have added immeasurably to the stock of knowledge and research from which the curriculum can be informed but it is still very much vocational and action orientated. This obviously provides a robust starting point for providing education to meet the needs of some, if not the majority, of stakeholders, particularly the industry and potential employers. However, there are two questions which it leaves open. First, by not entering more fully into the other parts of the curriculum space, is only a partial picture of the issues raised by hospitality management being presented? Second, if hospitality management is to continue its successful development as an area of serious study can it do so without exploring territories outside the vocational and then bringing these into the curriculum? In the final analysis the curriculum in higher education has to be informed by knowledge which in turn has to be informed by research. The successful development of the curriculum and the subject needs new knowledge and new research. This is as true of hospitality management as it is of any other discipline of field of study. The real challenge for hospitality management education is the origins and creation of this new knowledge.

Hospitality knowledge

Again, Tribe's (1997) work in tourism provides a framework for considering the development of knowledge about hospitality management. He describes tourism as a field of knowledge which calls upon a number of disciplines to investigate and explain their area of interest and quoting Hirst (1965, p.130) he describes fields as being 'formed by building together round specific objects, or phenomena, or practical pursuits, knowledge that is characteristically rooted elsewhere in more than one discipline'. This immediately positions fields of study like tourism, and hospitality management, as multidisciplinary in origin in that they draw upon more than one discipline. But also they are potentially interdisciplinary in that they can serve as a focal point in which disciplines can come together to present new insights or new knowledge. This provides the basis for Tribe, drawing upon the work of Gibbons *et al.* (1994), to identify the areas where knowledge about tourism is developed: in the contributing disciplines themselves and in the interdisciplinary areas where two or more disciplines come together. Traditionally this is knowledge that is developed within universities and other HEIs and Tribe (1999, p.103) suggests that 'Disciplinary-based methodology and peer review are the hallmarks of quality control' of such knowledge.

Tribe also identifies a second area of knowledge generation which he labels *extradisciplinary* knowledge. He quotes Gibbons *et al.* (1994, p.vii) to explain that extradisciplinary knowledge:

> ... operates within a context of application in that problems are not set within a disciplinary framework ... It is not being institutionalised primarily within university structures ... [and] makes use of a wider range of criteria in judging quality control.

Much of this form of extradisciplinary knowledge for tourism, according to Tribe, is generated not in higher education but in the business world and the sites of such knowledge production include 'industry, government, think tanks, interest groups, research institutes and consultancies' (1999, p.103). He gives examples of such knowledge production in tourism as including 'developments and applications of information technology for tourism such as smart hotel rooms, yield management systems and computerised reservations developments – developed in the industry for the industry' (1999, p.103). He concludes on this point:

> The important points to note about [this] knowledge production are first that it occurs outside higher education, the traditional centre for knowledge production. Second that it is developing its own epistemology. ... [This] knowledge ... judges its success by its ability to solve a particular problem, its cost effectiveness and its ability to establish competitive advantage, that is its effectiveness in the real world.

In many ways Tribe's comments about multidisciplinary, inter-disciplinary and extradisciplinary knowledge generation can be related to a wide range of fields of study. For example housing, media studies, leisure management as well as hospitality management all demonstrate similarities with tourism. They are also similar in that they are relative newcomers to the education repertoire. It is perhaps this latter point which provides the common clue to their current state of knowledge. Academic research is a slow process and the accumulation and dissemination of knowledge takes place over generations of scholars. For this reason it is in many ways unsurprising that fields of study such as hospitality management have relied heavily on the third of Tribe's types of knowledge, i.e. that generated outside the academic community. This factor is additional to the natural wish to use knowledge that has industry relevance. An indication of the nature of the type of early production of knowledge can be seen in the policy of the CNAA which interpreted research in a very wide sense to include consultancy and professional practice (Glew, 1991). The sheer importance of this kind of knowledge can also been seen in some of the early writings about the hotel industry. For example the very comprehensive reference list for one of the early and influential textbooks (Medlik, 1972) on the subject is dominated by government and other official reports and studies. This says as much about the state of knowledge at the time as it does about the industry focus of the author.

To a certain extent this extradisciplinary knowledge still plays an important role in hospitality management and is reflected in research, writing and course content. But the size and experience of the academic community means that the knowledge base is in a process of rapid change. One indication of this is the growth of the research conference conducted annually by the UK-based Council for Hospitality Management Education. The publication from the most recent conference (Lockwood, 1999) includes 75 papers and while many of these have a clear industry focus many substantially draw upon discipline-based research which makes a contribution to the knowledge base of the subject from a multidisciplinary and interdisciplinary basis.

The important point here is that hospitality management is arriving at a point, as an area of study, where with the development of academic alongside professional knowledge, it is well capable of moving out of the narrow territory framed by the *vocational action* area of the curriculum. The development of the knowledge base and the work of the community of scholars in the field will permit it. However, there remains the question as to whether this is the right direction to take.

Future directions and dangers

The future of any field of study lies partly within itself and partly within the external world. As far as hospitality management is concerned it is certainly at a point where it could break out from its *vocational action* orientation and begin to explore new territories relating for example to the cultural, social, anthropological aspects of hospitality. This in turn would expose the students more to liberal thinking and lead them to reflection. Lashley has provided further examples of this thinking in Chapter 1 of this book by exploring the social and private domains of hospitality activities. However, the external world is also important for hospitality management. In part, as Tribe has suggested (1999, p.104), this is influenced by a view that knowledge creation in general is led by functionalism, and, as he says 'the aim of knowledge production becomes not an impartial uncovering of the truth but a search for truths which are useful in terms of marketability and efficiency'. For hospitality management in particular the link with the successful operation of a sector of the economy is perhaps stronger than for education in general. The original rationale for hospitality management education lay with management preparation for the industry and, as identified earlier, the vocational orientation and links with industry remain strong. Indeed this is often seen as one of the strengths and successes of this aspect of education.

Clearly there are strong arguments for and against the broadening of the hospitality management curriculum. Confined to *vocational action*, and using the kind of framework developed by Nailon (1981) hospitality management provides a coherent, robust and industrially relevant area of education which can justify its existence in vocational terms and can certainly demonstrate appropriate levels of challenge for students in higher education. Without this clear focus there is the danger that it would cease to justify its existence separate from business and management studies or from the contributing disciplines. However, there is an important argument that if it is restricted too tightly to the *vocational action* area of the curriculum the education provision does not do justice to the individual students, to the industry or to the subject area itself. As far as the students are concerned the other quadrants of the curriculum space provide important ingredients of education. *Liberal reflection* has long been a key component of higher education in what Tribe (1999, p.125) refers to as 'the Oxbridge tradition of developing the person and their powers of mind' providing the opportunity for a critique not only of society but in this case for a critique of hospitality within that society. In a similar way *reflective vocational*, again in Tribe's words (1999, p.128), encourages the individual 'to find his or her own voice for development and critique of the vocational action' while *liberal action* sets the student on a path of critiquing the wider world of action relating to hospitality management and developing the skills and knowledge to put critical ideas into practice. Clearly each of these areas of the curriculum space has an important contribution to make in the education of the individual students, many of whom will be preparing for a lifelong career, whether in hospitality or elsewhere, as well as for their life outside their careers. They can also make a vital contribution to the hospitality industry itself by producing future managers who are able to think outside the existing practices and paradigms. And as far as the subject itself is concerned it is only by exploring new areas and coming up with new knowledge and solutions that it will refresh itself and maintain its relevance, whether for the world of work or beyond.

Echoing the CNAA report on tourism studies (1992), in many ways hospitality management education has now 'come of age'. Apart from a large cohort of undergraduate and postgraduate students there has been a substantial growth of teachers, textbooks, journals, conferences, organizations, and, possibly most importantly, of research and knowledge. Up to now there has also been a fair measure of agreement about the content of the hospitality curriculum. The challenge for hospitality educators now is how to use the research and knowledge in the further development of the curriculum. The *vocational* and *action* orientation is likely to remain important but beyond the boundaries of this corner of the curriculum there is also new territory to explore.

References

Council for National Academic Awards (1992) *Review of Hotel and Catering Degree Courses.* London, CNAA.

Council for National Academic Awards (1993) *Review of Tourism Studies Degree Courses.* London, CNAA.

Gibbons, M., Limoges, C., Nowotny, H., Schwartsman, S., Scott, P. and Trow, M. (1994) *The New Production of Knowledge.* London, Sage.

Glew, G. (1991) *Research and Scholarly Activities in Support of Honours Degree Teaching (with special reference to consumer and leisure studies courses).* London, CNAA.

Her Majesty's Inspectorate (1992) Higher education in the polytechnics and colleges. *Hotel, Catering and Tourism Management.* London, Department of Education and Science.

Higher Education Funding Council for England (1998) *Review of Hospitality Management Education.* Bristol, HEFCE.

Hirst, P. (1965) Liberal Education and the Nature of Knowledge. In: *Philosophical Analysis and Education* (R.D. Archambault, ed.). Henley, Routledge and Kegan Paul, pp.113–40.

Hotel, Catering and Institutional Management Association (1977) *The Corpus of Professional Knowledge in Hotel, Catering and Institutional Services, HCIMA Research Fellowship Final Report.* London, HCIMA.

Lockwood, A. (ed.) (1999) *CHME Hospitality Research Conference Proceedings 1999.* Guildford, University of Surrey.

Medlik, S. (1972) *Profile of the Hotel and Catering Industry.* London, Heinemann.

Medlik, S. and Airey, D.W. (1978) *Profile of the Hotel and Catering Industry.* London, Heinemann.

Nailon, P. (1981) *Theory and Art in Hospitality Management.* University of Surrey, Inaugural Lecture, 4 February 1981.

Tribe, J. (1997) The Indiscipline of Tourism. *Annals of Tourism Research*, **24**, No. 3, 628–57.

Tribe, J. (1999) The Philosophic Practitioner: Tourism Knowledge and the Curriculum. PhD thesis, University of London.

Index

Hospitality, Leisure & Tourism Series